Adolf Grünbaum

THE CAUSES AND CURES
OF NEUROSIS

By H. J. Eysenck

DIMENSIONS OF PERSONALITY
THE SCIENTIFIC STUDY OF PERSONALITY
THE PSYCHOLOGY OF POLITICS
THE DYNAMICS OF ANXIETY AND HYSTERIA
CRIME AND PERSONALITY

Edited by H. J. Eysenck

EXPERIMENTS IN PERSONALITY
(in two volumes)

THE CAUSES
AND CURES OF
NEUROSIS

An Introduction to Modern Behaviour Therapy
Based on Learning Theory and the Principles
of Conditioning

by
H. J. EYSENCK
and
S. RACHMAN

ROBERT R. KNAPP, *Publisher*
San Diego California USA 92107

FIRST EDITION 1965
SECOND IMPRESSION 1967
THIRD IMPRESSION 1972
LIBRARY OF CONGRESS CATALOG CARD NUMBER 64-21700
ISBN 0-912736-03-8
MANUFACTURED IN GREAT BRITAIN

CONTENTS

FIGURES

vii

TABLES

INTRODUCTION

THIS book is an introduction to post-Freudian methods of diagnosing and treating neurotics. For convenience of reference these methods are known collectively as 'behaviour therapy', a term which indicates their derivation from modern behaviourism, learning theory, and conditioning principles. Almost half a century ago John B. Watson pointed out that 'psychology, as the behaviourist views it, is a purely objective experimental branch of natural science. Its theoretical goal is the prediction and control of behaviour.' Behaviour therapy attempts to extend this control to the field of neurotic disorders, and in doing so it makes use of experimental laboratory findings, and of theories based on these.

It will be seen that in this way it proceeds in a manner which is exactly opposite to that adopted by psychoanalysis. Like all other applied sciences, behaviour therapy bases itself on existing knowledge of a fundamental kind and attempts to derive methods of treatment from these along lines of deduction which are as rigorous as possible. Freud, on the other hand, explicitly rejected academic psychology and tried instead to build a new general psychology on the basis of his experiences in treating patients. We shall have occasion in the course of this book to examine the relative success of these two methods of procedure.

In speaking about 'cures' in the title of this book we have intended not only to follow alliterative convenience, but to indicate our firm belief that it is in principle possible, and in many cases feasible even at this early stage of development, to eradicate completely specific neurotic disorders from the behaviour repertoire of the patient. Freud, it will be remembered, became very pessimistic towards the end of his life about the therapeutic possibilities of psychoanalysis, and declared that he would be remembered as the originator of a method for investigating mental life rather than as the creator of a method for treating neurosis. We believe that the general failure of psychotherapy to effect cures, a failure which has led many people to abandon the use of this term altogether in connection with mental illness, is not due to the impossibility of achieving cures but rather to erroneous methods of setting about this task. We would agree that the evidence available to date is conclusive only with respect to certain types of disorder and that for many others the evidence suggests promise rather than definitive achievement. In view of the short period during which behaviour therapy has been practised at all widely this is, of course, inevitable. Nevertheless, the methods described in this book have already been widely adopted by psychiatrists and clinical psychologists, particularly in England and the Commonwealth, and there is evidence also of considerable interest in the United States. The routine use of these methods is undoubtedly not yet feasible; it must await further improvement of techniques and definitive evidence of superiority over other available techniques. We are sanguine enough to believe that these developments are only a matter of time and that within the next decade or two behaviour therapy will be firmly established as one of the most important, if not *the* most important, weapon in the hands of psychiatrists and clinical psychologists.

H.J.E.
S.R.

Institute of Psychiatry,
The Maudsley Hospital.

Sedulo curavi humanas actiones non ridere,
non lugere, neque detestari, sed intelligere

SPINOZA

Chapter *1*

THE NATURE OF NEUROSIS

IN this book we are concerned with the problem of the *diagnosis* and the *treatment* of neurotics, as well as with the problem of the reasons why they develop their neurotic disorders. Problems of nosology, aetiology, and therapy may be approached along three different lines. The first of these we may call 'notional'. By this is meant that the proposed solution is based on a notion or a hunch, that it has not received empirical verification, and that its propagation owes nothing to proof but much to persuasion and emotional appeal. Solutions of this type may be highly systematized and may often be susceptible to disproof only with the greatest difficulty. Phrenology, or the belief that character may be read from the bumps on a person's head, may be a good example of a notional theory in psychology. It hardly needs saying that notional solutions to problems are pre-scientific and of little practical importance, although very occassionally later research may be able to substantiate some of the hunches or notions underlying these approaches.

Much more useful is a second category which we may call 'empirical'. Here we are dealing with methods which have originated in some notion or belief, or which may have been discovered by chance. They are characterized by the fact that there is some empirical support for their validity and usefulness. In psychiatry, electro-shock is a method of treatment which clearly fits into this category. Empirical methods may be practically useful and valuable, but they fall short of what scientists would be willing to accept as truly scientific because as long as the rationale of the methods is not known it is likely to prove inconsistent and only of partial value.

I

The third category may be called 'rational', meaning by that simply that the answers to practical problems are derived by a rigorous process of deduction from certain general laws or principles, independently established and constituting the main body of theories, axioms, and postulates of the science in question. It is this last method which alone deserves the name 'scientific', and the whole history of applied science is evidence that no problem can be considered solved until it is brought into direct relationship with a rational system of thought in this manner.

We may ask ourselves what precisely is the present position in the field of psychiatry and clinical psychology, as far as the treatment and diagnosis of neurotic disorders are concerned. The following three statements would probably present a true picture of the situation. (1) With the exception of electro-shock, the only method of treatment at all widely used is psychotherapy. (2) In practically all of its manifestations, psychotherapy is based on Freudian theories. (3) With the exception of intelligence testing, psychological contributions consists almost entirely in the administration and interpretation of projective tests, usually along psychoanalytic lines. We thus find a situation in which psychologists lay stress on *projective tests* in diagnosis, and on *psychotherapy* in treatment. In relation to both there is considerably evidence that they belong to the *notional* group of methods, having no empirical support and not deriving in any way from the main body of psychological theory.

It is not the purpose of this book to document these criticisms or to deal at any length with current practices, except incidentally. Evidence for the brief statements made above will be found in the Handbook of Abnormal Psychology (Eysenck, 1960a), Critical Essays on Psychoanalysis (Rachman, 1963), and in many other books and articles quoted in these sources. Here we shall be concerned entirely with the development of a completely different type of approach to the problem of neurotic disorder, one which stems from Pavlov and modern learning theory rather than from Freud and 'dynamic' psychology, and which has been attracting a great deal of attention, particularly in England, but also, in recent years, in the United States. We call this approach *rational* because its methods and theorems are derived from the large body of knowledge which has been accumulated by experimental psychologists over the past fifty years or so, and which, in its systematized form, we call learning theory or, perhaps better, behaviour theory. The exposition of these methods of treatment is the primary purpose of this book: they will be referred to by the generic term "behaviour therapy'.

We may perhaps begin by very briefly stating the main points which characterize modern behaviour therapy and the theories on which it is based. In the first place, we regard neurotic behaviour as being *learned* behaviour. In this way, it is set off from innate or instinctive behaviour, on the one hand, and behaviour due to lesions of one kind and another in the central autonomic system, on the other. This hypothesis will not be readily disputed by many psychologists or psychiatrists because the importance of learning and conditioning in the growth and development of neurotic behaviour is probably admitted nowadays by almost everyone who has had any experience in this field; we do not believe that psychoanalysts or orthodox psychiatrists would in any sense disagree with this stress on the importance of learning and individual experience.

As nearly all human behaviour may be said to be learned, how do we distinguish neurotic behaviour from other types of behaviour? The answer must be that neurotic behaviour is *maladaptive;* the individual who adopts neurotic behaviour patterns fails to achieve what he is trying to do and succeeds in doing what in fact is highly disadvantageous to him. Mowrer (1950) refers to this as the 'neurotic paradox'. 'Commonsense holds that a normal, sensible man, or even a beast to the limits of his intelligence, will weigh and balance the consequences of his acts: if the net effect is favourable, the action producing it will be perpetuated; and if the net effect is unfavourable the action producing it will be inhibited, abandoned. In neurosis, however, one sees actions which have predominantly unfavourable consequences; yet they persist over a period of months, years, or a lifetime. Small wonder, then, that commonsense has abjured responsibility in such matters and has assigned them to the realm of the miraculous, the mystical, the uncommon, the preternatural.' Maladaptive habits thus present a paradox and seem to go beyond the simple rules of learning theory; it will be our task to show that in actual fact learning theory can encompass such activities.

We believe that the paradigm of a fully developed neurosis can be postulated to be something like this (Eysenck, 1960*b*, 1964*a*). In the first instance, we have a single traumatic event, or else a series of sub-traumatic events producing unconditioned but strong autonomic reactions, mainly of the sympathetic nervous system. These strong emotional reactions may themselves be such as to disorganize the behaviour. There is much evidence that such disorganization may follow from strong emotional involvement, and the history of neuroses occurring during war, particularly in the front line, is replete with examples of such direct consequences. It is doubtful, however, whether we should regard such immediate consequences as being in any sense 'neurotic', because although probably maladaptive in some way, they are not necessarily persistent, and they are so universal as to make a special term for them a rather unnecessary refinement.

At the second stage we find that in a large number of cases conditioning takes place, in the sense that a previously neutral stimulus, through association, becomes connected with the unconditioned stimuli which give rise to the traumatic, emotional reactions. From now on it will be found that the conditioned stimulus, as well as the unconditioned stimulus, produces the original, maladaptive, emotional behaviour. This, it seems to us, is the essential learning process which takes place in the development of a neurosis. Single traumatic events are frequently implicated in the development of phobic fear reactions, whereas in the case of more widespread anxiety, it is likely that large numbers of sub-traumatic events may have played a more important part. However that may be, we postulate that Pavlovian conditioning is involved in the great majority of neurotic illnesses characterized by anxiety, phobic fears, obsessional reaction, and other dysthymic responses.

Conditioned responses which are not reinforced begin to extinguish, and we would expect, therefore, that conditioned autonomic responses of the type described above would extinguish as the individual concerned encounters many examples of a conditioned stimulus which are not followed by reinforcement, i.e. by traumatic events accompanying the original presentation. This would lead us to postulate that the great

4

majority of neurotic reactions of this type should show what is often called 'spontaneous remission', and the evidence is indeed very strong that such remission takes place. Eysenck (1960*a,g*) has reviewed the literature and has derived a formula showing the degree to which X, the proportional improvement, depends on N, which denotes the number of weeks elapsing from the beginning of the experiment. This formula is shown in Figure 1, which also contains a plot of the data derived from a study by Denker (1946), in which 500 severe cases of neurosis which were not treated by any form of psychotherapy but were merely seen by their ordinary G.Ps. were followed up over a period of many years. It will be seen that some 70 per cent recovered after two years, and over 90 per cent after five years. We can see, therefore, that the evidence strongly supports our hypothesis of extinction of conditioned neurotic

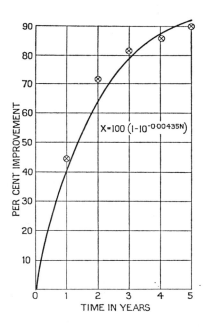

$$X = 100 \left(1 - 10^{-0.00435N}\right)$$

FIG. 1. Proportion of 500 severe neurotics recovered after 1, 2, 3, 4 and 5 years respectively, without receiving any form of psychotherapy. In the formula, X denotes the percentage improved, N denotes the number of weeks elapsed from the beginning of the experiment (Eysenck, 1960*a*).

responses. Indeed, it may be said that of all the phenomena characterizing the neuroses, spontaneous remission is probably the most obvious, the most impressive, and the least frequently mentioned in psychiatric textbooks.

The fact that not all cases show spontaneous remission, however, must make us suspect that there is, in many cases, a third stage in the development of neurotic disorders. This third stage may be said to owe its existence to the fact that human beings differ in one very important particular from the animals on whom Pavlov originally demonstrated the existence of extinction. The animal is strapped in his stand, and when the conditioned stimulus is presented to him without reinforcement following, he has no choice but to observe the stimuli as they are presented to him. A human being, however, has a very important choice indeed; he can choose to watch the stimuli and let extinction occur, or he can choose to avoid the stimuli, or indeed run away from them. Consider, as an example, the case of a woman suffering from a cat phobia, which is quoted in more detail later in this book. This phobia developed from a very traumatic event in the past history of the patient, when her father drowned a favourite kitten in front of her eyes. This traumatic event caused a conditioned fear response to cats, and this fear response would, in the normal course of events, have extinguished, had not the patient made use of her freedom of choice in situations involving cats, by turning and running away from them. In this way, she succeeded in reducing the conditioned fear responses produced by the cat, through eliminating the cat from her field of vision, and through putting a larger distance between herself and the cat. In other words, through a process of operant conditioning, the woman was effectively reinforced, or rewarded, for running away from the phobic object, and thereby acquired a secondary conditioned habit, namely that of avoiding the cat. In this way she made it impossible for extinction to occur.

The three-stage theory here developed is applicable to all the disorders we have called *dysthymic*, i.e. to phobic reactions, anxiety states, obsessional and compulsive disorders, and so forth; these may be called *disorders of the first kind*, and our general hypothesis is that they are caused by conditioned autonomic fear responses and the reactions, skeletal, muscular and hormonal, of the organism of these conditioned responses.

6

There is, however, according to our theory a second group of disorders, and these may be called *disorders of the second kind*. In these disorders we postulate not the occurrence of a conditioning process leading to maladaptive habits, but rather the failure of a conditioning process to occur which would produce socially desirable habits. Psychopathic behaviour would be a good illustration of this point. Mowrer (1950) has pointed out that the development of socially desirable behaviour patterns in children can be accounted for only through a process of Pavlovian conditioning. According to this theory, it may be postulated that whenever the child indulges in some form of activity which is disapproved of by his parents, or his teachers, or his peers, then immediate punishment of one kind or another will follow. The behaviour in question is the conditioned stimulus, the punishment the unconditioned stimulus leading to autonomic pain and fear responses. In this way conditioning is set up, and in due course the conditioned stimuli, i.e. the behaviour patterns to be discouraged, would be directly connected with the conditioned response (the fear and pain reactions of the autonomic system). This whole process we may imagine to be greatly facilitated by a process of generalization, making use of verbal identification of the acts in question as being naughty, bad, or wicked. In this way, a whole system of *mores* is built up in the growing child through conditioning, taking ultimately the form of a 'conscience' (Eysenck, 1960*h*, 1964*b*). Failure to acquire this conscience, for whatever reason, may then lead to psychopathic activities, also sometimes called 'moral imbecility', i.e. behaviour patterns characteristic of the inveterate liar, the person unable to resist any form of temptation or to refuse to indulge every appetite or whim regardless of the consequences which will inevitably follow. (Such persons are now often called 'sociopaths', particularly in the United States.) *Enuresis nocturna* is another disorder where there has been an apparent failure of the proper conditioning to take place, and where the enlargement of the bladder and the beginning of urination fails to trigger off the appropriate conditioned response of waking up and going to the toilet.

A rather different sub-section of this group of disorders is formed by those where there is not a failure of desirable conditioning which is postulated to have taken place, but where

7

there may have taken place a type of positive, appetitive conditioning which is contrary to the rules and laws of the country in question. Thus, homosexual, fetishistic, or other perverse erotic behaviour patterns may have become fixated through a process of conditioning in which these undesirable behaviour patterns were in fact reinforced through orgasm or in some other way, so that the problem for the therapist is now one of breaking down the positive conditioning and of establishing instead a negative conditioned response to these stimuli. In some cases it may not always be clear whether the particular behaviour pattern is innate, or whether there has been a failure of socially desirable conditioning to take place, or whether the behaviour is not innate but has in fact been created through a special process of positive conditioning. Homosexuality is a case in point; there is considerable evidence that homosexual patterns of behaviour may be innate in many people, but there is also considerable evidence to show that in many people it may have been triggered off by a process of social learning and conditioning. However that may be, it will be seen that disorders of the second kind are, in many ways, differentiated from disorders of the first kind, and it will also be seen that theory does not predict the occurrence of spontaneous remission in these disorders.

In disorders of the first kind there has been a process of conditioning which, through non-reinforcement, should lead to spontaneous remission. In disorders of the second kind there has been a failure of conditioning to occur, or, when conditioning has occurred, it may be expected to be reinforced in any accidental evocation of the conditioned stimulus; neither of these conditions would lead to extinction, and consequently we cannot expect spontaneous remission to occur. There is a dearth of evidence on this point, but psychiatric opinion is certainly in good agreement with the view that psychopathic and perverted behaviour patterns are very must less liable to spontaneous remission than are the dysthymic behaviour patterns discussed previously.

It might be objected that surely society tends to punish behaviour patterns of this second kind, and that psychopathic behaviour, homosexuality, fetishism, and so on, in so far as they violate the law of the land, will call forth punishment which has been designed specially by society to produce precisely such a dissociative effect between the conditioned stimulus and reinforcement. It is, of course true that by imprisonment, beating, or torturing homosexuals, fetishists and others society is substituting negative reinforcement for a positive one. Nevertheless, such punishment cannot be expected to lead to extinction, and indeed it has been shown in practice, by the failure of these methods throughout recorded history, that they are relatively useless. No one nowadays assumes that the habits of the homosexual, for instance, are altered by putting him into prison, even though such punishment may restrain the expression of these habits for a while (in other words, punishment may affect $_sE_r$ but not $_sH_r$). Even more important, Mowrer (1950) has shown both theoretically and experimentally ' . . . that the consequences of a given act determine the future of that act not only in terms of what may be called the quantitative aspects of the consequences but also in terms of their temporal pattern. In other words, if an act has two consequences—the one rewarding and the other punishing—which would be strictly equal if simultaneous, the influence of these consequences on later performances of that act will vary depending on the *order* in which they occur. If the punishing consequence comes first and the rewarding one later, the difference between the inhibiting and the reinforcing effects will be in favour of the inhibition. But if the rewarding consequence comes first and the punishing one later, the difference will be in favour of the reinforcement.' Punishment, therefore, coming much later than the rewarding consequences of the guilty act, is not likely to lead to extinction of behaviour in the long run.

How does our theory compare with the psychoanalytic one? In the formation of neurotic symptoms, Freud emphasizes the traumatic nature of the events leading up to the neurosis, as well as their roots in early childhood. Learning theory can accommodate with equal ease traumatic 'single trial' learning, for which there is good experimental evidence, but it can also deal with repeated sub-traumatic pain and fear responses which build up the conditioned reaction rather more gradually. As regards the importance of childhood, the Freudians' stress seems to be rather misplaced in allocating the origins of *all* neuroses to this period. It is possible that many neurotic symptoms find their origin in this period, but there is no

9

reason at all to assume that neurotic symptoms cannot equally easily be generated at a later period, provided conditions are arranged so as to favour their emergence.

The point, however, on which the theory here advocated breaks decisively with psychoanalytic thought of any description is in this. Freudian theory regards neurotic symptoms as adaptive mechanism which are evidence of repression; they are "the visible upshot of unconscious causes." Learning theory does not postulate any such 'unconscious' causes, but regards neurotic symptoms as simply learned habits; there is no neurosis inderlying the symptom, but merely the symptom itself.[1] *Get rid of the symptom (skeletal and autonomic) and you have eliminated the neurosis.* This notion of purely symptomatic treatment is so alien to psychoanalysis that it may be considered the crucial part of the theory here proposed. We would like to explore its implications a little further later on.

From the point of view of learning theory, treatment is, in essence, a very simple process. In the case of *surplus* conditioned responses treatment should consist in the extinction of these responses; in the case of *deficient* conditioned responses treatment should consist in the building up of the missing stimulus-response connections. Yet this apparent simplicity should not mislead us into thinking that the treatment of neurotic disorders offers no further problems. It is often found, in scientific research, that the solution of the problems posed by applied science is as complex and difficult as is the solution of the problems posed by pure science; even after Faraday and Maxwell had successfully laid the foundations of modern theories of electricity, it needed fifty years and the genius of Edison to make possible the actual application of these advances to the solution of practical problems. Similarly here: a solution in principle, even if it be correct, still needs much concentrated and high-powered research in the field of application before it can be used practically in the field of cure, amelioration, and prophylaxis.

Several methods of treatment have already been worked out and have been used on quite large numbers of patients of various types. These methods will be discussed in considerable detail in the main body of the book, which has been sub-

[1]The term 'symptom' is retained in our discussion, although there is no implication that it is symptomatic of anything. A better term might be C.M.R. (conditioned maladaptive response).

divided according to the main diagnostic criteria currently used in psychiatry. We would like to say at this point simply that we believe that these methods constitute an alternative to the Freudian, that they are based on a theory which claims to account for the facts at least as satisfactorily as does psychoanalysis, and which, in addition, puts forward quite specific suggestions about methods of treatment. We have called these methods 'behaviour therapy' to contrast them with methods of 'psychotherapy' (Eysenck, 1959a). This contrast of terms is meant to indicate two things. According to psychoanalytic doctrine, there is a psychological complex situated in the unconscious mind underlying all the manifest symptoms of neorotic disorders; hence the necessity of therapy for the psyche. According to learning theory, we are dealing with unadaptive behaviour, conditioned to certain classes of stimuli; no reference is made to any underlying disorders or complexes in the psyche. Following on this analysis, it is not surprising that psychoanalysts show a preoccupation with psychological methods involving mainly *speech*, while behaviour therapy concentrates on actual *behaviour* as most likely to lead to the extinction of the unadaptive conditioned responses. The two terms express rather concisely the opposing veiwpoints of the two schools. Below, in summary form, is a tabulation of the most important differences between psychotherapy and behaviour therapy.

We have given, in this Chapter, a very brief outline of the general theory which we are putting before the reader in this book; a detailed development of the various types of therapy based on this theory constitutes the main body of the book, and will not be anticipated here. We would like, however, at this point to explain why we are not going on directly to a discussion of the methods of treatment, but will discuss, in the next Chapter, something that, at first sight, may seem to be rather irrelevant to the main purpose of this book, to wit, the structure of personality. We believe that the study of individual differences, dimensions of personality, and the measurement of non-cognitive variables in general are extremely relevant to behaviour therapy, and we hope to indicate, in the next Chapter, just why this is so. Nevertheless, we would agree that it is possible to practise behaviour therapy, and to agree with its main postulates without necessarily agreeing with the theories regarding personality structure which are developed in the

TABLE I

The most important differences between psychotherapy and behaviour therapy

Psychotherapy	Behaviour therapy
1. Based on inconsistent theory, never properly formulated in postulate form.	1. Based on consistent, properly formulated theory leading to testable deductions.
2. Derived from clinical observation and made without necessary control observations or experiments.	2. Derived from experimental study specifically designed to test basic theory and deductions made therefrom.
3. Consider symptoms the visible upshot of unconscious causes ('complexes').	3. Consider symptoms as unadaptive conditioned responses.
4. Regards symptoms as evidence of *repression*.	4. Regards symptoms as evidence of faulty learning.
5. Believes that symptomatology is determined by defence mechanisms.	5. Believes that symptomatology is determined by individual differences in conditionability and autonomic lability, as well as accidental environmental circumstances.
6. All treatment of neurotic disorders must be *historically* based.	6. All treatment of neurotic disorders is concerned with habits existing *at present;* the historical development is largely irrelevant.
7. Cures are achieved by handling the underlying (unconscious) dynamics, not by treating the symptom itself.	7. Cures are achieved by treating the symptom itself, i.e. by extinguishing unadaptive C.Rs and establishing desirable C.Rs.
8. Interpretation of symptoms, dreams, acts, etc. is an important element of treatment.	8. Interpretation, even if not completely subjective and erroneous, is irrelevant.
9. Symptomatic treatment leads to the elaboration of new symptoms.	9. Symptomatic treatment leads to permanent recovery, provided autonomic as well as skeletal C.Rs are extinguished.
10. Transference relations are essential for cures of neurotic disorders.	10. Personal relations are not essential for cures of neurotic disorders, although they may be useful in certain circumstances.

next Chapter. It is necessary to state this quite explicitly, because otherwise it might seem that behaviour therapy stands and falls by the success or failure of the personality theories outlined here. This is not so; we believe that the personality theories given here form an important adjunct to behaviour therapy, and make intelligible many of the facts which have been unearthed by research in recent years, Others, however, may not share this view, and future research may indeed disprove our theories in this field. This would not necessarily imply that behaviour therapy as such was at fault; new theories could presumably be found on the personality side to supplement the systematic views about the genesis and treatment of neurotic disorders which we have developed in this book. We believe that the evidence is already extensive enough to suggest that any such wholesale failure of our personality theories is perhaps unlikely; nevertheless, we considered it our duty to point out that this part of the general theory is more easily expendable than many of the points dealt with so far.

Chapter 2

DIMENSIONS OF PERSONALITY

ALL that has been said in the first Chapter may perhaps be regarded as fairly orthodox, behaviouristic doctrine; it simply constitutes the application of certain conditioning and learning principles to the abnormal field. In this Chapter we are proposing to introduce the concept of personality, and it will immediately be obvious that here we are departing, to some extent at least, from orthodox behaviourism. Most writers of that school adopt the position that the very notion of personality is unnecessary; considering that all learning proceeds on the orthodox principles of stimulus-response connection formation, they argue that personality, if the term is to be used at all, will simply correspond with the sum total of the person's behaviour. As Watson (1930) once put it quite clearly, personality 'is the sum of activities that can be discovered by actual observation for a long enough period of time to give reliable information.' For many behaviourists, therefore, there is no room for personality in a natural science type of psychology.

However, it is becoming more and more widely recognized that between stimulus and response interposes an organism, and the formula S-O-R has pretty well superseded the old S-R paradigm. The recognition of the existence of an organism intervening between stimulus and response is made necessary by the very simple fact that identical stimuli applied to different organisms frequently lead to different responses, and even identical stimuli applied to the same organism do not always lead to similar responses. There are two possible causes for this, both involving the concept of an intervening organism. In the

14

first place, individual organisms may differ with respect to their past reinforcement schedules; on this hypothesis, we are simply saying that past learning determines in part the reactions which we now make to different types of stimuli. There is nothing very novel in this, of course, and even commonsense recognizes the importance of past learning in present activities. However, the fact that this is so is incompatible with a simple-minded application of the principles of stimulus-response psychology. Equally interesting and important, and perhaps less widely recognized nowadays, is the fact that individual organisms differ innately with respect to many variables which may determine the responses to certain classes of stimuli. It is perhaps a little unfashionable to stress the importance of innate hereditary factors in behaviour, but the evidence regarding their importance is quite conclusive. We will return to this point in the next Chapter; it is raised here mainly to indicate the direction in which our discussion will be going. For the moment, therefore, let us simply note that the organism is an absolutely essential part of any stimulus-response type of psychology, because it is the organism which intervenes between the stimulus and the response, and organisms differ, both with respect to past reinforcement schedules and also with respect to innate potentiality and other variables.

Assuming, then, for the moment that the concept of personality may have some scientific value, we may go on to search for the main dimensions of personality in the hope that these may be related to different types of neurotic behaviour which we have discussed in the first Chapter. We may also hope that the discovery of these main dimensions of personality will help us in the problem of *nosology*, or classification of neurotic disorders. Classification is an absolutely fundamental part of the scientific study of human personality; a satisfactory typology is as necessary in psychology as was Mendeleyeff's Table of the Elements in physics. This has, of course, always been recognized by psychologists, and almost everyone is acquainted with the famous typological classification into melancholics, cholerics, sanguines, and phlegmatics dating back to Galen and even earlier. As this system still has much to teach us, we will present it here as Figure 2; it immediately confronts us with one of the main problems of classification. The first of these may be phrased in terms of the question:

'Categorical or dimensional?' The famous German philoso-
pher, Immanuel Kant, to whom this system owed much of its
popularity during the last two hundred years, was quite
specific in maintaining the categorical point of view, i.e. the
notion that every person could be assigned to a particular
category; he was a melancholic, or a phlegmatic, or a sanguine,
or a choleric, but any mixtures of admixtures were inadmissible.

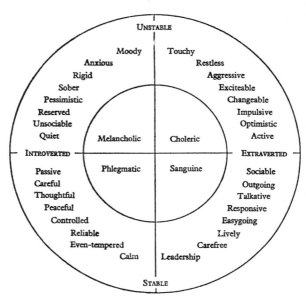

FIG. 2. The inner ring shows the 'four temperaments' of
Hippocrates and Galen; the outer ring shows the results of
modern factor analytic studies of the intercorrelations between traits by Guilford, Cattell, Eysenck and others (Eysenck,
1963b).

This notion of categories is, of course similar to the psychiatric
notion of disease entities and their corresponding diagnoses;
hysteria, anxiety state, paranoia, obsessional illness, and so on
are often treated as categorical entities in this sense.

Opposed to this notion, we have the view that any particular position in this two-dimensional framework is due to a
combination of quantitative variations along the two con-
tinua labelled 'introversion-extraversion' and 'stable-unstable'.

Wundt (1903), who is the most notable proponent of Galen's system in modern times, favoured the dimensional view; he labelled the one axis 'slow-quick' instead of introversion-extraversion, and the other 'strong-weak' instead of unstable and stable.

It may be interesting to quote Wundt's very modern-sounding discussion:—'The ancient differentiation into four temperaments . . . arose from acute psychological observation of individual differences between people . . . The fourfold division can be justified if we agree to postulate two principles in the individual reactivity of the affects: one of them refers to the *strength*, the other to the *speed of change* of a person's feelings. Cholerics and melancholics are inclined to strong affects, while sanguinists and phlegmatics are characterized by weak ones. A high rate of change is found in sanguinists and cholerics, a slow rate in melancholics and phlegmatics.

It is well-known that the strong temperaments . . . are pre-destined towards the *Unluststimmungen*, while the weak ones show a happier ability to enjoy life . . . The two quickly change-able temperaments . . . are more susceptible to the impressions of the present; their mobility makes them respond to each new idea. The two slower temperaments, on the other hand, are more concerned with the future; failing to respond to each chance impression, they take time to pursue their own ideas.' (pp. 637-638).

There is no reason to believe that the notion of the *typology* presupposes a categorical system; both Jung and Kretschmer, who were probably the best-known typologists of the inter-war period, postulated a dimensional rather than a categorical system. The widespread notion that typologies implied discontinuities, bimodal distributions, and the like does not accurately represent the writings and views of modern typologists (Eysenck, 1960c).

Most writers on the subject of personality come down in favour of either the categorical or the dimensional point of view, without basing themselves on any experimental demonstration. It is, however, not impossible to devise experimental and statistical means for verifying the one and falsifying the other hypothesis. Eysenck (1950) has tried to do this in terms of the method of *criterion analysis*, which relies on separate factor analyses of intercorrelations between tests administered to two or more criterion groups (say, normals and psychotics), and a

17

comparison of the factors emerging with the criterion column derived by biserial correlation between the tests and the criterion. The results of this method have, in every instance, supported the doctrine of continuity, and failed to support the doctrine of categorization, even when the latter seemed most firmly entrenched, as in the case of psychosis (Eysenck, 1952).

Assuming for the moment, therefore, the doctrine of dimensionality, we are required to build up, on an experimental and statistical basis, a quantitative system of personality description (Eysenck, Eysenck and Claridge, 1960). The most widely used tool for this purpose is, of course, factor analysis, and the main results of the application of this tool are shown in Figure 2. The outer ring in this Figure shows the results of a large number of factor analytic studies of questionnaires and ratings (Eysenck, 1960c). As is customary in these diagrams, the correlation between any two traits is equal to their scalar product, that is to say, in this case, the cosine of their angle of separation. The closer the two traits are together in the diagram, the higher is the observed correlation between them; the further apart are any two traits in this diagram, the lower is the correlation. If the angle between them exceeds ninety degrees, the correlation becomes negative.

Factor analysis has often been criticized on the grounds that different practitioners achieve different results, and that a method which is unreliable in the sense of failing to produce agreed results cannot be taken very seriously. Whatever may have been true twenty or thirty years ago, there can be no doubt that nowadays there is comparatively little disagreement between investigators in this field. Cattell's most recent book (Cattell and Scheier, 1961) shows him in firm agreement with the above-mentioned system first put forward in 1947 (Eysenck, 1947), and Guilford, too, now appears to recognize the existence of these two main factors in personality description which we have used as the major axes in Figure 2. Vernon (1953, p. 13) also puts forward a similar scheme, and factor analyses of a variety of questionnaires such as the MMPI (Kasselbaum *et al.*, 1959), the Gough California Personality Inventory (Mitchell and Pierce-Jones, 1960; Nicholls and Schnell, 1963) and the Murray List of Needs (Stern, 1962) all result in factors very closely resembling those noted in Figure 2. The agreement present nowadays is indeed impressive, and if failure to agree could be used as a criticism of the method of factor analysis, then the almost universal agreement existing at the present time can perhaps rightly be claimed as strong support for the usefulness of the statistical method in question.

Terms such as extraversion and introversion are used in our discussion in a sense strictly derived from empirical studies such as mentioned above; they should not be taken as having the same meaning here as they do in Jung's discussion. Jung, who is often erroneously credited with originating these terms which had been in use on the continent of Europe for several hundred years before he wrote his famous book on psychological types, has put forward a very complicated scheme of personality description; there would be no point in criticizing his scheme here. We merely wish to point out that our own use of these terms must stand and fall by empirical confirmation, and owes more to the work of factor analysts and early experimentalists like Heymans and Wiersma, than to Jung and his followers (Eysenck, 1960c). A brief description of typical extreme extraverts and introverts may be useful at this point, to show the reader precisely what we mean by these terms.

The typical extravert is sociable, likes parties, has many friends, needs to have people to talk to, and does not like reading or studying by himself. He craves excitement, takes chances, often sticks his neck out, acts on the spur of the moment, and is generally an impulsive individual. He is fond of practical jokes, always has a ready answer, and generally likes change; he is carefree, easygoing, optimistic, and 'likes to laugh and be merry'. He prefers to keep moving and doing things, tends to be aggressive and loses his temper quickly; altogether his feelings are not kept under tight control, and he is not always a reliable person.

The typical introvert is a quiet, retiring sort of person introspective, fond of books rather than people; he is reserved and distant except to intimate friends. He tends to plan ahead, 'looks before he leaps', and mistrusts the impulse of the moment. He does not like excitement, takes matters of everyday life with proper seriousness, and likes a well-ordered mode of life. He keeps his feelings under close control, seldom behaves in an aggressive manner, and does not lose his temper easily. He is reliable, somewhat pessimistic and places great value on ethical standards.

These descriptions, of course, sound almost like caricatures because they describe, as it were, the 'perfect' extravert and the 'perfect' introvert; needless to say, few people closely resemble these extremes, and the majority of people undoubtedly are somewhat in the middle. This does not necessarily detract from the importance of these typological concepts, just as little as the fact that 50 per cent of the total population have I.Qs of between 90 and 110 detracts from the importance of intelligence as a concept in psychology.

It is perhaps less necessary to give a detailed description of the typology implicit in the second major dimension of personality shown in Figure 2. We have there labelled the one end 'unstable'; this has often in the past been called a factor of *emotionality* or of *neuroticism*, and these terms adequately designate its meaning. At the one end we have people whose emotions are labile, strong, and easily aroused; they are moody, touchy, anxious, restless, and so forth. At the other extreme we have the people whose emotions are stable, less easily aroused, people who are calm, even-tempered, carefree, and reliable. Neurotics, needless to say, would be expected to have characteristics typical of the unstable type, normal persons typical of the stable type.

If we accept the principle of continuity, then we should be able to find a place for the major psychiatric classifications of neurotic disorders within our Figure 2. The theory has been put forward that dysthymic neurotics suffering from anxiety, reactive depression, obsessions, phobias, and so on would be found in the 'melancholic' quadrant, while hysterics, psychopaths, and perhaps juvenile delinquents and criminals generally, would be found in the 'choleric' quadrant (Eysenck, 1960c). Descriptively, there seems little doubt about the truth of this hypothesis; it is only necessary to look at the traits characterizing people in these two quadrants to realize that they might almost have been quoted from a psychiatric text-book, rather than being the result of factor analytic studies of normal people. Nevertheless, experimental support would seem to be required. Figure 3 shows the relative positions of different groups of neurotics and criminals, with respect to scores on various questionnaires of extraversion and neuroticism; the scales most frequently used in these studies have been the Maudsley Personality Inventory (Eysenck, 1959d), the Cattell

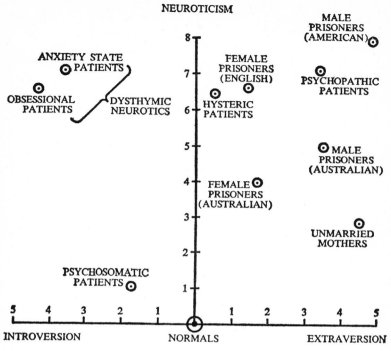

FIG. 3. Position of various neurotic and criminal groups on the two factors of neuroticism and introversion-extraversion (Eysenck, 1964*b*).

Personality Inventory (Cattell, 1957), and the Eysenck Personality Inventory (Eysenck and Eysenck, 1963). To make scores comparable, these have been turned into standard scores before plotting them in Figure 3. It will be seen that indeed, as expected, patients suffering from anxiety, obsessional disorders, phobias, and so on, i.e. patients who have been called dysthymic by Eysenck (1947), do indeed fall into the melancholic quadrant and are strongly introverted, whereas psychopaths and criminals generally tend to fall into the choleric quadrant and be strongly extravert. Hysterics fall in between these two groups and are not significantly differentiated from normals with respect to extraversion-introversion, although they do, of course, have high scores on neuroticism. The position is well illustrated in Figure 4, which shows the results of a factor analysis of

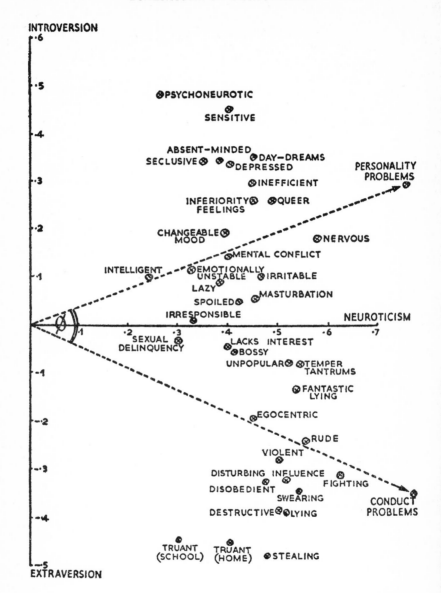

FIG. 4. Results of a factor analysis of various conduct and personality problems shown by children (Eysenck, 1960c).

behaviour patterns observed in large groups of children referred to a child guidance clinic (Eysenck, 1960c). It will be seen that all the notations involved correlate together to define a factor of neuroticism, but that there is also another factor dividing the (introverted) *personality problems* from the (extraverted) *conduct problems*. Extraverted children swear, fight, are disobedient, destructive, play truant, steal, lie, are violent, rude, and egocentric, whereas introverted children are sensitive, absent-minded, depressed, seclusive, inefficient, have inferiority feelings, daydream, and are nervous. This is a very important and fundamental distinction, and is probably more useful in practice than the much more detailed psychiatric diagnostic nomenclature which is notoriously unreliable.

It may be asked just how closely psychiatric diagnosis, when reliably made by experienced psychiatrists, correlates with the results of psychological measurement, using questionnaires of the type described and short objective tests. The answer is given in an experiment carried out by Eysenck and Claridge (1962), who gave six such tests to sixteen normal, sixteen dysthymic, and sixteen hysteric patients. The results were treated by means of multiple discriminant function analysis. The theory we are dealing with predicts that if we carry out such an analysis, it should give us two significant latent roots; further, if we derive variance scores for the forty-eight subjects of our experiment, then these should be situated in a prescribed manner in a two-dimensional plane generated by the two significant variants. To put this prediction in its simplest form, we may say that the mean variance scores for the three groups should lie at the corners of an equilateral triangle. Figure 5 shows the outcome of the experiment. It will be seen that the prediction is verified, and that the first variant discriminates completely between the dysthymics and the hysterics. The second variant, with only slightly overlap, discriminates between the normal group on the one hand, and the neurotic group on the other. Similar success in achieving a 100 per cent agreement between diagnostic test and psychiatric diagnosis attended an earlier experiment by Eysenck, Eysenck and Claridge (1960).

The discrimination between melancholics and cholerics, or, in modern terminology, between dysthymics and psychopaths, obviously corresponds, in some degree, with that made in the

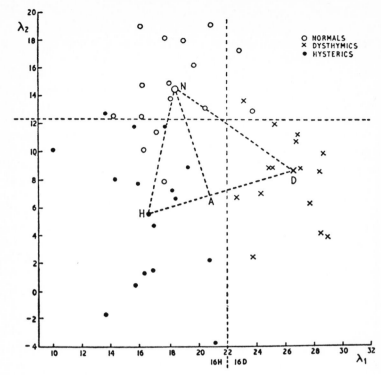

FIG. 5. Position of 16 normal subjects, 16 dysthymic and 16 hysteric patients in a two-dimensional framework generated by a discriminant function analysis of their performance on 6 objective tests (Eysenck and Claridge, 1962).

first Chapter between neurotic *disorders of the first kind*, and neurotic *disorders of the second kind*. Agreement is not quite complete, however; we have postulated that certain types of disorders, such as fetishism, homosexuality, and so forth are disorders of the second kind, yet we would, for reasons which will become apparent in the next Chapter, regard people afflicted with these disorders as being more likely to be introverted than extraverted. To anticipate a little, we may say that in our general system introverts are postulated to condition more easily and, therefore, to acquire the conditioned anxieties and fears characteristic of the dysthymic more easily than other people, whereas psychopaths and prisoners generally are people

24

who condition poorly and who, therefore, fail to acquire the conditioned responses characterizing the socialization process. Fetishists, homosexuals, and so on have acquired conditioned responses which are contrary to the social mores; it is quite likely that it is because they acquire conditioned responses easily that they have fallen prey to these perverted practices, and as introverts are postulated to condition more easily, it seems likely that they must be regarded as introverted. Unfortunately, there is very little empirical evidence regarding the personality traits of people in these groups, and very little can, therefore, be said about them from this point of view.

We have said nothing so far about the psychotic disorders. It is well known that for many psychoanalysts these are but an exteme form of neurotic disorders, and it is postulated that normal, neurotic, and psychotic states form a single continuum of 'regression'. Opposed to this is an alternative and perhaps more orthodox view, according to which neurotic and psychotic disorders differ fundamentally in aetiology, treatment, and prognosis. These two hypotheses are shown diagrammatically in Figures 6 and 7. In Figure 6, the one-dimensional hypothesis is shown, according to which normal, neurotic, and psychotic groups are discriminated only along one single dimension. Figure 7 shows the two-dimensional hypothesis. It is possible to decide between these two hypotheses by means of factor analysis, and examples of this approach are given in the Handbook of Abnormal Psychology (Eysenck, 1960a, f). These results strongly favour the two-dimensional approach; two clear-cut orthogonal factors appear, one having high loadings on all the typical psychotic notations, the other on all the typical neurotic ones. Multiple discriminant function analysis, too, can be used to answer this question. In one such experiment, twenty normal controls, twenty neurotics, and twenty psychotics were tested on four objective laboratory tests (Eysenck, 1955a). Multiple discriminant function analysis disclosed two significant latent roots, thus rendering impossible the assumption that one dimension was sufficient to incorporate the results. Figure 8 shows the actual position of the members of the three groups; the correlation ratio between the three groups and the two variants was 0·84, which indicates a refreshingly high validity for the tests used in predicting these psychiatric criteria. That this figure is not higher still is probably due to lack of reliability

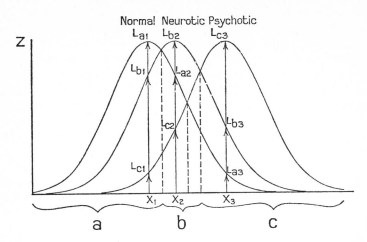

FIG. 6. Diagrammatic representation of the one-dimensional hypothesis of mental abnormality (Eysenck, 1955*a*).

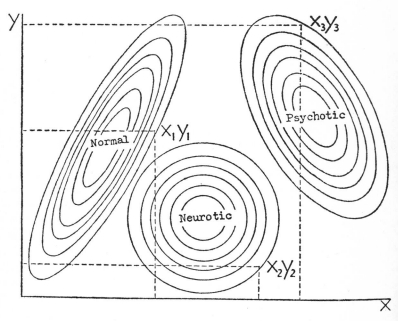

FIG. 7. Diagrammatic representation of the two-dimensional hypothesis of mental abnormality (Eysenck, 1955*a*).

of the criterion. It will be seen in Figure 8 that two of the neurotics, labelled A and B, were grouped with the psychotics by the tests. Both were re-admitted later and diagnosed as psychotic. A similar study was carried out by S. B. G. Eysenck (1956), using a much larger population of subjects and a greater variety of tests; her results were similar to those just mentioned. It is interesting to note that cultural differences do

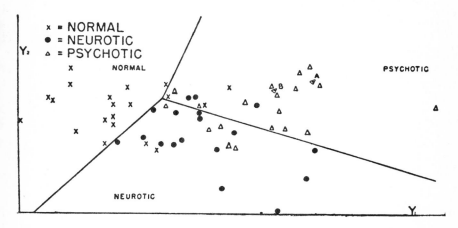

FIG. 8. Distribution of 20 normal subjects, 20 neurotic and 20 psychotic patients in a two-dimensional framework generated by discriminant function analysis of objective test performance (Eysenck, 1955a)

not seem to affect the applicability of methods or conclusions to any considerable extent; Devadasan (1963) has duplicated many of the details of S. B. G. Eysenck's study on an Indian population in Kerala (Trivandrum) with almost identical results.

There are, of course, other ways in which theories of this type can be tested. One of these is the genetic method. If it is true that psychotic and neurotic disorders are orthogonal to each other, then we would expect that the children of psychotic parents should not show any greater degree of neuroticism than would the children of normal parents. This very interesting hypothesis was tested by Valerie Cowie (1961), and her results leave no doubt that the genetic implication of neuroticism in the children of psychotic parents is non-existent; if anything, they tended to be less neurotic. This finding may also serve as a warning to those who would overstress the impoitance of environment in giving rise to neurotic disorders; it is difficult to imagine a more servere stress to a child than having psychotic parents. All these studies, then, are in good agreement in stressing the complete separation between psychotic and neurotic disorders.

We can now summarize the main results of the discussion by saying that there are two main factors or dimensions which between them account for a good part of the non-cognitive aspect of personality. These two factors may be labelled extraversion-introversion, and neuroticism or emotionality as opposed to stability or normality. Psychotic behaviour trends are orthogonal to these dimensions and they may, therefore, be left out of account in a discussion of neurotic behaviour. Dysthymic neurotics, i.e. those exemplifying neuroses of the first kind, are found largely in the 'melancholic' quadrant, i.e. are both high on neuroticism and high on introversion. Psychopaths, criminals, and others exemplifying neuroses of the second kind tend to be high on extraversion as well as on neuroticism, with certain possible exceptions which were mentioned in the text. Hysteric patients tends to be inter-mediate between the dysthymic and the psychopathic groups, with introversion-extraversion scores on questionnaires which are not very much different from those of normals. On objec-tive tests, however, as shown in Figure 5, hysterics tend defi-nitely to group themselves on the extraverted side. For the purpose of the discussion, therefore, we shall henceforth treat them as extraverts, which is permissible perhaps also in view of the fact that, as compared with the dysthymic groups, they are always significantly more extraverted on questionnaires.

Chapter 3

THE BIOLOGICAL BASIS OF PERSONALITY

BEHAVIOUR of human beings is determined by biological as well as by social factors. It is notable that during the last twenty or thirty years, the attention of clinical psychologists has been largely attracted by social factors, to the virtual exclusion of biological ones. This is unfortunate, because any tendency to over-stress one aspect of human personality must lead to a disregard for important and relevant factors. It is not the purpose of the book to deny the importance of social factors and to over-stress in turn the influence of biological ones; what we are trying to do in this Chapter is to adduce some evidence to show that biological factors are indeed important and should not be dismissed out of hand in a discussion of the causes and cures of neurosis; it will become apparent that only by using these factors appropriately will it be possible to work out a proper scheme of treatment which shall be less one-sided and perhaps more successful than those currently in favour.

Any proof for the existence of a biological basis of personality must begin with a discussion of the influence of hereditary factors. Most of the work done in this field has, of course, made use of the convenient appearance of certain types of twins (identical or monozygotic twins) who share completely identical heredity, and whose similarities and dissimilarities may be compared with those appearing in fraternal or dizygotic twins, i.e. twins who share heredity only to the extent of 50 per cent, which is, of course, not different from that shown by ordinary siblings. The notion underlying all work with twins may be simply put in the following way. If individual differences in a particular trait or ability are due entirely to environmental causes, then the fact that identical twins show more common heredity than do fraternal ones will not affect degree of similarity or dissimilarity between twins, and consequently identical twins will be no more alike with respect to this trait or ability than will fraternal twins. If, on the other hand, heredity plays a part in producing individual differences in this trait or ability, then identical twins will be more alike than fraternal ones. The early studies of Eysenck and Prell (1951) and Eysenck (1956), using objective tests as well as questionnaires, showed that identical twins were much more alike, both with respect to neuroticism and with respect to introversion, than were fraternal twins, and it was argued that the degree of heredity of these personality traits was probably not far different from that shown by abilities such as intelligence. Later work by Wilde (1962) and Gottesman (1963) supported this view, as did work along rather different lines of familial descent by Lienert and Reisse (1961). No systematic review will be made of all the studies carried out in this field, because the results tend to be rather similar. We will note, however, certain objections which have been made to work with twins. In particular, it has been suggested that identical twins may perhaps be treated more alike, because of their greater similarity, than will be fraternal twins whose lack of outward similarity may lead to their being treated rather differently. Thus, there may be a kind of interaction effect which may falsely suggest the greater hereditary determination of personality variables in identical twins as compared with fraternal twins.

This objection is conclusively answered in a recent study by Shields (1962). He administered two intelligence tests, a non-verbal test and a vocabulary test, as well as questionnaires of extraversion and neuroticism, to twenty-eight pairs of dizygotic twins as well as forty-four pairs of monozygotic twins brought up apart (the S group) and the same number of monozygotic twins brought up together (the C group), obtained from the same source—mostly volunteers responding to an appeal made on television and matched for sex and age. Table 2 shows the intra-class correlation coefficients for these various groups on the tests. It will be seen that not only are the monozygotic twins much more alike than the dizygotic ones, but it will also be seen that the monozygotic twins brought up separately are if anything more alike than are the monozygotic twins brought up together. It is perhaps unlikely that this difference between twins brought up separately and twins brought up together would be duplicated in a second investigation, and we would not stress it unduly, except to point out that there is here no evidence at all for any influence of environment in making identical twins more alike than fraternal twins. Identical twins, whether brought up separately or brought up together, come out as decisively more alike than fraternal twins brought up together; this finding would seem to be conclusive in suggesting the great importance of hereditary variables in determining individual differences with respect to extraversion, neuroticism, and intelligence.[1]

TABLE 2

Intraclass correlations of monozygotic twins brought up together and separately, and of dizygotic twins. (From Shields, 1962)

	C	S	DZ
Intelligence	+0·76	+0·77	+0·51
Extraversion	+0·42	+0·61	−0·17
Neuroticism	+0·38	+0·53	+0·11

The fact that both extraversion and neuroticism apparently have a strong hereditary component suggests a search for the physiological or neurological substratum for this component. We may conveniently begin with the search for such a component in the field of neuroticism, because a candidate for this position can be readily identified, and because for many years psychiatrists have indeed recognized the relevance of the autonomic system, particularly the sympathetic part, to the behaviour of neurotics. Putting it formally, we might perhaps postulate that the behaviour of neurotics and, quite generally, people who have high scores on neuroticism, is causally related to an excessive lability of their autonomic nervous system. More precisely, we may postulate that some people are innately

[1] The greater concordance of identical twins with respect to criminal behaviour has been documented many times; a detailed discussion will be found in Eysenck's (1964) book on 'Crime and Personality'. There appears to be strong evidence for the appearance of a hereditary factor in predisposition to crime.

predisposed to respond more strongly, more lastingly, and more quickly with their autonomic system to strong, painful or sudden stimuli impinging upon the sense organs. A detailed discussion of this hypothesis has been given by Eysenck (1960c), and we will not enter into the complex physiological arguments surrounding this area. It will, however, be necessary to discuss one very important qualification which concerns the so-called law of autonomic response stereotypy or response specificity (Lacey, 1950; Lacey et al., 1952, 1958). Lacey recorded a number of different autonomic responses to a variety of stimuli and found that his subjects responded 'with a hierarchy of activation, being relatively over-active in some physiological measures, under-active in others, while exhibiting average reactivity in still other measures. These patterns of response seem to be idiosyncratic, each subject's pattern is different. For a single stressor patterns of response have been shown to be reproducible, both upon immediate re-test and over a period of nine months. Moreover, the pattern of response obtained with one stimulus condition tends to be reproduced in other, quite different stimulus conditions.' Lacey stated his findings in the form of a general principle, which reads as follows: 'For a given set of autonomic functions subjects tend to respond with an idiosyncratic pattern of autonomic reactivation in which maximum activation is shown by the same physiological function, whatever the stress.' Lacey also postulated and found 'that continuous quantitative variation exists in the degree to which they exhibit stereotypy (reproducibility) of their pattern of response.' Similar findings have been reported by Malmo et al. (1950) and also by Sainsbury and Gibson (1950) with respect to the specificity of electromyographic responses. There seems to be no doubt that a considerable degree of response specificity exists in this field.

However, we also have the work of Wenger (1948) and others, showing that moderate but positive correlations exist between response strength of the autonomic system in its various parts to different types of stimuli. We may perhaps try to bring all these findings together by saying that there is some evidence for an exaggerated lability of the autonomic system as a whole, in some people, but that this lability is shown more particularly in one or other of the many parts of the autonomic rather than by the system as a whole. This is an important conclusion, because it may be in part responsible for the different types of symptoms developed by different people. Persons who, on being stressed, show marked contraction of the frontalis muscle have been found to react with headaches to psychological stresses, whereas persons reacting with contraction of the back muscles will tend to show backache under conditions of neurotic breakdown. Similarly, specific autonomic reaction on the part of the heart or some other organ to experimental stress may be strongly related to a tendency on the part of that person to react with over-activity of the same organ to neurotic stress and breakdown. However that may be, we think that there is ample evidence to implicate the autonomic system as a whole and, in particular, the sympathetic branch of the autonomic system in the personality trait labelled neuroticism or emotionality, and we shall use this hypothesis in the rest of this book for making a variety of predictions. It should be noted, however, that such an implication is not necessary or essential for the empirical success of the method of treatment suggested; if the hypothesis should be shown to be faulty this would not necessarily disprove the effectiveness of the types of treatment we have suggested below.

Whereas the position is rather simple and straightforward with respect to neuroticism, it is rather more complex and confused in the case of extraversion-introversion. The theory here adopted was first put forward by Eysenck (1957), who suggested that cortical processes of 'excitation' were more readily elicited in introverts, whereas cortical processes of 'inhibition' were more readily elicited in extraverts. The theory thus postulates the existence of two processes entitled 'inhibition' and 'excitation'. The first writer to use these terms and concepts in roughly the way here intended was, of course, Pavlov (1927). Among those who have clarified their meaning and added experimental content, Hull (1943) must be particularly singled out. Many other writers from Dodge (1931) to Teplov (1959) have contributed to the gradual clarification of these notions, but it would not be correct to say that any agreed and unambiguous definition of these terms would be possible even now. By and large, 'excitation' refers to the arousal of the cortex and the general facilitation of processes of learning, remembering and performing. Inhibition, in its broadest of meaning, refers to a process within the central nervous system which interferes with the ongoing perceptual, congnitive and motor activities of the organism.[1] The type of interference intended can best be clarified by reference to the two main types of inhibition which may be called *temporal inhibition* and *spatial inhibition*. Temporal inhibition refers to the accumulation of a performance decrement as a result of the performance itself; it is usually associated with massed practice and can be elicited experimentally in those situations giving rise to what Pavlov has called 'internal inhibition', and Hull, 'reactive' inhibition. Spatial inhibition refers to the production of the performance decrement through some other form of action occurring simultaneously, or almost simultaneously; it is sometimes called 'distraction' in common parlance, and is similar to Pavlov's notion of 'external inhibition'. The terminology here suggested is preferred to that of Pavlov or of Hull because these authors have given to their own terms excess meaning by incorporating them in a wider theoretical system, so that the use of Hullian or Pavlovian terms might seem to imply acceptance of that system as a whole.

The postulated process of 'inhibition' may be illustrated by means of certain experimental paradigms. One phenomenon, for instance, which would appear to demand an explanation in terms of inhibition is that of *vigilance*, or rather the decline of vigilance. Whenever a long-continued and monotonous visual or auditory task is being carried out, such as a continued inspection of a series of dials, one of which may occasionally indicate danger, or the continued listening to a series of numbers, one of which may require occasionally some action to be performed, then it is usually found that performance is only perfect or near perfect at the beginning of the experiment and declines after a while to an altogether lower level. This decline in vigilance may be supposed to be due to temporal inhibition, and the recovery after rest may be considered analogous to 'reminiscence'.

Another phenomenon which may be relevant is that of adaptation. Whenever a stimulus is presented to an organism, certain non-specific reactions occur, such as the orienting reflex (Berlyne, 1960; Razran, 1961a), changes in the electrical conductivity of the skin (Martin, 1960a), and various other auto-

[1]One important activity of the cortex is the inhibition of sub-cortical centres (Diamond *et al.*, 1963). Inhibition of the cortex therefore *disinhibits* subcortical centres.

nomic reactions. On repetition, particularly on rapid (massed) repetition of the stimulus, these reactions grow less strong and may in time die out completely. While peripheral events may play some part in this process of adaptation, there is no doubt that central factors are involved also, and it is the involvement of these which may make the series of phenomena relevant to the notion of temporal inhibition.

With respect to spatial inhibition we may perhaps refer to the well-known process called 'extinction' by Bender (1952), which he defines as a 'process in which the sensation disappears or the stimulus becomes imperceptible when another sensation is evoked by simultaneous stimulation elsewhere in the sensory field.' Bender's own work and that of the authors quoted by him is rather poorly controlled and of an all-or-none character, but the more recent studies of Uttal (1960) and Ingham (1959) show that corresponding phenomena can be obtained in well-controlled and properly quantified experiments.

As mentioned before, Eysenck (1957) has postulated that there is a close relationship between the personality dimension of extraversion-introversion and the processes of excitation and inhibition, in the sense that high degree of extraversion are found in people in whom inhibitory processes occur quickly, strongly, and persistently, and in whom excitatory processes occur slowly, weakly, and non-persistently; high degrees of introversion are found in people of whom the reverse is true. Clearly, this hypothesis lends itself very easily to experimental proof, and all that is required is the performance of experiments in which extraverted and introverted people, as diagnosed by means of ratings or questionnaire responses, are contrasted with respect to their performance on experimental tests of vigilance, reminiscence, extinction, and so forth. There is now a considerable literature on this summarized in books by Eysenck (1957, 1960d, 1963a) and it cannot be the purpose of this book to go into this question in any detail. Suffice it to say that many investigations have found very significant support for the theory in question, although, of course, the support has fallen far short of being complete and one hundred per cent. The evidence, however, is sufficient by now to suggest that essentially the hypothesis outlined above may be along the right lines and that, tentatively at least, it may be accepted as reasonable and tenable. (Cf. Table 3, below.)

Of all the predictions made and tested, one stands out as being particularly important in relation to the general system of theories, hypotheses, and deductions with which we are here concerned. Our theory predicts that introverts would form conditioned responses more quickly, more strongly, and more lastingly than would extraverted people; this follows both from the attribution of higher excitation to introverts

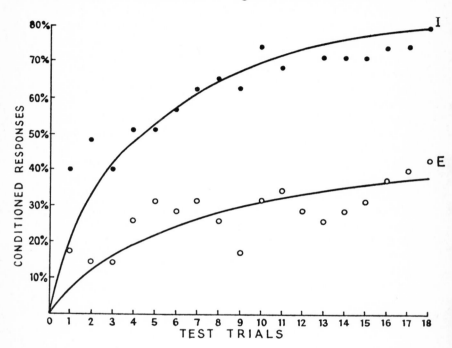

FIG. 9. Eye-blink conditioning performance of introverted and extraverted groups of subjects, showing the superior performance of the introverted group (Eysenck, 1962a).

and of the attribution of greater inhibition to extraverts. A detailed discussion of this particular prediction has been given by Eysenck (1962a), who outlines several of the possible ways mediating the prediction. He also gives a Figure which summarizes the researches done by Cyril Franks (1956, 1957) on normal and neurotic subjects. His results have been reproduced here as Figure 9; neurotic and normal subjects have been combined, as there were no noticeable differences between them. It will be seen that on the eye-blink conditioning test which Franks used, the introverted group shows, at all stages, approximately twice as many conditioned responses as does the extraverted group. There are thirty-five extraverted and thirty-five introverted subjects who took part in these experiments, and the results clearly, and at a very high level of statistical significance, support the hypothesis. Barendregt, (1961) following Franks, found a correlation of ·29 between eye-blink conditioning and introversion, and Kerenyi (1959) and Shagass and Kerenyi (1958) report correlations between eye-blink conditioning and extraversion (Guilford's R scale) of —,36, introversion (Guilford's S scale) of ·34, and the Taylor MAS of ·12.

Brebner (1957) and Symon (1958), using extreme groups of introverts and extraverts, both duplicated Franks's original results on eyeblink conditioning, finding introverts to condition twice as strongly as extraverts. Franks and Leigh (1959) found a correlation of —·26 between eyeblink conditioning and extraversion. Three investigators (Das, 1957; Field and Brengelmann, 1961; Willett, 1960b) only succeeded in finding low negative correlations between eyeblink conditioning and extraversion; it is notable, however, that in these studies the population of subjects used was in each case such as to make the application of the questionnaire used doubtful. Das used a mixed white and coloured group, with his coloured subjects coming from quite a different cultural background; Field and Brengelmann used prisoners, for whom the many sociability questions used in extraversion inventories must be largely meaningless; Willett used adolescents below the age for which the questionnaire used was designed. Sweetbaum (1963), Farber, Bechtoldt and Spence (1957), and Spence and Spence (1964) failed to find correlations with extraversion on the eyeblink conditioning test, while Al-Issa (1961, 1964) obtained significant results only in one of three conditions. These apparently contradictory results can be clarified when we realize that Eysenck's original hypothesis specifies that the inferiority of extraverts on conditioning tests is due to reactive inhibition accumulating more speedily and strongly in them than in introverts; hence the conditions of the test must be so arranged as to facilitate the occurrence of inhibition. One way of achieving this is the use of *partial reinforcement* (Eysenck, 1957), and a survey of the studies mentioned above will demonstrate that positive results have nearly always been achieved with this form of reinforcement, while experiments using complete (100%) reinforcement have usually failed to show significant negative correlation between extraversion and conditioning. Other means of producing reactive inhibition might of course be employed, such as the massing of trials, or discrimination conditioning, but these have not to date been used. From the clinical point of view it may perhaps be stated that experiments using partial reinforcement are much more likely to resemble life situations which might give rise to the formation of conditioned neurotic 'symptoms', or to the elaboration of a 'conscience'; such life situations are extremely unlikely to provide reinforcement every time the conditioned stimulus is applied!

When we turn to GSR conditioning, we find again that positive results predominate; Franks (1956), Lykken (1957), Vogel (1960, 1961), and Halberstam (1961) have provided very convincing evidence of a negative correlation of considerable size between extraversion and conditioning. Others, such as Becker (1960), Martin (1960b), Becker and Matteson (1961), and Davidson, Payne and Sloane (1964) have failed to find a significant relationship. Again it is possible to specify the reasons for this apparent discrepancy. Successful experiments have on the whole combined conditions likely to produce reactive inhibition, such as partial reinforcement and discrimination conditioning, with unconditioned stimuli which were not so strong as to produce vehement arousal, thus raising excitatory potential and making impossible the accumulation of inhibition. In testing the inhibition theory of extraversion in the field of conditioning it is of the utmost importance to specify clearly the experimental parameters required; it is fatally easy to set up experiments which fail to give rise to inhibitory potentials, and thus do not in fact provide any relevant evidence for the theory in question.

It is interesting that a similar position has arisen with respect to another theory also linking personality and conditioning. Spence (1956) and Taylor (1956) have argued that eyeblink conditioning should be stronger in persons high on neuroticism, as this personality variable would act as a drive; in terms of Hull's theory drive multiplies with habit to produce performance, and the performance measured in the test should therefore be superior in subjects high on neuroticism (or anxiety, as Spence and Taylor prefer to call it). Here also there are many studies in favour of the hypothesis, but also some which contradict it (King *et al.*, 1961; Hilgard *et al.*, 1951). Spence (1964) has argued that positive results can only be expected when conditions of administration are emotion-arousing, and his survey suggests that this generalization does indeed account for the observed facts. Thus Spence's hypothesis of a positive correlation between neuroticism and conditioning requires a set-up in which there is some arousal of the sympathetic system, just as Eysenck's hypothesis of a negative correlation between extraversion and conditioning requires a set-up in which there is some arousal of reactive inhibition. When conditions are arranged in such a way as to arouse neither emotion nor inhibition, conditioning would not be expected to (and apparently does not in fact) correlate with either neuroticism or extraversion.

Our interest in this relationship between personality and conditioning stems fundamentally from a very simple consideration. As pointed out before, we have postulated that disorders of the first kind, i.e. the dysthymic disorders, are essentially due to a process of conditioning, whereas disorders of the second kind, i.e. the psychopathic and criminal types of reaction, are essentially due to a failure of conditioning to occur. It is, of course, possible to take a purely social or a purely biological point of view and to argue as follows. From a social point of view, it might be said that the failure of the one group to condition and the ready conditioning of the other group are both due to differences in reinforcement schedules presented to the individual by society. To put it in a slightly different way, the dysthymic forms conditioned anxiety responses, phobic and obsessional responses because, in his particular history, there have occurred certain events which have reinforced and conditioned these reactions, while similar events have not occurred in the past history of other people. Similarly, a person develops psychopathic or criminal tendencies because there has been a failure in his environment of suitable reinforcements to occur for law-abiding and moral types of conduct. There is undoubtedly some truth in the hypothesis of this kind, but it clearly does not account very well for many of the facts. Thus, one person may suffer neurotic breakdown under conditions which are much less stressful than those under which other people survive without a breakdown. Similarly, it has often been found among siblings that one becomes a criminal, the other one a law-abiding citizen, although the conditions of upbringing are very similar indeed. It is, of course, always open to the protagonist of the social point of view to postulate very fine and undiscoverable differences between one type of upbringing and another, but as long as these cannot in fact be specified and experimented upon, this is clearly not a very useful type of explanation. A theory which is not, in principle, falsifiable by empirical means is not a scientific theory (Popper, 1948, 1963). The biological view might be stated in the following way. Reinforcing events occur more or less at random in the histories of the people who constitute the population of a particular country. Those who are biologically predisposed to form conditioned responses quickly, strongly and lastingly will easily develop dysthymic disorders because these are by hypothesis simply conditioned autonomic reactions. On the other hand, those who are biologically predisposed to form conditioned responses only weakly, poorly, and with great difficulty will fail to form very readily those conditioned responses which underlie the process of socialization. They will, therefore, show conduct characterized as psychopathic or criminal.

Clearly, neither hypothesis in its extreme form is tenable. It is undoubtedly an exaggeration to say that reinforcing events are distributed at random over the population; simple consideration of the sociological evidence relating to the differences in upringing between different classes is sufficient to show that this is not so. We would, therefore, be quite willing to admit the importance of differences in social reinforcement situations in producing different types of conduct; but we would also stress the importance of biological factors such as the degree of conditionability of the individual. We would postulate that both social and biological differences are essential to account for the observed phenomena. We do not believe it is necessary to make a choice between these two hypotheses, but would regard them both as necessary to account for the facts.

The general nature of our theory reconciling the social and the biological aspects of personality can perhaps best be seen from Figure 10, which shows, in diagrammatic form, the

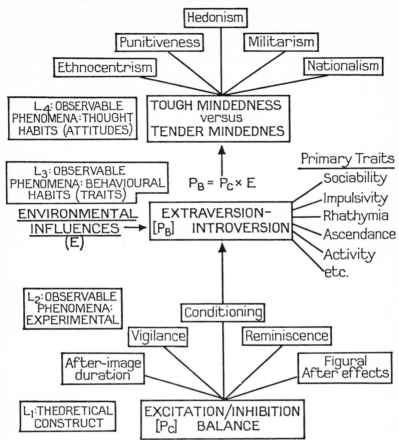

FIG. 10. Diagrammatic picture of the interaction between genetic and environmental influences giving rise to phenotypic behaviour patterns. For explanation see text. (Eysenck, 1960e.)

various levels assumed to be causally related to one another (Eysenck, 1960e). At the most fundamental level, we have the concept of the excitation/inhibition balance; we will try and show in the next Chapter that these concepts have a physiological basis, but for the time being they are simply to be regarded as hypothetical constructs or intervening variables in a system of postulates and theorems which mediate and explain a large number of experimentally well-authenticated phenomena.

Some of these phenomena have been listed at the second level (L_2). Thus, conditioning, vigilance, reminiscence, after-image duration, figural after-effect, and many other experimental phenomena are causally related to the excitation-inhibition balance. The number of experimental phenomena which could be listed at this level is very large indeed, and those given in Figure 10 are only a few selected examples. For the interest of the reader, we have listed a few more in Table 3.

TABLE 3

Experimental studies of introversion-extraversion

Variables	Introversion	Extraversion	Reference
Neurotic syndrome	Dysthymia	Hysteria: psychopathy	Eysenck (1947)
Body build:	Leptomorph	Eurymorph	Eysenck (1947)
Intellectual function	Low I.Q.— vocabulary ratio	High I.Q.— vocabulary ratio	Himmelweit (1945) Foulds (1956)
Perceptual rigidity	High	Low	Canestrari (1957)
Persistence:	High	Low	Eysenck (1947)
Speed:	Low	High	Foulds (1953)
Speed/accuracy ratio:	Low	High	Himmelweit (1946)
Level of aspiration:	High	Low	Himmelweit (1947) Miller (1951)
Intra-personal variability:	Low	High	Eysenck (1947)
Sociability:	Low	High	Eysenck (1957)
Repression:	Weak	Strong	Eriksen (1954)
Social attitudes:	Tender-minded	Tough-minded	Eysenck (1954)
Rorschach test	High M%	High D	Eysenck (1956)
T.A.T.:	Low productivity	High productivity	Foulds (1953)
Conditioning:	Strong	Weak	Franks (1956, 1957)
Reminiscence:	Low	High	Eysenck (1962b)
Figural after-effects:	Small	Large	Eysenck (1955b)
Stress reactions:	Overactive	Inert	Davis (1948) Venables (1955)
Sedation threshold:	High	Low	Shagass (1956)
Perceptual constancy:	Low	High	Ardis et al. (1957)
Time judgment:	Longer	Shorter	Claridge (1960) Eysenck (1959)
Verbal conditioning:	Good	Poor	Eysenck (1959b) Sarason (1958)

Variables	Introversion	Extraversion	Reference
Response to therapy:	Good	Poor	Foulds (1959)
Visual imagery:	Vivid	Weak	Costello (1957)
Necker cube reversal:	Slow	Fast	Costello (1957)
Perception of vertical:	Accurate	Inaccurate	Taft & Coventry (1958)
Spiral after-effect:	Long	Short	Claridge (1960) Willett (1960c)
Time error:	Small	Great	Claridge (1960)
Vigilance:	High	Low	Claridge (1960) Bakan (1957)
Motor performance decrement:	Little	Much	Ray (1959)
Problem solving; performance decrement:	Little	Much	Eysenck (1959e)
Smoking:	No	Yes	Eysenck, Tarrant & England (1960) Eysenck, Claridge & Eysenck (1960)
Car-driving constancy:	High	Low	Venables (1955)
Cheating:	No	Yes	Keehn (1956)

So far we have been dealing with what is called P_C in the diagram, i.e. the constitutional aspects of personality. We now turn to the third level, to wit, that of behavioural habits or traits, and to P_B, i.e. behavioural personality. As is shown in the formula there, $P_B = P_B \times E$; that is to say, behavioural personality is a product of constitutional personality and environmental influence. It is at this level that the social and the biological determinants of behaviour meet and produce the observable phenotypic behaviour patterns of sociability, impulsiveness, ascendance, and so forth.

The diagram extends this theory to a further level, namely that of thought habits or attitudes. The tough-minded attitudes of the extravert and the tender-minded attitudes of the introvert, just like their behavioural habits, grow out of the interaction between environmental influences and biological predetermining factors; this aspect of the theory has been discussed in The Psychology of Politics (Eysenck, 1954) and will not be dealt with again here, as this level is probably less relevant to the concept of neurosis than are the phenomena dealt with at level three.

A consideration of the joint influence of constitutional and environmental factors on the observable personality pattern suggests that observed correlations between experimental tests taken from Level Two, and personality traits taken from Level Three would not be very high, unless corrected by partialing out environmental influences or using some convenient numerical estimate of the environmental variable. This prediction is reinforced by consideration of the probable lack of reliability of individual test scores on experimental measures of conditioning, reminiscence, and so forth, and the also far from perfect reliability of personality measures at Level Three. In fact, correlations usually run between ·2 and ·4, with only very few correlations going up to ·6; it is not infrequent to find correlations below ·2. It is very rare indeed, however, to find that the direction of the correlations obtained is contrary to prediction.

Our formula is rather static and applies to the fully developed personality; it will be clear that in our conception, childhood and adolescence are the primary periods where E interacts with P_C. It is commonplace to regard this as a period of growth in which socialization takes place; there are still to be found psychologists who argue that the essential process takes place in 'the first five years', while others would extend this period until considerably later. The baby and the very young child are clearly completely 'extraverted' in the sense of lacking all internal barriers to immediate satisfaction of impulses, and the growth of introversion and socialization is a rather gradual one. If this notion be accepted, then it should be possible to derive some kind of 'personality quotient' by analogy with the I.Q.; this would then make it possible (as it is not at present) to compare children of different ages with respect to personality.

Our formula does not only apply to introversion-extraversion of course, but equally well to the concept of neuroticism and indeed also to that of intelligence. Our terms P_B and P_C correspond for instance to Hebb's notions of Intelligence A and Intelligence B. Altogether, of course, this distinction between genotypic and phenotypic conceptions is very much central to modern biology, and in principle is a distinction which cannot be by-passed by any serious personality theorists.

It is interesting to note that a leading Russian psychologist in the personality field has arrived at a somewhat similar formulation to ours. Teplov (1957, p. 155) has this to say. 'On peut considérer comme démontré le fait que chez les animaux les tableaux typiques du comportement ne sont pas des indices directs des propriétés typologiques du systéme nerveux. Ces propriétés ne peuvent ètre connues avec précision qu'à l'aide de procédés expérimentaux spéciaux. Chex l'homme, les propriétés typologiques du systéme nerveux se manifestent moins directement encore dans le comportement, le caractére ou les traits de la personnalité; l'influence de l'éducation sur la formation des traits de la personnalité chez l'homme est trés grande; il y a là une différence qualitative d'avec ce qui se passe chez l'animal lors de la formation des modes de comportement typiques.' There are many other similarities between the work of Teplov and that of Eysenck; many of these are brought out in the recent summary of Teplov's work by Gray (1964).

Chapter 4

DRIVE, DRUGS AND PERSONALITY

IN the last Chapter, we have stressed the biological determination of certain aspects of behaviour, and, in particular, in relation to introversion-extraversion, we have concentrated on such hypothetical constructs or intervening variables as excitation and inhibition. Is it possible to go a little further still and identify some actually recognizable physical structures in the brain as, in turn, underlying these variables? Eysenck (1963*b*) has suggested the possibility that different parts of the so-called reticular formation may be in part responsible for the phenomena of excitation and inhibition, and a brief presentation of this theory will now be given.

The reticular formation can be regarded as a pathway for the conduction of impulses, additional to the classical long afferent and efferent pathways. Peripheral stimulation of the neural pathways causes impulses to be sent via the direct route along the long sensory tracts to the appropriate cortical projection area; at the same time, impulses are sent through collaterals from the long sensory tracts into the brain stem reticular formation, through which they are transmitted and eventually also projected to the cortex. Impulses arriving at the cortex from the reticular formation are not necessarily confined to the specific sensory projection area, as are those arriving from the long afferent tracts. If the stimulus is of such a nature as to give rise to generalized alerting responses, widespread projection of impulses from the reticular formation is produced when the latter is subjected to bombardment via the sensory collaterals (Figure 11).

Impulses travelling through the reticular formation appear

46

CORTEX

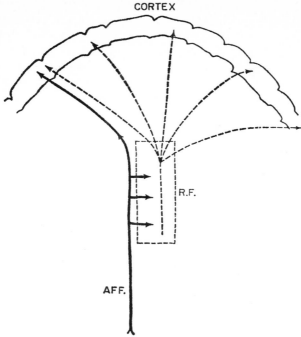

R.F.

AFF.

FIG. 11. Diagrammatic picture of the reticular formation (R.F.), receiving impulses from collaterals of the major afferent pathways and sending impulses to various part of the cortex (Eysenck, 1963a).

to be concerned mainly with facilitatory or suppressor efforts capable of modulating the transmission of impulses through other centres including reflex centres, the 'relay stations' related to the long classical pathways, and the cortical integrating mechanisms. These facilitatory and suppressor influences may be of a general tonic kind, or of a more specific, discrete and phasic nature. A diagrammatic representation of the reticular formation is given in Figure 12. It shows the brain stem reticular formation which gives rise to facilitatory impulses of a non-specific kind arising from areas of the medulla, pons, and mid-brain; these are directed upwards through the diencephalic reticular formation. These activating impulses arising from the brain stem are of a tonic kind, whereas impulses arising due to stimulation of the thalamic reticular

47

formation within the diencephalon give rise to a phasic activation. Also lying in the reticular formation are synchronizing elements, particularly within the medulla, pons, and recruiting system of the thalamic reticular formation, which give rise to impulses directed at the cortex *antagonistic* in effect to the influence of the activating system. It is our belief that the impulses arising from the activating system are at the basis

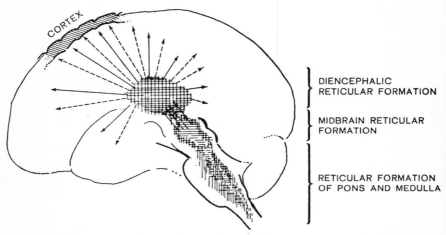

DIENCEPHALIC
RETICULAR FORMATION

MIDBRAIN RETICULAR
FORMATION

RETICULAR FORMATION
OF PONS AND MEDULLA

Fig. 12. Position of the reticular formation and its various parts in relation to the brain (Eysenck, 1963*a*).

of what we have called 'excitation', whereas the impulses arising from the synchronizing and recruiting systems are at the basis of what we have called 'inhibition'. A detailed discussion of this hypothesis has been given by Gooch (in Eysenck, 1963*a*), whose account we have followed in some detail.

In trying to clarify the differential uses of the terms excitation and inhibition by physiologists and psychologists, Gooch points out that 'the words "excitation" and "inhibition" as applied by the psychologist are hypothetical constructs and must not be confused with the same words as used in a technical sense by the neurophysiologist. The neurophysiologist uses "excitability" to describe a definite property of a single neurone. The word "excitation" is used by the physiologist in a related sense, when speaking of the influence of a stimulus on a single neurone or small groups of neurones. The word "inhibition" is used to describe the lowering of the level of excitability which occurs in a single neurone or group of neurones under certain circumstances (e.g. the inhibitory influence of the Renshaw cell on the spinal cord motor neurone). However, when describing the functional activity of a large number of neurones composed of both neurones having an "inhibitory" influence and an "excitatory" influence interacting in a complex fashion, the physiological terms "excitation" and "inhibition" as applied to units become meaningless, so that when speaking about molar activity the physiologist tends to apply the words "facilitation" and "suppression" in regard to the gross influence of one part of the nervous system on another.'

These physiological terms, facilitation and suppression, are nearest in meaning to our use of the terms excitation and inhibition.

It is difficult to prove or disprove a very general hypothesis of this kind linking complex behaviour patterns like extraversion and introversion with the respective dominance of different parts of a physiological structure such as the reticular formation. Nevertheless, it is possible to derive deductions from such a theory which are susceptible to experimental test, and some of these deductions are of considerable importance and relevance to our later treatment of the mechanisms of causation of the neuroses and also certain methods of treatment. There is a good deal of evidence to suggest that the Central Nervous System stimulant and depressant drugs such as amphetamine and caffeine, on the one hand, and the barbiturates and hypnotics, on the other, act through the reticular formation (Bradley, 1958), and the hypothesis has been advanced by Eysenck (1957) that central nervous system stimulant drugs have an introverting effect and increase 'excitation', whereas the central nervous system depressant drugs shift personality and behaviour patterns in the direction of greater extraversion, and increase 'inhibition'. A great deal of supporting evidence has been produced and discussed in 'Experiments with Drugs' (Eysenck, 1963a), and this is not the place to attempt an assessment of the status of this particular theory. Let us merely note that, on the whole, there is considerable evidence that the following equation gives rise to testable and verifiable predictions:

$$E \div I = D \div S;$$

49

i.e. on experimental tests relevant to the excitation-inhibition hypothesis, extraverted people when compared with introverted people score in the same way as people administered a depressant drug when compared with people administered a stimulant drug. To quote just one example, we may note Figure 13, which shows the influence of a depressant and a stimulant drug as compared with a placebo condition on a test of eye-blink conditioning; it will be seen that the stimulant drug facilitates conditioning, whereas the depressant drug suppresses it. (These results may be compared with Figure 9 which shows the conditionability of extraverted and introverted groups.)

Some other examples to illustrate the application of Eysenck's drug postulate are given in Table 4 below; this table is quoted from 'Experiments with Drugs' where many other examples and references will be found.

TABLE 4

Drug Studies

Topic	Prediction:		References
	Stimulant	Depressant	
1. Conditioning	Increased	Decreased	Willett (1960b)
			Franks & Laverty (1955)
			Franks & Trouton (1958)
2. Sedation threshold	Raised	Lowered	Shagass & Naiman (1956)
			Eysenck (1963a)
3. Vigilance	Increased	Decreased	Mackworth (1948)
			Felsinger, Lasagna &
			Beecher (1953)
			Treadwell (1960)
4. Rotation spiral after-effects	Increased	Decreased	Eysenck, Holland & Trouton (1957)
			Eysenck & Easterbrook (1960c)
5. Suppression of primary visual stimulus	Decreased	Increased	Eysenck & Aiba (1957)
6. Nonsense syllable learning	Improved	Worsened	Willett (1960c)
			Eysenck (1957)
7. Motor responses	Smaller	Larger	Rachman (1961a)
8. Time perception	Increased	Decreased	Costello (1961)
9. Kinaesthetic figural after-effects	Decreased	Increased	Poser (1958)
			Eysenck & Easterbrook (1960d)
10. Pupillary responsiveness	Increased	Retarded	Eysenck & Easterbrook (1960b)

50

Topic	Prediction:		References
	Stimulant	Depressant	
11. Static Ataxia	Decreased	Increased	Eysenck & Easterbrook (1960a)
12. Adaptation (palmar skin resistance)	Weakened	Strgth'nd	Martin (1960b)
13. Critical Flicker Fusion threshold	Depressed	Elevated	Holland (1960a)
14. Alternation behaviour	Decreased	Increased	Sinha, Franks & Broadhurst (1958)
15. After-image duration	Length'd	Shortened	Eysenck (1963a)
16. Visual field sensitivity	Height'd	Reduced	Holland (1960b)
17. Pursuit rotor performance	Increased	Decreased	Eysenck, Casey & Trouton (1957)
18. Apparent movement threshold	Increased	Lowered	Eysenck (1963a)
19. Visual masking effects	Decreased	Increased	Eysenck (1963a)
20. Set	Increased	Decreased	Martin (1960c)
21. Risk taking	Decreased	Increased	Cohen et al. (1958)
22. Performance accuracy	Increased	Decreased	Drew et al. (1959)
23. Retroactive interference	Increased	Decreased	Summerfield & Steinberg (1957)
24. C.E.R.	Increased	Decreased	Singh (1959; 1961) Singh & Eysenck (1960)

Our example of drug effects on conditioning has been given because, as we shall see later on in the text, conditioning plays a very important part in our theory of the origin and treatment of neurotic disorders, and it may frequently be extremely useful and necessary to control the rate of conditioning during therapy. As will be seen, there are several instances where a treatment of a person who conditioned poorly and weakly could only accomplish its purpose when the introduction of a stimulant drug increased the patient's conditionability. Conversely, many behaviour problems, both among children, adolescents, and adults, which are characterized by extreme extraversion, as shown in Figure 4, demonstrate quite a marked transformation of behaviour when the patients are given an injection of a stimulant drug and are, therefore, temporarily shifted over to a condition of greater introversion.

One typical study was reported by Cutts and Jasper (1949). They investigated twelve behaviour problem children, giving them doses of benzedrine. Half of these children showed

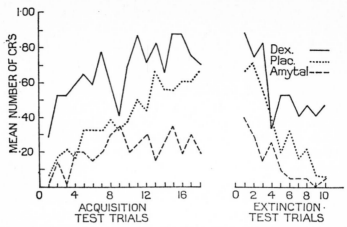

FIG. 13. Acquisition and extinction of eye-blink conditioned responses for groups having received dexedrine, amytal, or a placebo (Franks and Trouton, 1958).

marked improvement in behaviour. When the children were given phenobarbitone their behaviour was definitely made worse in nine out of twelve cases. A similar study has been described by Lindsley and Henry (1942), who studied thirteen behaviour problem children with the mean age of ten and a half years and of average intelligence. They write, 'Behaviour disturbances were of sufficient degree of intensity to render the children distinct problems in management at home, at school, or in the community, and to make their admission to the hospital for treatment advisable. The behaviour of each child was characterized by a number of undesirable traits such as negativism, hyperactivity, impulsiveness, destructiveness, aggressiveness distractibility, seclusiveness, sex play, stealing, lying and a variety of other characteristics. These varied in combination, number, and degree for each child.'

The behaviour of the children was rated in the ward, in the playground, and in the schoolroom, with particular reference to the kind of behaviour complained of. Having established a baseline, as it were, during an initial control period, during which no drugs were given, the children were then administered some benzedrine over a period of a week; during this time they were again rated. Finally, during the third week each subject received phenobarbital, which is a depressant drug and which we would, therefore, expect to exacerbate their symptoms. Finally, after an interval of two weeks, the children were rated again under conditions of no drugs, this constituting the terminal control.

The authors state that 'Under the influence of benzedrine marked improvement of behaviour was noted by all observers. Phenobarbital resulted in an exacerbation of symptoms. . . . Behaviour scores on the sixth week of the study during the final control period . . . were reduced considerably below the leval of the initial score.' The authors of this report also took electroencephalographic recordings, and they state that, 'During the preliminary preparations an unique opportunity for observation of each subject was afforded under conditions which required co-operation. During the period of benzedrine medication, sociability, co-operation, attention, and alertness all seemed to be improved. Phenobarbital generally resulted in quite opposite reactions and attitudes. Under its influence practically all subjects were glum, irritable, uncommunicative, and annoyed by requests for co-operation.' It is also stated that, 'Under benzedrine medication all subjects show better than ten per cent improvement in their behaviour scores over those of the initial control periods; nine subjects show better than fifty per cent improvement.' In view of the short periods during which the medication was applied the results seem to be remarkable.

In another study, Bradley and Bowen (1941) studied the effects of amphetamine on one hundred behaviour problem children. Of these, they found that fifty-four became more 'subdued'. By this term they mean, 'That in some conspicuous way a child became less active than before. . . . Many children began to walk and move quietly in contrast to previous running and rushing about. A number spoke in a normal or lower tone of voice instead of shouting raucously. Some of these same children, instead of quarrelling and arguing boisterously, began to avoid expressing differences of opinion or conducted their discussions in tones which were not offensive. In certain instances, children appeared subdued because they began to spend their leisure time playing quietly or reading, whereas formerly they had wandered aimlessly about, antagonizing and annoying others. The general impression given by all the children who became definitely subdued was that they were

53

effectively exerting more conscious control over their activities and the expression of their emotions. In general, they were conducting themselves with increased consideration and regard for the feelings of those about them.'

As an example, Bradley and Bowen quote the case of John, a ten-year-old boy who was admitted to the hospital because of hyperactivity, destructive behaviour, poor school progress, and failure to mingle satisfactorily with other children. It appears that he teased his companions incessantly, quarrelled with them, pushed them, and took their toys. This overactivity had been noted since earliest childhood but, of course, the social problems arising from it became exaggerated when he entered school. Although he was under psychotherapeutic treatment for fifteen months, he was over-active, irritable, noisy, and disturbing in the ward, in the playground, and in the classroom where he made little progress. He demanded a great deal of attention in school, worked acceptably only when given individual instruction, but was unreliable when the teacher left the room. He was restless and distractible in all activities. At mealtimes he stuffed food in his mouth, laughed and talked noisily, and constantly teased children. He gave no evidence of profiting from suggestion or training. When amphetamine was started, 'There was immediately a definite change in his behaviour. On the ward, John was much quieter and none of his usual hyper-activity was noted. He was prompt for meals and school, and became pleasant and congenial with children and adults. He co-operated well in all matters of routine; no longer restless, but applied himself to daily tasks. In the class room he accomplished a great deal every day and showed excellent initiative. During leisure periods he was frequently busy with school work which he requested be given to him to do in his free time. He also occupied himself with reading and became interested in jig-saw puzzles. Several times John remarked spontaneously that he was glad he was receiving "the pills", because they made him "do better in school and ward work". . . . Following discharge from the hospital John received amphetamine sulphate periodically. At times it produced dramatic improvement in his behaviour in school and at home. At other times, when unfavourable environmental conditions existed, little effect was observed.'

The most recent report available (Eisenberg *et al.*, 1963)

describes the effects of dextro-amphetamine on delinquent boys, compared with the effects of placebo and no medication. Using a symptom check list and a sociogram procedure, they found it 'possible to demonstrate a statistically significant reduction in symptoms among subjects given dextro-amphetamine' when contrasted with the other two groups. Here, as in most such studies (Bender and Cottington 1942; Bradley, 1937, 1950; Hill, 1947; Lauber et al., 1954, 1957; Pasamanik, 1951; Shorvon, 1945, 1947) there was no attempt to link drug-induced introversion and conditionability with a programme of behaviour therapy designed to take advantage of the neural changes produced by the drug; consequently effects were largely transitory. It is noteworthy, however, that delinquent and psychopathic patients have been found to be very tolerant of amphetamine, even in very large doses, and not to develop as addicts with it. This fact is in line with our drug postulate, and is indeed simply the reverse of the low sedation thresholds of such subjects when *depressant* drugs are concerned. This whole area of combining drugs and behaviour therapy is crying out for development along the theoretical lines discussed here.

Another factor which should theoretically interfere with the reciprocal exchange of neural impulses between cortex and activating reticular system would be brain damage, particularly in the prefrontal region, and we would expect that operations such as lobotomy would have the effect of making people more extraverted by increasing inhibitory potential and reducing excitatory potential. The first to produce evidence of an experimental kind along these lines was Petrie (1952); her results were very much in line with the hypothesis, and later work has fully supported the prediction (Willett, 1960a). While it is admitted, of course, that the effects of brain injury are not entirely general but may be quite highly specific to the particular area of the brain involved, nevertheless the results are positive enough to suggest that the theory is on the right lines.

The notions of 'excitation' and 'facilitation' are often used in connection with such psychological terms as 'activation' or 'arousal'. This concept has been put forward recently by a number of people, including Malmo (1959) who, in a recent review, considers the level of consciousness as a function of the degree of 'cortical activation' which is attained in response to corticopetal impulses derived from lower centres. 'The continuum extending from deep sleep at the low activation end to "excited" states at the high activated end is a function of the amount of cortical bombardment by the A.R.A.S. (ascending reticular activating system), such that the greater the cortical bombardment, the higher the activation.' He also points out that there is a relationship between the level of 'activation' and the level of performance, such that as activation increases performance rises towards an optimum, but once this optimum is reached, increase in 'activation' is reflected in a fall in performance. (Cf. also Hebb, 1955.) This so-called inverted U hypothesis is, of course, simply a more recent formulation of the well-known Yerkes-Dodson law (Broadhurst, 1959), relating drive to performance in a similar curvilinear fashion. Altogether, the Hullian notion of a single generalized drive state has considerable similarity to Malmo's notion of 'activation', and we would perhaps go not too far wrong in considering the two as identical from a theoretical point of view.

If this were so, then we should be able to make certain predictions as to the reactions of typical extraverted and introverted subjects as compared to people working under conditions of high and low drive. If indeed introverts are characterized by greater excitatory potentials and extraverts by greater inhibitory potentials, and if excitation and 'activation' or arousal are physiologically similar and may, provisionally at least, be identified with 'drive', then the following relationship should hold:

$$E \div I = L \div H:$$

in other words, extraverts, as compared with introverts should on a particular type of objective test behave like subjects working under low drive compared to subjects working under high drive. Much work has been done along these lines, and a report has been published under the title 'Experiments in Motivation' (Eysenck, 1964c). Again, there would be little point now in reviewing all the evidence; let us again concentrate on eye-blink conditioning, and compare the results of an experiment in which subjects working under high drive have been compared with subjects working under low drive. The results are given in Figure 14, and it will be seen that, as predicted, the high drive group resembles the introverts in showing a considerable degree of conditioning, whereas the low drive group resembles the extraverts in showing relatively little conditioning. We may conclude that, by and large, introverted people, on a given task, are likely to be characterized by higher drive than are extraverts. It should, of course, be noted that this does not necessarily mean a superiority of performance of introverts as compared with extraverts; it will be remembered

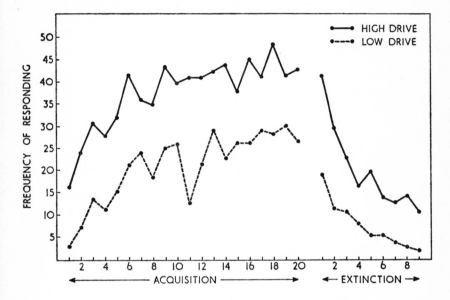

Fig. 14. Acquisition and extinction of conditioned eye-blink responses for groups working under high drive and low drive respectively (Eysenck, 1964*c*).

that there is a *curvilinear* relationship between performance on the one hand, and activation or drive on the other; consequently, overhigh drive may lead to poorer performance. Many examples of this are given in 'Experiments in Motivation'.

This completes the brief and necessarily inadequate account of the general theory of personality which we believe facilitates understanding of the phenomena of neurotic behaviour, and leads eventually to an understanding also of the methods of treatment. It is obviously a bio-social theory, in the sense that it stresses both the biological inherited nature of the organism and the social influences which impinge upon this organism and lead to certain types of responses. If, in these introductory Chapters, we have stressed the biological aspect more than the social, this has been because, in modern writings, there has been a distinct tendency to underplay the biological and over-stress the social; it seemed important to us to redress this balance, at least to some extent. To summarize our description, we see human beings as being equipped innately with an auto-nomic system which is more or less labile, more or less ready to react strongly and lastingly to the various physiological and psychological stresses of everyday life, thus predisposing its possessor to have strong or weak emotional responses. We also see human beings as being equipped, through the processes of hereditary transmission, with an ascending reticular forma-tion, the different excitatory and inhibitory parts of which are working with differential effectiveness to produce an excess of either excitation or inhibition in a given person, or else, of course, producing a rough and ready equilibrium; excesses along one line or the other will be reflected in a variety of laboratory phenomena, particularly conditioning, and also in personality traits which cause individuals to be labelled extravert or introvert, as the case might be.

We see introverted and highly emotional people as being constitutionally predisposed to develop dysthymic neuroses, that is to say anxiety states, obsessional and compulsive habits of behaviour, phobias, and so forth; we see extraverted and highly emotional people as predisposed to develop psychopathic criminal, and hysterical reactions. Whether these predispositions are to be translated into actual behaviour patterns or not depends, of course, on the particular environment in which the person finds himself, and the schedule of reinforcements which he encounters during his life. Thus, both biological-hereditary and social-environmental influences come into play in determin-ing the final conduct which we observe and which, in the case of the neurotic or the criminal, brings him in touch with some social agency or other.

Given that a particular behaviour pattern, whether neurotic or criminal, has in fact developed, our approach would now be quite ahistorical. We are not particularly concerned, in the majority of cases, with the particular reasons for the emergence of this pattern, but we are vitally concerned with the problem of how this pattern is to be changed. Such change must clearly take the form of deconditioning in the case of the dysthymic disorders, and one of reconditioning in that of the criminal and psychopathic disorders. We do not postulate any underlying complexes or even 'neuroses'; in our account, these are unnecessary hypotheses not called for by the facts in question. Thus, our theory and our treatment are purely symptomatic; the symptom in each case is a conditioned, unadaptive, autonomic or skeletal response, and our task is to abolish this particular maladaptive pattern of behaviour. Once this is accomplished our task is over; there is no anticipation of any recrudescence of the symptom itself or any emergence of new symptoms, as would be expected if there were any hypothetical complex or underlying cause for the behaviour outside the field of conditioning. It is here that our theory parts most clearly from the psychoanalytic account, and it is here that the facts must pronounce their judgement as to the adequacy of these two hypotheses.

The implications of this general theory for the treatment of neuroses will be spelled out in considerable detail in the succeeding Chapters. Here, we would like to stress one further point, however, which will not come out very much in the later portions of this book, and that is the function of diagnosis. Having attempted to provide a rational theory of the aetiology and treatment of neurotic disorders, we must, of course, also provide a rational theory of their diagnosis. As will have become clear in what we have said before, our view of neurotic disorders as conditioned responses of a maladaptive type takes us far away from the current psychiatric habit of referring to different types of symptom patterns as different disease entities. Psychiatric nosology is, in principle, categorical; a patient is an hysteric, or an anxiety state, or an obsessional. In our view, this is an erroneous taking over into a psychological field of medical concepts which do not properly apply. As pointed out above, we would prefer an interpretation and a description in terms of a person's standing on the two major dimensions of personality, to wit his degree of neuroticism and his degree of extraversion or introversion. We have already shown that the diagnostic categories of the psychiatrist define certain areas within this two-dimensional space generated by our two main axes, so that statements from the one field can be translated into statements in the other. The disadvantages of a psychiatric approach are that the precise area of the two-dimensional field which is occupied by patients enjoying a similar diagnosis is ill-defined and differs from person to person; hence the great unreliability of psychiatric diagnosis. Furthermore, there is inevitably a considerable part of the space which is outside the areas claimed for each particular diagnostic group, thus giving rise to large numbers of neurotics who cannot be fitted easily into one or other of these groups. Hence our preference for the dimensional system and for the measurement of relevant personality variables in terms of neuroticism and extraversion-introversion.

Such measurement, it will be remembered from Figure 5, and also from Figure 10, can best be undertaken in terms of experimental laboratory tests of conditioning, reminiscence, satiation, and so forth. These tests, it must be stated again, give us some insight into the genotypic background of the patient; this will not, in all respects, agree with phenotypic observations which we may make. Thus, the psychopath may be characterized by an inherited tendency to condition poorly, but given a reinforcement schedule which presents him a large number of times with a conditioned stimulus followed by a strong unconditioned stimulus, even he will learn, and he will learn more so than the dysthymic who is not presented more than once or twice by a similar reinforcement contingency.

Our reasons for stressing knowledge of the genotypic aspects of personality as a diagnostic aid are, of course, very simple. The patient has acquired certain maladaptive conditioned responses, or he has failed to acquire certain desirable conditioned responses. The reasons for either of these two undesirable contingencies do not any longer concern us; they are merely of historical interest. Our concern is with a change in the general position in which the patient finds himself, and this will call for some form of deconditioning or reconditioning. In either case it is vital to know whether the patient conditions quickly or poorly before any rational system of therapy can be prescribed. Consequently, tests of conditionability will constitute an important and indeed vital aid in diagnosis. If the patient's innate propensities do not make him a good subject for a particular type of therapy, we can have recourse to drugs which, as we have shown above, can change his propensities

either in the direction of greater introversion and conditionability, or in the direction of greater extraversion and speedy
extinction of conditioned responses.

It will not be necessary to elaborate this point any further;
the reader will see what kind of diagnostic procedures we are
advocating, and how we propose to fit them into the general
picture. What does perhaps need emphasizing, however, is that
at the present time few psychiatric institutions are well equipped
for allowing the psychologist to carry out procedures of this
kind. What is required is clearly a large, sound-proof, air-con-
ditioned laboratory, furnished adequately with apparatus of a
rather refined nature which makes possible the recording of
autonomic and skeletal responses as well as the controlled
administration of a great variety of different stimuli. It is still
too frequently the case that the psychologist is regarded as the
person who works entirely with pencil and paper or, at best,
with a batch of ink blots and a couch; the clinical psychologist
must be first and foremost an experimental psychologist, and as
such he must insist on being furnished with the tools of his trade.

It will also be realized that in the kind of scheme we are
outlining here we are assuming a certain educational background for the clinical psychologist, which stresses experimental
psychology, learning theory, and physiology far more than has
hitherto been the case, and which lays little stress on proficiency
in the administration of projective techniques and so forth.
We believe that an unfortunate division has occurred in the
last twenty years between experimental and academic psychologists, on the one hand, and clinical psychologists on the other,
leaving the former relatively isolated from the problems and
challenges presented by neurotic and other mentally ill individuals, and leaving the latter separated from what should
be his main source of ideas and methods. We believe that one
of the great advantages of the general outlook which has
informed this book is the opportunity which it gives for a
reconciliation between these two great groups of psychologists. It is our belief that experimentalists will find challenging
projects in the clinical field, and that clinicians, in turn, will
find inspiration for their work in the theories and practices of
the experimentalist. Psychology cannot remain half experimental and half clinical; it is clearly time for a reconciliation
and integration.

Chapter 5

ANXIETY STATES—I

IT is generally agreed that anxiety plays a central role in the majority of neurotic conditions. Although anxiety may be analysed into three major components—autonomic, ideational, and motor responses (Metzner, 1961)—it is the autonomic aspects which are of primary interest when considering those disorders which are classified as anxiety states. Anxiety can be produced by noxious stimulation or by conflict and numerous factors determine both the degree and the persistence of the anxiety reactions which are evoked. The variables which are known to influence anxiety reactions are: (1) personality factors (e.g. neuroticism); (2) degree of confinement; (3) intensity of the unconditioned stimulus; (4) age; (5) past experiences; (6) type of conflict; (7) strength of the competing responses.

The nature of the personality dimensions of neuroticism and introversion has been discussed in Chapter 2 above. It was shown how both of these factors exert an influence on anxiety reactions. In people who have a high degree of neuroticism, few exposures to noxious stimulation will be necessary before observable anxiety reactions are produced. On the other hand, those people who are low on the neuroticism dimension will not display excessive anxiety reactions except under conditions of persistent and/or extreme stress. When a high degree of neuroticism is combined with a high degree of introversion then the person is likely to be prone to dysthymic disorders, of which anxiety states are the best examples. Those people who are low in neuroticism and high in extraversion can be expected to show a considerable degree of 'resistance' to dysthymic disorders.

Several research workers in the field of experimental neurosis have emphasized the importance of physical restriction in the production of these disordered behaviour patterns. Liddell (1944), in particular, has drawn attention to the significant role which physical confinement plays in the onset of neurotic conditions in animals. Similarly, the work described by Wolpe (1952), on the production of experimental neurosis in cats, indicates in a very clear manner how it is possible to produce neurotic behaviour by the application of relatively simple noxious stimuli when the animal is confined in a small cage. The factor of confinement operates differently in human beings than in animals. In human beings, the confinement is most commonly of a psychological rather than a physical nature. There are circumstances, nonetheless, where simple physical restriction may play some part in the genesis of neurotic behaviour, even in human beings.

While it is true that neurotic anxiety reactions can be produced by unconditioned stimuli of a mild type, such a result is only obtained after the animal has been persistently exposed to the mildly noxious stimulus (Liddell, 1944). It has been conclusively shown, nevertheless, that when a severe noxious stimulus is presented to an animal in conditions of physical restriction, the anxiety reactions can be produced even with a single exposure.[1] It is known, moreover, that stronger conditioned responses are established in the presence of high-intensity unconditioned stimuli (Solomon and Wynne, 1953; Kimble, 1961). Sanderson et al. (1963) have recently provided a striking demonstration of the rapid acquisition of a strong and persistent anxiety reaction to a traumatic stimulus in human subjects.

Pavlov and his co-workers showed that conflict can produce anxiety reactions and neurotic breakdowns in animals (Broadhurst, 1960). Miller (1944) skilfully combined the Pavlov's findings with the theoretical analyses of Lewin and Hull to produce a comprehensive analysis of the nature and effects of conflict.

[1]In their report on combat neuroses, Grinker and Spiegel (1945) found that neurotic breakdowns were precipitated by four types of experience (in combination or alone): (1) breakdowns caused by a single catastrophe; (2) those caused by several specific traumata; (3) those caused by a gradual accumulation of mild anxiety; (4) those caused by severe and long-lasting anxiety.

Miller's theoretical model incorporates one of Lewin's notions concerning the differential effects of the four basic types of conflict. Lewin suggested that approach-avoidance conflicts would be more anxiety-provoking and disruptive than approach-approach conflicts. Miller developed this idea into a sophisticated schema, and was able to draw on the experimental results obtained by Hovland and Sears (1948) and by Barker (1941). These experimenters found that approach-avoidance conflicts produced greater disturbances of behaviour than approach-approach conflicts. Similarly, Rachman (1956) was able to obtain evidence which indicates that approach-avoidance conflicts produce greater tension and anxiety than approach-approach conflicts. In a series of unpublished experiments carried out at the same time, he was also able to obtain evidence which showed that the degree of anxiety, tension, and behaviour disorders increased with increases in drive-level.

In these experiments, subjects were observed in semi-realistic conflict situations, under conditions of high and low drive-level. Observations were made of the subjects' overt anxiety manifestations, such as trembling, sweating, and dryness of the mouth, while their drive-levels were manipulated by post-hypnotic suggestions. The subjects were placed in a conflict situation after having received a post-hypnotic suggestion that the consequences of their behaviour in the conflict situation would be unimportant, and then re-introduced into the same conflict situation at a later time, after having received a post-hypnotic suggestion to the effect that their reactions to the conflict situation would be of considerable importance. The manifest signs of anxiety observed under these two conditions were clearly different, and in the case of the high drive situations, the subjects displayed a very considerable degree of anxiety. Miller has summed up the effect of drive level on conflict behaviour in this way: 'An increase in drive raises the height of the entire (approach-avoidance) gradient.' This generalization is illustrated in Figure 15 below (Miller, 1944).

The person's age influences not only the degree of anxiety which is evoked, but also the type of stimuli which will produce the anxiety. The evidence on which this statement is based is provided primarily by the surveys which have been conducted into the fears experienced by children (see Chapter 14). It has been shown that the frequency of fears experienced by children

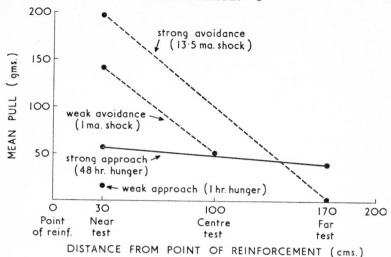

Fig. 15. Effect of strength of drive upon height of gradient. The two avoidance gradients represent the strength of pull on near and far shock tests of two groups of rats that had received shocks of different strengths. The approach gradient represents the strength of pull at near and far points of the runway tested after 48 hours of food deprivation; weak approach represents a test at the near point in another group of animals which had been deprived of food for one hour. (From N. Miller *Experimental Studies of Conflict*, Ronald Press, 1944.)

varies with their age—the greatest number of fears being experienced in the younger age-group. It has been shown, in addition, that the type of fear experienced by children also varies with their age. Younger children tend to fear intense and concrete stimuli, whereas the older children experience anxiety in relation to less tangible stimuli. There is also evidence to show that the degree and frequency of fears experienced by children, is, to some extent, determined by their physical strength and their ability to cope with the environment, so than one might expect a decline in the number of fears displayed by children as they increase in size and age.

The importance of the person's previous experiences with the conditioned and unconditioned stimuli concerned is attested to by various sources of evidence. Liddell and his co-workers, for example, have shown that experimental neuroses can be produced by the cumulative effect of repeated exposure to mild noxious stimulation. Grinker and Spiegel (1945) have described numerous cases of neurotic breakdowns, particularly anxiety states, in the field of combat; according to their observations, one of the most common causes of war neuroses is the cumulative effect of repeated exposure to intensely dangerous situations. On the other hand, it should be remembered that a careful and gradual exposure to anxiety-producing situations can, under certain circumstances, produce a form of immunity to anxiety reactions. This immunity has been observed directly by Miller (1960) and indirectly by observations on school phobias in children who have had previous experience of a nursery school situation. School phobias are less common in children who have had the immunizing experience of nursery school attendance.

It will be apparent from the above discussion that the genesis of anxiety states is by no means shrouded in mystery, although, of course, there is still a good deal which needs to be known. In this discussion we have been speaking of anxiety states in a very general sense. A closer and more detailed examination of a specific form of anxiety state, namely phobias, is provided on page 80 below.

The majority of patients who have received behaviour therapy so far have been classified as suffering from anxiety states of one kind or another. The technique which has been shown to have particular value in handling these disorders is the method of systematic desensitization developed by Wolpe (1958). He arrived at this method, which may be described as a gradual deconditioning of the anxiety responses, in the following way. Dissatisfied with the results which he was obtaining with the prevailing conventional forms of psychoanalytically influenced psychotherapy, he decided to turn to experimental psychology for assistance. At that time, the two most promising leads were those provided by the work of Pavlov and his successors on experimental neuroses, and the early but neglected work of Watson and Jones on the genesis and elimination of children's fears. Wolpe carried out his experiments on the artificial induction of neurotic conditions in cats, and came to the conclusion that the most satisfactory way of treating these neurotic animals was by gradual deconditioning along the lines proposed by Jones in 1924. He started off by feeding the neurotic cats in an environmental situation which was distinctly dissimilar from the original traumatic environment. Wolpe then proceeded gradually, through a series of carefully worked-out stages, to situations which approximated more and more to the original traumatic situation. He found that in this way he was able to overcome the animals' neurotic reactions in the original situation and restore them to apparent normality. It was obvious, however, that feeding responses would not be particularly effective in the treatment of adult neurotic patients. His search for a response which would be antagonistic to anxiety led him on to the work of Jacobson (1938), who recommended the use of relaxation in the treatment of patients with neurotic conditions. Wolpe decided then to substitute relaxation for feeding as the major incompatible response which would dampen the anxiety reactions.

At first Wolpe attempted to relax his patients in the presence of the actual objects. This method, he soon discovered, was both tedious and impractical, as it involved amassing a large collection of objects for the treatment of each patient. Furthermore, as some patients did not experience anxiety in the presence of discrete and tangible objects, it meant that he would either have to refuse such patients treatment, or develop some new method. He then began experimenting with the imaginary evocation of the anxiety-producing stimuli, and soon found that it provided a very effective substitute for the real object. In other words, instead of attempting to treat a patient complaining of a phobia of dogs with an accumulation of photographs and models of dogs, he simply asked the patient to imagine these objects while relaxing in the consulting room. This method produced results and was easy to manipulate in the consulting room. It also allowed the therapist a high degree of flexibility in the planning of treatment. Very simply, this is how the method of systematic desensitization works. The patient is requested to imagine the anxiety-producing stimuli in a very mild and attenuated form. When the image is obtained vividly, the therapist relaxes the patient, causing the small amount of anxiety which the image has produced to dissipate. This process is repeated with the same stimulus or a stimulus which is slightly more disturbing. The patient is again relaxed and the next stimulus is then presented and dissipated. With each evocation and subsequent dampening of the anxiety response, conditioned inhibition is built up. Eventually the patient is able to imagine even the previously most anxiety-provoking stimulus with tranquillity, and this tranquillity then generalizes to the real-life situation. The transfer of improvements from the consulting room to real-life situations usually accompanies each stage of the treatment programme in a regular, temporal fashion. When the person is able to envisage the previously disturbing stimulus in the consulting room without anxiety, he generally finds that he is able to cope with the actual stimulus in the real-life situation without any time delay. Naturally, before the systematic desensitization proper commences, various preliminary steps have to be taken. In the first place, a full and complete history of the patient's current disorder and his general life history are obtained. Secondly, an attempt is made to reduce or eliminate any conflicts or anxiety-provoking situations which prevail at the time of treatment. Thirdly, the patient is trained in the methods of progressive relaxation, as described by Jacobson. Fourthly, a hierarchy or group of hierarchies containing the anxiety-producing stimuli is established by the therapist and patient, as a result of detailed therapeutic discussions. In these discussions, the therapist, with the aid of the patient, builds up a series of situations which might produce anxiety in the patient, and the patient is then required to rank them from the most disturbing to the least disturbing situations. When all these steps have been completed, the desensitization itself may proceed.

The method of desensitization, and the other therapeutic procedures used by Wolpe, are all based on the following general principle, as stated by him: 'If a response antagonistic to anxiety can be made to occur in the presence of anxiety-evoking stimuli so that it is accompanied by a complete or partial suppression of the anxiety responses, the bond between these stimuli and the anxiety responses will be weakened.' The entire process of systematic desensitization is best illustrated by reference to a case history.

The patient, Miss A. G., was a 24-year-old female teacher who complained of an inability to undergo injections of any kind. On those few occasions when she had been unable to avoid them, she had always fainted during or immediately after the injection. She requested therapy at the time she did because of an impending trip for which she would be required to have a yellow fever injection and smallpox vaccination. Her fear of injections was of long standing, dating back to either six or seven years of age. She experienced a moderate reaction (slight trembling and 'butterflies in the stomach') when asked to imagine a person receiving an injection, and ordinarily preferred not to talk about injections or related topics, e.g. visits to the dentist. She also complained of 'a sexual problem' and a fear of using internal sanitary pads.

In addition to a symptom history, the patient was given the Willoughby Neurotic Tendency Inventory (Willoughby, 1934) and a form of the Incomplete Sentence Test during the first interview. Her Willoughby Score was moderately high (44) and the I-S Test, which was only partially answered, revealed a slightly disturbed childhood, an exaggerated need for company and acceptance by other people, and vague fears about her future. Her relationships with her parents, with whom she lived, appeared to be unsatisfactory, but no serious difficulties seemed to be present. The general picture was one of mild insecurity.

In view of the nature and history of the chief symptom, it was decided to employ systematic desensitization therapy and to attempt at the same time to relieve the feelings of insecurity by discussion and reassurance.

Treatment

General procedure

In desensitization therapy, an enquiry is first conducted in order to ascertain which stimulus situations provoke anxiety in the patient. The patient is told that he can add to or modify this list at any time. The stimuli are then categorized by the therapist, and the patient is asked to rank the categories of stimuli in order from the most to the least disturbing. This ranked list of anxiety-provoking conditions is referred to as the hierarchy. In the present case, for example, one would refer to the 'injection hierarchy' and the 'sanitary pad hierarchy'. Hierarchies typically contain from five to twenty-five items. The construction of the relevant hierarchies generally takes from one to three interviews, and the patient is concurrently given practice in hypnotic and relaxation procedures. Hypnosis is not an essential requirement, and, in those cases where the patient refuses to be hypnotized or requires prolonged practice, the procedure can be omitted and deep non-hypnotic relaxation employed instead.

When the hierarchies have been worked out, the subject is told which stimuli are to be presented in the individual session and is advised to signal with his hand if a stimulus presentation disturbs him unduly. This is an important instruction and is on no account to be omitted, because the arousal of excessive anxiety during the session can be disruptive. With most patients, it seems possible, by observing facial expressions, bodily tension, respiration, etc. to perceive such disturbances before the patient actually signals. When such disturbances occur, the therapist immediately withdraws the stimulus and calms the patient. No session is concluded when a disturbance occurs, but before rousing the patient, the therapist presents an 'easy' stimulus which has already been successfully overcome.

When the preliminary instructions have been given the patient is relaxed (hypnotically or otherwise) and then told to visualize the various stimuli, e.g. 'Picture a hospital in the distance . . . Now stop picturing that and go on relaxing.' Each visualization of this kind is referred to as a 'presentation'. Each stimulus is visualized for five to ten seconds, and from two to four different items are presented each session. Each item is generally presented two or three times. When the requisite number of stimuli have been presented, the patient is slowly roused and then asked for a report on his reactions. If the items were visualized vividly and without undue disturbance, the therapist then proceeds to the next stimuli in the following session. The items lowest in the hierarchy (i.e. the least disturbing ones) are introduced first, and the therapist proceeds slowly up the list, depending on the progress achieved and the patient's reactions. In this way it is possible for the patient eventually to imagine formerly noxious stimuli without any anxiety whatever. This ability to imagine the noxious stimulus with tranquillity then transfers to the real-life situation.

As the purpose of this technique is to decondition anxiety reactions, it is necessary for the patient to experience *some anxiety* during the stimulus presentations. The total inhibition of the neurotic anxiety is achieved by inhibiting small degrees of anxiety in a gradual and systematic progression.

Interview No. 2. A discussion of A. G.'s responses to the Incomplete Sentence Test revealed that some 18 months earlier, she had unsuccessfully attempted to use an internal sanitary pad. On the first attempt she fainted after the pad had been inserted. She left it in when she had regained consciousness, but it felt uncomfortable, and she was anxious lest she would not be able to extract it. The second attempt, a day later, was unsuccessful. She only managed to place the pad half way in after much effort. Her hand seemed to be stiff and almost paralysed, and she was perspiring and trembling. This failure left her very upset. A third attempt on the following day was also unsuccessful, and the emotional upset recurred. Since that time she had used external pads exclusively. The patient also reported that she experienced pain during intercourse. This sexual difficulty had been present from her first experience of sex and was consistent. Her menstrual periods were regular, and she rarely experienced pain or other difficulties.

During this second interview the patient was given her first lesson in relaxation, to which she responded very well and achieved a calm state within 15 minutes. She was instructed to practice relaxation for 15 minutes every day.

Interview No. 3. As the reaction to internal sanitary pads was judged to be less disturbing than that of injections, it was decided to commence with this problem. The following hierarchy was constructed: a box of Tampax, an opened pad, holding a pad, holding a pad next to the vagina, seeing someone else using a Tampax, placing a pad at the vaginal entrance, sliding it in slowly, completely inserted. The patient was given a second lesson in relaxation and again responded well.

Interview No. 4. After a discussion about her ambitions and future plans, the patient was relaxed and asked to visualize each of the first three items in the hierarchy twice (i.e. box of pads, opened box of pads, holding a pad). She reported afterwards that the images had been slightly disturbing but not very vivid.

Interview No. 5. In the fifth session, A. G. revealed the history of her protracted relationship with her lover. She expressed doubts about the wisdom of marrying him and also about his attitude towards her. After some discussion, her feelings and motives became more lucid and she experienced some relief.

Items 3, 4, and 5 in her anxiety hierarchy were successfully presented but again were not very vividly perceived.

Interview No. 6. The patient reported that she 'felt better' since the last interview and had been practising relaxation regularly. In view of her inability to visualize the hierarchy items vividly, she was given some instruction and practice to remedy this. She was then relaxed and Items 5 and 6 were presented three times each. The images were reported as slightly disturbing and a bit clearer.

Interview No. 7. A. G. said that she had been feeling tense for the past two days, but no incident or other cause for this upset could be located. She had seen a bullfight film after the development of this tension and reported that the bullfighting and darting of the bulls, previously upsetting to her, had left her unaffected. Desensitization of Items 6 and 7 (placing a pad at the vaginal entrance, sliding it in slowly) was proceeded with. Each item was presented three times, and A. G. reported vivid images and a slight disturbance.

Interview No. 8. The patient's menstrual flow had started the previous afternoon, and she decided to try an internal sanitary pad. She reported, 'I had a bath, felt a bit nervous, and then tried to insert a Tampax in the bathroom. I started perspiring, felt very hot, and got terribly upset. I tried to relax myself, then managed to put the tip of the pad in. Just then I had a "thing" (near panic, almost fainted). I should have stopped but could not. I pushed and pushed and got terribly upset. I felt scared and started crying. Then C. (a friend) came in and tried to help me. I could not do it and eventually gave up. I felt dizzy and weak and was extremely upset.'

The patient was given deep relaxation for 15 minutes and then the last two items were presented twice each (sliding pad in, pad fully inserted). The last item was more than usually disturbing, She was then given another five minutes of relaxation and told to attempt an actual insertion in an adjoining room, in the presence of a friend. This she managed to do with some difficulty after three minutes. When she had succeeded, however, she felt extremely pleased and had no dizzy spells of feelings of weakness.

She was instructed to insert a pad by herself that night after relaxing for ten minutes, and also to relax for a further ten minutes after insertion.

Interview No. 9. A. G. reported that she had successfully inserted the sanitary pads on four occasions and had experienced two failures, nether of which had upset her very much. She said that she was now able to insert them more quickly and with little or no pain.

During this interview, an injection hierarchy was constructed. The items were (in ascending order): seeing a hypodermic syringe, holding a syringe, filling a syringe, seeing a cinema slide of a person receiving an injection, seeing a bull receive an injection, seeing a dog receive an injection, another person being injected, being injected at home, being injected in the district surgeon's rooms. The first three items in this hierarchy were then presented twice each. They were visualized vividly and were not disturbing.

Interviews 10 *and* 11. These sessions were mainly devoted to systematic desensitization. By this time, all the items up to and including No. 8 (seeing another person being injected) had been successfully presented.

Interview No. 12. The patient having received a setback in her love affair, this session was restricted to a sort of non-directive, cathartic discussion. No desensitizing was undertaken because of A. G.'s depressed mood and obvious desire to 'just talk'.

Interview No. 13. The cathartic process of the last interview was continued, and the patient was subsequently relaxed. Item 7 (dog being injected) was given once, Item 8 (person being injected) three times, and Item 9 (A. G. being injected at home) presented once very briefly. This last item caused some disturbance and was, therefore, not repeated in this session.

Interview No. 14. In anticipation of the patient's menstrual period, the sanitary pad image was reinforced under deep relaxation three times. Item 8 of the injection hierarchy (person being injected) was also visualized three times. In the meantime, various difficulties regarding A. G.'s projected trip had arisen and were fully discussed.

Interview No. 15. Since the onset of her menstrual flow, two days earlier, A. G. had successfully inserted sanitary pads on three out of four attempts. She was put under deep relaxation and then instructed to insert a pad while alone in the relaxation room. She managed perfectly in very rapid time, with no disturbance whatsoever.

73

She reported that she had attempted sexual intercourse a week earlier but had been forced to give up because of the pain and anxious feelings engendered. She added hesitatingly that she was worried lest she had some physical defect which would always prevent her from experiencing anything but pain in sexual activities. Analysis of the unsuccessful sexual attempt indicated that a contributing factor was inadequate foreplay. The patient was given information and advice about loveplay and was told to relax fully before lovemaking. It was also suggested to her that there would probably be a spontaneous transfer of relaxation effect, and, therefore, success in sex was likely once the other two anxiety areas had been desensitized.

Interview No. 16. The menstrual flow had ceased and the 'score' for the month was that six out of seven attempts at insertion of sanitary pads were successful. A. G.'s realization of this success had a marked beneficial effect, and she was quite elated about a long behaviour difficulty which had at last been remedied.

The patient was then desensitized to Items 8 (person being injected) and 9 (self injected at home). Each item was presented three times, and the patient reported no disturbance but inadequate visualization of the images.

Interview No. 17. A. G. stated that her trip was almost certainly cancelled and expressed considerable disappointment. She was also experiencing further uneasiness about her love relationship, as a result of some action on the part of her partner which had given her cause to doubt his positive, affectionate feelings towards her.

Desensitization of the last two items in the hierarchy were carried out successfully. Each image (self being injected at home, being injected at district surgeon's rooms) was presented three times. They were vividly pictured and caused little disturbance, the patient being very deeply relaxed and extremely calm.

Interview No. 18. A. G. reported that she had experienced sexual intercourse two days previously. For the first time in her life, it had been completely free of even the slightest pain. She had felt slightly anxious but had managed to control this reaction and to indulge in pre- and post-coital loveplay unhindered. The fear of some physical defect had disappeared

74

entirely, and she felt reassured about her sexual adequacy.

The last two items of the injection list were presented again, three times each. They were vividly imagined and caused no disturbance.

Interview No. 19. In reply to A. G.'s queries, information regarding the aetiology of neurotic behaviour was supplied, and her own case was then discussed in some detail. She was told that phobias such as hers develop out of painful experiences and that despite their apparent senselessness they nevertheless persist. The usual reason for the persistence of the phobia, she was informed, is that it produces an avoidance of the painful situation. Because of her fear of injections, she had successfully managed to avoid having any form of injection for many years. Both the fear and avoidance reactions were reinforced over the years because they were never followed by pain and were, in this way, satisfying patterns of behaviour.

The patient was desensitized to injections at the district surgeon's (three times) and to the sanitary pad situation (three times) in anticipation of the menstrual period again. Both items were seen vividly and without disturbance.

Interview No. 20. The patient reported that sexual intercourse had again been successful. She had experienced minimal anxiety and no pain. She also felt a change in her attitude to injections: 'They no longer seem to bother me when I think about them.'

After a final three presentations of the district surgeon situation under relaxation, it was agreed to test her reaction to injections. It was accordingly arranged that she would receive an injection of chemically pure water at the next interview.

Interview No. 21. After ten minutes of deep relaxation, A. G. received an intramuscular water injection in the left arm. She experienced considerable pain but did not faint, despite a strong feeling of 'butterflies' and excessive sweating. She was relaxed for a further fifteen minutes, but her arm continued to ache and she felt 'shaken up'. The sanitary pads were now being used when necessary and provoked no anxiety or other untoward reactions.

Interview No. 22. Four days after the water injection, A. G. received her yellow fever injection at the district surgeon's rooms. She relaxed on a couch before and after the injection and experienced no disturbance, despite her marked fear just prior to the event. She was extremely glad about this success and reported feeling 'a lot better all round'. As A. G. had been desensitized to the full hierarchies of noxious stimuli and her behaviour difficulties overcome, this interview brought to an end the formal desensitization treatment. The patient was instructed to return for follow-up interviews at two-month intervals unless, of course, she felt the need to return before the stated time had elapsed.

Six weeks later, A. G. reported that she had received a smallpox vaccination in the interim and had experienced no ill effects, although she had been apprehensive for a while prior to her visit to the district surgeon's rooms. All the other improvements effected during therapy had been maintained.

Six weeks later, A. G. reported feeling well and 'over her troubles'. She was given the Willoughby Neurotic Tendency Scale again. Her score was 26, a decrease of 18 points since the first interview. Therapy was terminated, as A. G. seemed improved in terms of Knight's criteria (1941) of symptom improvement, improved adjustment and pleasure in sex, and increased stress tolerance. The other two criteria of improved interpersonal relationships and increased productivity were not relevant to the case, as A. G.'s behaviour in these areas had never been disrupted.

The patient was seen again nearly five years after the completion of treatment. None of her symptoms had recurred despite the fact that she had been exposed to a stressful conflict situation lasting for nearly two years. She also reported other general improvements in her behaviour, but was still a little indecisive.

Discussion

The twenty-two therapeutic interviews were spread over a period of three months, averaging two per week. Perhaps the most striking feature of the case was its smooth progression. The therapeutic programme proceeded from interview to interview in a regular, predictable way, with behaviour changes following therapy in a manner almost perfectly consistent with theoretical expectations.

At only two points was therapy every threatened with disruption. In interview No. 12, A. G. arrived for her appointment depressed and perturbed about her love relationship. This mood prevented a desensitization session, and had it not cleared as rapidly as it did, could have delayed further progress for weeks or even months. The second difficulty occurred towards the end of therapy as a result of the therapist's avoidable error in using water in the trial injection (Interview No. 21). The injection of water is ordinarily painful. The pain experienced by A. G. on this occasion fortunately did not reinforce her fear of injections unduly. She still underwent the yellow fever injection successfully a few days later. These two obstacles to progress have, of course, no general lesson or application, other than the observation that therapeutic planning and procedure must be carried forward with caution on the part of the therapist.

It seems likely that the improvement in A. G.'s sexual performance resulted from a transfer of her progress in relaxation and in the sanitary pad procedure. Before the anxiety associated with the insertion of sanitary pads had been fully overcome, she unsuccessfully attempted to have intercourse (in the period between Interviews 13 and 14). By Interview 16, she was managing the sanitary pad insertions with very little anxiety and, soon after the following interview, had her first painless experience of sexual intercourse. Prior to the inhibition of the sanitary pad anxiety she had been unable to have normal sexual intercourse. Spontaneous recovery of sexual functioning accompanying general psychological improvement is not unusual, but, in the present case, the transfer effect occurred rather early. The probable reason for this occurrence was the close similarity in this case between the symptom under treatment at the time (internal sanitary pads) and the pain experienced during sex.

The present case study indicates practically the point stated elsewhere that 'while a knowledge of the causative process and genesis of the individual neurosis can be of considerable value in therapy, improvement can nevertheless be obtained in many cases without such knowledge' (Rachman, 1958). In the present case, no certain 'cause' could be found for the development of the anxiety and phobic reactions. A. G. said that when she was a young child she had experienced some painful injections. This may well account for her neurotic reaction to injections, but the sanitary pad and sexual difficulties were never ade-

77

quately traced backwards. The possibility that these problems arose out of the fear of injections as a prototypical fear of penetration seems far-fetched. The reverse explanation, that all three 'reactions to penetration' were of a sexual nature, is also not supported by the evidence. The phobic response to injections antedated the sexual difficulties by twelve years, and the penetration analogy cannot be assumed to be relevant in the absence of any supporting evidence. In any event, A. G. was assisted, without either her or the therapist discovering adequate reasons for the development of her behaviour problems.

A useful refinement which Wolpe has now added to his technique of systematic desensitization[1] is the construction of what may be called a 'fear thermometer'. The patient is asked to imagine the most disturbing situation which he can think of, and to rate it at the top of the thermometer, i.e. 100 per cent. The total absence of anxiety in the situation would be rated as zero. Once the high and low points on the thermometer have been established, various examples of situations which would fall on the intermediate range are elicited from the patient. For example, in the case of A. G., described above, it is probable that she would have ranked the image of her having a series of painful injections in rapid succession as being at the top of the scale, i.e. 100 per cent. She was not, however, disturbed by the printed word 'injection' and would have rated that at zero. Imagining a situation in which she was observing someone else receiving an injection would probably have been rated at 70 on the scale. Once the fear thermometer has been constructed for each anxiety hierarchy, it is possible for the therapist and patient to communicate more freely during each therapeutic session. It provides some kind of quantitative estimate of the degree of anxiety experienced during each presentation of a disturbing item in the hierarchy, and it also provides a form of shorthand which facilitates the progress of the treatment. This fear thermometer was used in the treatment of L. H., a school phobic boy, described in Chapter 14 below.

Most of the case reports by behaviour therapists deal with the treatment of patients suffering from various kinds of anxiety

---

[1] Further information about this technique is provided by Wolpe (1958) and Lazarus (1964).

states. Apart from the fact that dysthymic disorders appear to be the most frequent type of neurosis encountered nowadays, this preponderance of anxiety cases also reflects, to an important extent, the theoretical framework and rationale of behaviour therapists. Wolpe (1963*b*) has pointed out in a cogent manner the way in which behaviour therapists approach their patients and how their analysis of neurotic disorders tends to resolve most of these conditions into a consideration of the stimuli which are producing anxiety. In his definition of neurosis, he ascribes a crucial role to anxiety (Wolpe, 1958). He says: 'Anxiety is usually the central constituent of (neurotic) behaviour, being invariably present in the causal situations.' Wolpe (1963*b*) has provided a clear example of the way in which learning theorists analyse neurotic behaviour into its essential S-R relationships. He describes the theoretical analysis used in the treatment of a compulsive neurosis in an eighteen-year-old boy. This patient had a very severe hand-washing compulsion, the basis of which was a fear of contamination by urine, particularly his own urine. When first seen, he was in a serious psychological state; after urinating, he would spend up to forty-five minutes in carrying out an elaborate ritual of cleaning his genitalia and then washing his hands for up to two hours. Examination of the patient's history and the origin of the complaint led Wolpe to the conclusion that the primary anxiety-provoking stimulus was urine itself. Consequently, he treated the boy by systematic desensitization (see page 136 below for details).

In attempting to analyse the neurotic behaviour in terms of stimulus and response connections, it is almost invariably found that the response is a relatively pure anxiety response, or at least heavily coloured by anxiety. The problem then becomes one of isolating the trigger stimulus and tracing the connection between the stimulus and the anxiety which it produces. It also follows that when an analysis of this kind is carried out, many patients will be given the label of 'anxiety neurotics', when, viewed from another theoretical standpoint, they might be diagnosed in a different manner. Conventional therapists often remark that the cases described in the literature on behaviour therapy appear so often to be straightforward and, by their standards, uncomplicated. Wolpe argues that the simplicity or complexity of neurotic disorders is very often the function of the therapist, rather than the illness itself. For example, it is very difficult, if not impossible, to produce a clear-cut and straightforward account of a neurotic illness if one employs psychoanalytic terms and interpretations. There are very few people who would claim that simplicity is a Freudian virtue. Wolpe argues that unless one is predisposed to analyse neurotic disorders in terms of stimulus and response relationships, it is very difficult to produce clear-cut descriptions of the particular disorder under consideration. A behaviouristic analysis of a case frequently elaborates straightforward relationships between the trigger stimuli and the anxiety responses, which then give the neurosis a phobia-like appearance. 'The distinctive feature of a classical phobia is the presence of clearly ostensible sources of anxiety . . . A behaviouristic analysis aims at the liquidation of these sources in every case.' When viewed in learning theory terms, anxiety states and phobias (and, indeed, many other neurotic disorders) are seen to share many important characteristics. Consequently, many of the laboratory findings in the field of anxiety can be applied equally well to various types of neurosis.

Phobias

Phobias are anxiety states in which the focus of the anxiety-producing stimuli is sharpened. In monosymptomatic phobias, the trigger stimulus can be identified and specified in a precise manner, whereas in multiple phobias, several types of stimuli are found to elicit the anxiety reaction. In learning theory terms, it is even possible to regard most, if not all, anxiety states as complex, multiple phobias.

A theory to account for the genesis and treatment of children's phobias was proposed in 1960 by Wolpe and Rachman and by Rachman and Costello (1961). The present account is a development of earlier versions and only the alterations and additions will be discussed in detail. In terms of the behaviour theory, phobias may be regarded as conditioned anxiety (fear) reactions. 'Any neutral stimulus, simple or complex, that happens to make an impact on an individual at about the time that a fear reaction is evoked acquires the ability to evoke fear subsequently. If the fear at the original conditioning situation is of high intensity or if the conditioning is repeated a good many times the conditioned fear will show the persistence that is characteristic of neurotic fear; and there will be generalization of fear reactions to stimuli resembling the conditioned stimulus' (Wolpe and Rachman, 1960).

The experimental evidence supporting this view of phobias is discussed in Wolpe (1958), Wolpe and Rachman (1960) and Rachman and Costello (1961), and is derived from studies of the behaviour of children and of animals. The classical demonstration of the development of a phobia was provided by Watson and Rayner in 1920. Having first ascertained that it was a neutral object, the authors presented an 11-month-old boy, Albert, with a white rat to play with. Whenever he reached for the animal the experimenters made a loud noise behind him. After only five trials Albert began showing signs of fear in the presence of the white rat. This fear then generalized to similar stimuli such as furry objects, cotton wool, white rabbits. The phobic reactions were still present when Albert was tested four months later.

The process involved in this demonstration provides a striking illustration of the manner in which phobias develop, and may be represented in this way:

1. Neutral stimulus (rat)————————————→Approach R
2. Painful noise stimulus (UCS)————————→Fear (UCR)
3. Rats (CS) + noise (UCS)————————————→Fear
4. Rats (CS)—————————————————————→Fear (CR)
5. Rabbit (GS^1) ————————————————→Fear (GR)
6. Cotton wool (GS^2)————————————→Fear (GCR)

The essentials of the theory may be summarized in nine statements.

1. Phobias are learned responses.
2. Stimuli develop phobic qualities when they are associated temporally and spatially with a fear-producing state of affairs.
3. Neutral stimuli which are of relevance in the fear-producing situation and/or make an impact on the person in the situation, are more likely to develop phobic qualities than weak or irrelevant stimuli.
4. Repetition of the association between the fear situation and the new phobic stimuli will strengthen the phobia.

5. Associations between high intensity fear situations and neutral stimuli are more likely to produce phobic reactions.

6. Generalization from the original phobic stimulus to stimuli of a similar nature will occur.

7. Noxious experiences which occur under conditions of excessive confinement are more likely to produce phobic reactions.

8. Neutral stimuli which are associated with a noxious experience(s) may develop (secondary) motivating properties. This acquired drive is termed the fear-drive.

9. Responses (such as avoidance) which reduce the fear-drive are reinforced.

Each of these nine statements is based on experimental evidence and would also appear to be consistent with clinical experience (Wolpe, 1958; Eysenck, 1960a). It can be legitimately argued in fact that these propositions are supported by the full weight of almost all the evidence accumulated in research on the learning process. Some sources of this evidence include Metzner, 1961; Wolpe, 1958, 1962a; Eysenck, 1960a, 1960e; Liddell, 1944; Gantt, 1944; Kimble, 1961; Mowrer, 1960.

In considering the aetiology of a patient's phobia, it is often difficult to determine the nature of the original causal experience. Is it possible to trace phobias back to a single experience or even to date the onset of the disorder? Allport's (1951) view is that 'an experience associated only once with a bereavement, an accident or a battle, may become the centre of a permanent phobia or complex, not in the least dependent on a recurrence of the original shock.' He also points out that tracing a phobia back to its origin is not necessarily a profitable enterprise. Evidence suggesting the occurrence of one-trial learning[1] of fear was obtained by Woodward (1959). Of 198 children who had suffered severe burns two to five years previously, 81 per cent showed 'signs of emotional disturbance according to their mothers.' Their most prominent symptom was described as

---

[1] Other examples of one-trial learning are provided by Sanderson et al. (1963) who used human subjects, and by Gantt et al. (1962) who used dogs. In both of these experiments, the UCS was traumatic and the conditioned responses were extremely resistant to extinction. See also Eysenck, H. J., *Dynamics of Anxiety and Hysteria*.

'fear and anxiety'. Only 7 per cent of the siblings of these children showed similar symptoms.

Nevertheless, it is likely that the great majority of phobias develop after cumulative traumatic or sub-traumatic experiences. Even in Watson's experiment with Albert, five trials were required before the boy first showed fear in the presence of the neutral stimulus. In a replication of Watson's findings, Jones (1937) confirmed the cumulative of effect repeated trials. This cumulative effect has also been observed in experiments with animals. Repeated mild shocks 'which by themselves do not elicit great emotional disturbance' can eventually produce neurotic behaviour[1] (Metzner, 1961). Similarly, Kurtz and Walters (1962) demonstrated that 'experiences of intense fear predispose animals to react with increased fear in subsequent encounters with aversive stimuli.'[2] Furthermore, one of the firmest conclusions that research on the psychology of learning has yielded is that repetition fosters learning.

The importance of repeated exposures to noxious stimulation lies mainly in the relationship between the frequency of traumata and the *strength* of the fear. The mechanism which is thought to be primarily responsible for the *persistence* of the fear is the secondary fear-drive.

Determinants of strength of fear

Miller (1951) noted that the factors which determine the strength of fear-drives are similar to those which operate in generating and sustaining other learned drives. He accordingly proposed five major determinants which contribute to the strength of a fear. These factors may be summarized as follows (for present purposes, we have changed the emphasis from fear as a drive to fear as a response):

(i)   Repetition of exposures to the fear-inducing situation will increase the strength of the fear;

(ii) Strong noxious stimuli will produce strong fears (e.g. a powerful shock will produce greater fear than a weak one);

[1]Under carefully controlled experimental conditions, however, the gradual and graduated exposure of animals to sub-traumatic stimulation can lead to the acquisition of a type of immunity to later stresses (Miller, 1960).

[2]See also Walters (1963).

(iii) Stimuli which are closely associated, temporally and spatially, with a noxious experience will produce strong fears.

(iv) Generalized fear stimuli which resemble the original noxious stimuli closely, will produce strong fears;

(v) The summation of fear-inducing stimuli will increase the strength of the fear.

Fear as an acquired drive

Thus far, we have considered fear primarily as a *response.* Fear can, however, also act as a drive to motivate the learning of new responses. In 1939, Mowrer formulated the idea of fear as a learned, anticipatory response to painful stimulation. He argued that the presence of the conditioned pain response (fear) motivates 'escape' behaviour and that those responses which bring about a reduction of the fear are reinforced or strengthened. The development of an agoraphobic syndrome illutrates this process quite clearly. The patient undergoes painful experiences (in a public place) which then give rise to a conditioned anticipatory fear-drive. The fear-drive persists or increases when he enters the noxious (public) situation. He indulges in various attempts to escape from the fear and only obtains relief when he reaches his home. The response of returning home will be reinforced because it is followed by a reduction of the fear-drive. Further attempts to travel towards public situations result in a reactivation of the fear-drive. Returning home reduces the fear-drive and this behaviour pattern is reinforced still further. Eventually this process, if not checked, will restrict the person's movements to a narrow environment surrounding the home, or make him entirely housebound.

The critical importance of the fear-drive in *sustaining* phobic (and other) patterns of behaviour is amply supported (Mowrer, 1960; Metzner, 1961; Yates, 1962; Miller, 1951). Neurotic behaviour patterns persist, paradoxically, because they are unpleasant. Once he has acquired an unpleasant reaction to a particular situation, the person then tends to avoid further contact with that situation. As learned patterns of behaviour can only be extinguished by repeated unreinforced (or inhibited) evocations, the tendency to avoid the noxious situation often precludes the 'spontaneous' disappearance of the neurotic behaviour. This analysis would lead one to predict, for example, that the spontaneous remission rate in agoraphobic conditions would be lower than in most other phobias.

The typical reaction of a phobic person when he comes into contact with the phobic situation is to retreat. This withdrawal is generally followed by a reduction of the fear-drive, which in turn reinforces the avoidance behaviour. This, then, is what has been described as 'the vicious circle which protects the conditioned fear response from extinction' (Eysenck, 1960a).

The development of phobias may be summed up in this way. The fear is *generated* by a painful experience (or experiences) and is *sustained* by the operation of the acquired fear drive.

A note on the effects of confinement. Research on the production of experimental neuroses in animals has shown that the restriction of the subject's behaviour plays an important part in the development of these disorders (Liddell, 1944; Wolpe, 1958). The probable explanation of this finding is that confinement reduces the animal's chances of making an adaptive response in the face of noxious stimulation. If the experimental subject is prevented from making a response which will terminate the noxious stimulus, a greater degree of fear is observed (Mowrer and Vieck, 1948). Wolpe's (1958) views on the role of restriction of the aetiology of phobias are summarized by Metzner (1961), in this way. 'The factor of confinement works (a) by preventing an escape response; (b) by restricting . . . fear-conditioning to a few cues, and (c) by not allowing any consistent response to control shock. All of these factors would make for more fear and hence more severe neurotic break-downs.'

Obviously, in considering the significance of these experimental findings for phobias in humans it is necessary to interpret confinement in a broad manner. It is psychological confinement rather than actual physical restraint which is the important influence to be considered. Psychological confinement is no less real than physical confinement. The barriers which prevent a child from carrying out a particular response may as easily reside within himself as in an external object. A simple example of psychological confinement may be found in the relations between a child and her school-teacher. The number of responses which the child can make in reply to a scolding is very limited. She cannot shout back, nor can she kick, scream, bite, or run away. If she is subjected to frequent verbal attacks of this kind, the child is likely to develop social anxiety. The degree of generalization of the anxiety to situations outside the school will, of course, depend on the general circumstances of her life and her previous social experiences. Some interesting examples of the role of confinement in producing and sustaining anxiety states in adults are described by Erwin (1963).

The treatment of simple and multiple phobias has been described in considerable detail in numerous case-reports:[1] see Wolpe, 1958; Eysenck, 1960a. The most important method of treatment in this condition is undoubtedly systematic desensitization. This method is often supplemented by other procedures, notably assertive training in those patients who experience fears in interpersonal situations. The therapeutic approach to phobic patients is, in all important respects, similar to that employed in treating patients suffering from anxiety states in general (see the case described on page 68 above, for example).

[1]The treatment of two phobic patients is described in Chapter 14 below.

Chapter 6

ANXIETY STATES—II

Social anxiety

SOCIAL anxiety is an unadaptive emotional reaction which is evoked by the behaviour, attitudes, or appearance of other people. In many instances the anxiety reaction is of a generalized nature and can be aroused by any member of a particular category of people, e.g. authoritarian figures, females, and so on. In extreme cases, the patient may experience social anxiety in the presence of all but a very few trusted and intimate friends or relations. Fear of people may affect the patient's behaviour in diverse ways ranging from agoraphobia (see Lazarus and Rachman, 1960) to homosexuality (see Wolpe and Stevenson, 1960), and many inter-personal problems, when subjected to an analysis in terms of learning theory, resolve themselves into problems of social anxiety.

A response which is antagonistic to anxiety and which can be easily invoked in social situations is self-assertion. The method of *assertive training*, or expressive training, as it is sometimes called, was developed by Salter (1950). Despite the fact that some of Salter's theoretical notions are of doubtful validity, he has succeeded in treating a wide range of neurotic disorders by the method of assertive training, supplemented by negative practice in some instances. Assertive training has been widely adopted by behaviour therapists, and is frequently used in combination with systematic desensitization.

Salter argues that psychotherapy is concerned with the social relations of the individual and that the basis of all neurotic disorders is excessive inhibition. The purpose of therapy, therefore, is to increase the patient's excitation. In support of his argument Salter states that most, if not all, neurotic symptoms disappear when the patient imbibes alcohol. The sort of 'inhibitory personalities' who benefit from imbibing alcohol are typified by the following attributes. They consider themselves to be shy, they are very sensitive to criticism, they are very self-conscious, they worry over humiliating experiences, they blush very easily, and so on. Salter has sought to overcome these inhibitory habits not by the conventional clinical means but by behavioural re-training.

In all, he describes six techniques for increasing the excitation of the neurotic patient. The first technique he describes as 'feeling talk'. This means that the patient is encouraged to express his spontaneously-felt emotions in a clear and forthright manner. If you don't like something, then you must say, 'I don't like it!' If you like something, then similarly you should express your appreciation in a direct manner. The patient is also encouraged to use 'facial talk'—that is, to express his emotions with a free use of facial expression. When you are angry, look angry; when you are happy, look happy. The third part of the training is concerned with contradiction. The patient is encouraged to express differences of opinion with other people, rather than simulate agreement. Fourthly, the patient is encouraged to use deliberately the word 'I' as much as possible. Fifthly, the patient is told to 'express agreement when you are praised.' He is trained to accept praise rather than dilute or disown it. Finally, the patient is encouraged to improvise and act spontaneously. Indecision, slow and deliberate consideration of unimportant actions, and morbid introspection are all strongly discouraged. Stated in this form, Salter's exercises in expressive behaviour might appear to be trivial and naive. In practice, however, they are frequently of great effectiveness as Salter's own cases amply demonstrate.

At first examination, Salter's assumption that inhibition lies at the heart of all neurotic illnesses appears to be a gross over-simplification and over-generalization. As we have indicated in earlier Chapters, there are in fact other forms of neurotic disorders in addition to those which are described as dysthymic. Nevertheless, a large proportion of those people who seek psychological assistance for neurotic disorders are suffering from dysthymic conditions. Furthermore, it seems quite feasible that assertive responses reciprocally inhibit anxiety, particularly in social situations. Although assertive training undoubtedly has a place among the techniques of behaviour therapy, an exclusive reliance on this method is unwarranted, particularly in the treatment of those patients who do not experience social anxiety. In the case described below, assertive training was the sole method of treatment, but it should be remembered that Salter's methods have most commonly been used in combination with other behaviour therapy techniques, notable systematic desensitization.

Mr. A. B., a twenty-five-year-old engineer, complained of persistent headaches, excessive shyness, lassitude, and inability to concentrate. The patient, who was unmarried, lived at his parents' home. The household was dominated absolutely by the patient's mother, who was extremely over-protective and restrictive. She insisted that the patient obtain her permission before going out in the evening and she also set a time for his return; she insisted on meeting and vetting all his friends and made or cancelled his social arrangements without his know-ledge or permission. She had accompanied him to school until he was thirteen years of age and bathed him until he was fifteen years old. Any resistance or assertion on his part was met with anger, tears, or in extreme cases, pseudo-illnesses. Mr. A. B. also complained that he was uneasy in company and tended to blush frequently and easily. He experienced great difficulty in his relationships with women and rarely invited them out. The standard of his work had deteriorated and he had become slow and clumsy.

The patient was given instruction in assertive training and was encouraged to practise the techniques at work in the first instance. In the first month of treatment, he reported few successes with the method, and it was decided to assign him set tasks to accomplish. The tasks were graded for difficulty and he was instructed to begin with the simpler assignments, such as praising his secretary for some work she had completed, deciding where he and his friends should have lunch, telling a waiter that he required quicker service, and so forth. He soon began recording successes in these exercises, and became a little more cheerful. As his confidence increased he was given a series of tasks to carry out at home. After another slow start, he achieved some important gains which culminated in his moving to his own flat. This decision, which he made on his own initiative, followed an argument with his mother. His departure provoked an attack of pseudo heart trouble in the mother, to which he responded with sympathy and solicitude without, however, returning home. One month after leaving home, he reported an increase in energy and freedom from headaches. He also succeeded in establishing close relations with two girls whom he had admired for some years past. His weekly treatment sessions were reduced to monthly ones, and six months after the commencement of the assertive training he was discharged, very much improved. A follow-up, carried out eighteen months after the completion of treatment, showed that he had maintained his improvement and no symptom replacements had occurred.

It is virtually certain that some anxiety, particularly social anxiety, is inhibited in most interview situations. Practically all forms of psychotherapeutic treatment will, by design or by accident, cause a reduction in some of the patient's anxiety. When the patient describes and discusses some of the situations or problems which disturb him, a degree of anxiety may be aroused. This anxiety is then inhibited by the calm and reassuring influence of the therapeutic environment and the therapist himself. Wolpe (1958) has suggested that these non-deliberate forms of desensitization may account for the observation that many different forms of psychotherapy can produce roughly the same number of improvements. The non-specific desensitization of anxiety, which occurs in interview or face-to-face situations, can also be invoked in an attempt to explain the occurrence of spontaneous remissions. For it is clearly not only psychotherapists who have the power to reassure and comfort people experiencing anxiety. Grinker & Spiegel (1945) have argued that abreactions which occur in non-therapeutic environments and in the absence of a therapeutic figure are not beneficial. In their experience with sodium pentothal-induced abreactions in the treatment of war neuroses, they reached the conclusion that the presence of what may be described as an anxiety-reducing figure was of great importance. Direct evidence of the efficacy of speaking about emotionally-toned subjects in a therapeutic setting is to be found in the work of Dittes (1957). He reported that the emotional strength of certain topics (as measured by the GSR recordings) declined after the subject had spoken about them in an accepting and comforting situation. Closer study of these interview-induced reductions in anxiety will enable therapists to put this phenomenon to deliberate use.

Pervasive anxiety

A manifestation of anxiety which is of considerable clinical significance but little understood, is what is sometimes termed free-floating or pervasive anxiety. Certain patients report that they feel anxious under many circumstances and for large periods of every day, and yet it is extremely difficult to isolate the trigger stimuli. In some patients, even the repeated and detailed consideration and re-examination of their general anxiety fails to reveal the critical stimuli. It has been argued by Wolpe that pervasive anxiety differs from the more common forms of anxiety in quantity rather than quality. He states that there is no dichotomy between specific anxiety evoked by recognizable stimuli and pervasive anxiety which is evoked by stimuli which are not easily discernible. 'The pervasiveness of the latter (intangible stimuli) is a function of the pervasiveness of the stimulus element conditioned; and there are degrees of pervasiveness ranging from the absolute omnipresence of time itself through very common elements like room walls to rarely encountered configurations like hunchbacks.' Wolpe supports his view by two types of observation. In the first place, he reports that patients who complain of pervasive anxiety almost invariably experience a reduction in this anxiety when they lie down and close their eyes. Secondly, he quotes from his own case material the few instances in which patients with pervasive anxiety were eventually able, with the assistance of the therapist, to isolate and label various sources of anxiety production. In one case, it was discovered that the sense of largeness was the disturbing trigger for the patient's anxiety, and in another it was the sense of physical space. Both by their very nature and also because of their rarity, these stimuli were only uncovered with the greatest difficulty.

Wolpe posits two possible sources for the development of pervasive anxiety—although there is no reason to assume that these possibilities are mutually exclusive. It is possible that pervasive anxiety is conditioned when the circumstances in which the neurosis developed were not clearly defined. If the stimuli which were present at the time of the original trauma or traumata were fleeting or relatively imperceptible, the person may continue to experience anxiety in a range of meaningless and ill-defined situations.

A second possibility is that patients' level of anxiety at the time of the onset of the neurotic condition was extremely high. Under these conditions, it would be predicted that a larger number of stimuli would acquire the ability to act as cues for anxiety evocation on subsequent occasions.

The origins of pervasive anxiety are, at this stage, still obscure, and the treatment of this condition is also still in an unsatisfactory stage of development. In Wolpe's experience, the commonly used techniques for treating anxiety states are comparatively ineffective in handling pervasive anxiety. For this reason, he was persuaded to experiment with a variety of alternatives, and eventually obtained some degree of success with the method of carbon dioxide therapy. He finally settled for a refined version of the Meduna technique, as described by La Verne (1953). Briefly, in this method the patient inhales a gas mixture comprising 70 per cent carbon dioxide and 30 per cent oxygen and when his lungs are full he removes the anaesthetic mask and breathes heavily for about 15 seconds. He is then allowed to relax for a further minute before an additional three or four inhalations are given. The rationale which Wolpe proposes for this method is that such high concentrations of carbon dioxide produce deep muscle relaxation and, consequently, inhibit anxiety. This explanation, which differs from those proposed by Meduna himself and by Gellhorn (1953) will, of course, require substantiation. It is worth mentioning in passing, however, that Lazarus (1963) obtained comparatively poor results with his pervasive anxiety patients and would appear, from his own description, not to include carbon dioxide therapy among his therapeutic procedures.

Chapter 7

HYSTERICAL DISORDERS

THE earliest applications of conditioning principles to the study of hysteria appear to have been made by Russian workers (Hilgard and Marquis, 1961). They were mainly interesting in applying these methods for diagnostic purposes, but since 1933 a number of attempts have been made to treat hysterical patients by conditioning methods.

The methods which have been used so far include the following. Avoidance conditioning, operant conditioning, negative practice, desensitization, abreaction. It will be seen from the descriptions given below that many of the techniques which have been used in treating hysteria are simple yet extremely clever.

In 1933, Sears and Cohen described the successful treatment of a 45-year-old woman who had developed hysterical anaesthesia eight months before treatment was undertaken. The patient had been diagnosed as follows: 'Psychopathic personality, with hysterical anaesthesia to superficial touch, analgesia to superficial and deep pain, and astereognosis.' The authors decided to attempt to develop a conditioned avoidance reaction in the anaesthetic left hand. The conditioned stimulus which they chose was the movement of a wisp of cotton wool across the back of the anaesthetic left hand. The unconditioned stimulus was a strong electric shock. The patient's hands were placed palm down on a table, with the right hand resting on an electric grid. An attempt was made to eliminate extraneous sounds or other cues, and the patient's eyes were bandaged to prevent her from seeing when the stimulus was about to be presented. Having ensured that the movement of the cotton wool across the left hand was a neutral stimulus, in the sense that the patient did not perceive it, they commenced the conditioning regime. The unconditioned stimulus, a shock, acted on the right hand after the cotton wool stimulus had been applied to the left hand (see Fig. 16). The time-interval between the conditioned and unconditioned stimuli was approximately one second. In the first part of the experiment, fifty trials of this kind were given, but no conditioned reaction was evoked. In order to examine the possibility that irradiation had occurred, the authors transferred the conditioned stimulus (cotton wool) to the right hand, and the unconditioned stimulus to the anaesthetic left hand. A conditioned reaction appeared after two trials. As the authors point out, it is improbable that a conditioned response could ordinarily be developed in only three trials; one must therefore conclude that a degree of transfer had occurred from one hand to the other. They then attempted to produce a conditioned response by applying the conditioned stimulus to the anaesthetic hand once more. No conditioned response was evoked, although the application of the conditioned stimulus to the normal hand continued to evoke a consistent conditioned reaction.

1. CS ⟶ No response
(Cotton wool across LEFT hand)

2. UCS ⟶ RIGHT-hand withdrawal
(Shock)

3. CS ⟶ UCS ⟶ Right-hand withdrawal

4. CS ⟶ No response

5. CS^1 ⟶ No response
(Tap on LEFT hand)

6. CS^1 ⟶ UCS (shock) ⟶ RIGHT-hand withdrawal

7. CS^1 ⟶ CR (RIGHT-hand withdrawal)

8. CS (cotton wool) ⟶ CR

9. Return of sensation in LEFT hand

FIG. 16. The treatment of an hysterical patient by conditioning. (Adapted from Sears and Cohen. *Behaviour Therapy and the Neuroses* ed. H. J. Eysenck, Pergamon Press, 1960.)

Sears and Cohen thought that irradiation within the same sense modality might occur under these conditions, and the next step in the treatment programme was as follows. The patient's pressure sense in the anaesthetic hand had remained normal and they consequently decided to use a tap on the knuckles as the new conditioned stimulus. The conditioned stimulus (tap on the knuckles) was followed one second later by the unconditioned stimulus (electric shock to the normal hand). A conditioned response was evoked after one trial and remained strong for the next ten trials. On the twelfth trial, the cotton wool stimulus was substituted for the tap on the knuckles and produced, for the first time, a conditioned response. On the next trial, the cotton wool did not produce a conditioned reaction. Six more trials were given with the tap on the knuckles, and again the cotton wool stimulus was interspersed. A second conditioned response was evoked and after another six reinforcements, using the tap on the knuckles as the conditioned stimulus, the cotton wool stimulus was able to produce two further conditioned reactions. When the patient was re-tested, two days later, the conditioned reactions were found to have extinguished spontaneously. After only one reinforcement, however, the conditioned response to the cotton wool stimulus reappeared. When the patient was asked why she withdrew her hand before receiving an electric shock, she replied that she did not know and denied having felt the cotton wool on her anaesthetic hand. When the conditioned response to the cotton wool stimulus was again evoked, the patient not only withdrew he hand but also exclaimed in surprise. She stated that she had felt the cotton wool on her anaesthetic hand. Twenty further trials were given, and in fifteen of them the patient reported that she had felt the cotton wool stimulus and also withdrew her normal right hand before the electric shock was delivered. The cotton wool stimulus had become sensible to her and thereafter served as an easily perceptible warning signal. The anaesthesia disappeared completely at this time and, at follow-up six months later, there was no evidence of its return.

This conditioned avoidance technique was also used by Hilgard and Marquis (1940) in their treatment of a patient whose left arm was totally paralysed and anaesthetic. The hysterical reaction had occurred six years before conditioning treatment commenced and the arm and hand had undergone considerable atrophy from disuse. Previous attempts at psychiatric treatment had failed to bring about any improvement. In the first part of the treatment programme, a light shock to the anaesthetic left hand was used as the conditioned stimulus. The unconditioned stimulus was a severe shock delivered to the normal right hand (see Fig. 17). A certain amount of conditioning developed, and the anaesthetic left hand gradually regained its sensitivity. The procedure was then reversed, for purposes of developing voluntary control. Now the normal hand was given a light shock which acted as the conditioned stimulus, and the paralysed hand was given the severe shock (unconditioned stimulus). At this stage the anaesthetic left hand had become fully sensitive to the shock but the patient was not able to move the hand. 'Presently movement began to occur in the paralysed hand at the signal given to the normal hand. This was the beginning of control and voluntary movement was gradually restored. At this stage, the patient was given physiotherapy to strengthen the muscles which had been so long unused. The symptoms had not returned two years later, nor were any additional symptoms reported.'

1. CS (Light shock, LEFT hand)———————→ No response
2. UCS (Strong shock, RIGHT hand)———→ Hand withdrawal
3. CS———→ UCS———→ CR (Hand withdrawal)
4. Return of left hand sensitivity
5. Reversal of stimuli
6. CS ———————→ UCS ———————→ CR
   (Light shock,   (Strong shock,   (LEFT hand withdrawal)
   RIGHT hand)   LEFT hand)
7. CS ————————————————————→ CR
8. Return of voluntary control of left hand

FIG. 17. Treatment of a patient with hysterical paralysis by conditioning methods. (Adapted from Hilgard and Marquis *Conditioning and Learning*, New York: Appleton, Century, Crofts, 1940.)

Malmo *et al.* (1960) used the same technique in treating a patient with total hysterical deafness. The patient, a nineteen-year-old girl, was admitted to hospital with psychogenic deafness. After 2½ months of psychotherapy her hearing had not returned and she was treated by conditioning methods. The conditioned stimulus was a tone and the unconditioned stimulus was an electric shock delivered to the middle finger of her right hand. Prior to the first conditioning session, the therapist strongly suggested to the patient that the machine would cure her deafness. Conditioned finger withdrawal reactions were produced in the first session (see Fig. 18). At the conclusion of this session, the patient asserted that she still could not hear. The therapist repeated the suggestion that her hearing would return on the following morning. The next morning the patient was crossing a busy street when a driver who narrowly avoided hitting her blew his horn and shouted at her. 'Her hearing suddenly returned and has remained intact.' When the patient was followed up, some two years later, it was learned that her hearing was still intact and that that she was apparently symptom-free.

1. CS (tone) ————————————→ No response
2. UCS (shock to finger) ———————→ Finger withdrawal
3. CS —————→ UCS ——————→ CR (Finger withdrawal)
4. CS (tone) ————————————→ CR
5. Return of hearing

FIG. 18. Treatment of a patient with hysterical deafness by conditioning methods. (Adapted from Malmo *et al.* in *Behaviour Therapy and the Neuroses.* (ed. H. J. Eysenck) Pergamon Press, 1960.)

Malmo *et al.* also carried out some interesting investigations on this patient, and showed, among other things, that her deafness was psychogenic in nature and could not be regarded as malingering. While the patient was still deaf, they subjected her to intense auditory stimulation but could produce little or no reaction. After she had recovered her hearing she displayed an intense reaction to the same kind of stimulation.

Brady and Lind (1961) were able to cure a patient suffering from hysterical blindness by means of an operant conditioning technique. The patient had lost his sight after being involved in a motor accident. No organic basis for his loss of vision could be found and he had received various types of psychotherapy, without success. Two years after the onset of the illness, he was treated by a conditioning method. He was conditioned to respond to the presence of a light, in the following way. He was informed that he would be rewarded with tokens when he pressed a small lever. These tokens could then be exchanged at the hospital canteen for various articles. Another important type of reward which was introduced by the therapists was social approval.

The light stimulus was switched on at irregular intervals and when a lever-pressing response followed the presentation of the light, the patient was given a reward token and social approval. He gradually learned to respond to the light. As his conditioning score continued to improve, his adjustment on the ward and his social relationships with others also improved. This conditioned response was accompanied by vague visual sensations, until eventually he reported that he could see the light. Brady and Lind describe the recovery of vision in this way. 'The patient's operant behaviour changed abruptly in session forty-three. The percentage of responses during the correct time-interval dropped to half its previous value and the number of multiple responses rose sharply. At the end of the session the patient came out of the room exclaiming that he could see the light. He appeared both anxious and ex-hilarated and sought praise and approval for his accomplish-ment. He accounted for his poor score during the session, despite his awareness of visual cues, by stating that he felt almost paralysed by the light. His score improved rapidly over the next two sessions however, and he became less anxious.' Once the patient had recovered his raw visual sensitivity, Brady and Lind trained him in a series of discrimination tasks. The patient's performance was poor during his first few sessions, and then gradually improved. During this part of the treatment, the patient's clinical condition contined to improve as well. After the operant conditioning was discontinued, the patient received conventional therapy. When he was last seen, thirteen months after the completion of treatment, he was found to have retained his normal vision.

Walton and Black (1960) reported the successful treatment of a patient suffering from chronic, hysterical aphonia, by negative practice methods. The patient, a twenty-four-year-old female, had been aphonic for some seven years, and com-pletely mute for two of these years before behaviour therapy was instituted. She had been brought up under adverse circumstances and had suffered various psychological traumata before the aphonia actually developed. The precipitating event which heralded the onset of aphonia was a minor throat operation which she had undergone at the age of seventeen. When she regained consciousness, she found that she had lost her voice, and after her condition had been diagnosed as psychogenic in origin, she was admitted to a neurosis unit. During the seven years in which she had been aphonic, she had received numerous forms of treatment, including intensive psychotherapy, hypnosis, insulin treatment, and other drug treatments. When the patient was first taken on for behaviour therapy, she was unable to speak in more than a whisper. Her score on the Maudsley Personality Inventory showed that she was slightly extraverted and that her neuroticism score was within normal limits.

Walton and Black assumed that the aphonia had originally developed as a conditioned avoidance response because it had satisfied a temporary need. Thereafter, it persisted in its own right as a habit and, they argued, this habit should be amenable to unlearning. In view of the findings that extraverted-hysteric neurotics develop reactive inhibition quickly and that this inhibition dissipates slowly, Walton and Black decided to attempt a therapeutic procedure based on negative practice.

Initially the patient was required to read from a boring book into a tape recorder. She was told that as she required exercise in reading and in voice production, she would have to read for periods of fifteen minutes at a time. If she failed to maintain the volume of her speech throughout the fifteen minutes' trial period or to improve on the volume produced in the previous trial period, then she would be given an additional two minutes of practice at the end of the session. If, on the other hand, she made an improvement during the fifteen minutes' trial period, two minutes would be lopped off from the end of the session— i.e. she would only need to practise for thirteen minutes. This procedure was adopted on the assumption that hysterics, who develop reactive inhibition quickly, would be highly motivated towards achieving a shorter session.

The training sessions were carried out three times a week, in the presence of one psychologist. Within a short number of trials, the subject began to show marked improvement. The volume of her speech increased with each session but she complained that at the end of the long sessions she felt hoarse and extremely tired. In the second phase of the treatment, she was given two training sessions per day, and the sessions were increased to half an hour in length. In addition, a second psychologist was introduced at this point, in order to ensure that her ability to speak would generalize to other situations and to other people. During these thirty minutes' training sessions, the patient was interrupted at five-minute intervals and given encouragement by the therapist. These interruptions had a twofold purpose. Firstly, they introduced rest periods, during which the reactive inhibition was dissipated, and secondly, they rewarded the patient for good performance. The third phase of the treatment consisted of introducing more people into the situation. This transition was successfully accomplished and the patient was, by this time, speaking with a reasonable volume. The subject matter of the training sessions was also changed and the patient was required to participate in a play-reading instead of simply reading from a book. This change was instituted in order to give her practise in conversation. In the final part of the treatment, the patient was given 10 mg. of dexedrine before each training session. The purpose of using this stimulant drug was to produce an introverted type of behaviour pattern and to reduce the amount of reactive inhibition which was generated These changes in each phase brought about a smooth and continuous improvement in her symptom and also in her general behaviour.

When the patient was followed up, some two years after the completion of treatment, she was found to have maintained her ability to speak normally. There had been no recurrence of the symptom, despite two extremely stressful experiences which she had undergone. No substitute symptoms occurred at any time.

Another case of hysterical aphonia was successfully treated by one of the present authors. A thirty-four-year-old actress lost her voice ten days before the opening night of a play in which she was to take the leading part. She had been extremely anxious about the part and had experienced unusual difficulty in learning her lines. Her voice had disappeared overnight, and no organic basis for the aphonia could be detected. When she was first seen by the therapist, she was in a state of heightened anxiety, and could speak only in a hoarse whisper. Prior to this illness, she had never suffered from any psychological disorder. The Maudsley Personality Inventory scores showed her to be above the average on both the extraversion and neuroticism scales.

She was treated by desensitization, based on deep relaxation. The first five of the eleven treatment sessions were devoted to exercises and practise in progressive relaxation. Thereafter the patient was desensitized to various social situations and also to stage fright. Her voice gradually returned to normal, and at the end of treatment she was very much improved. She appeared in the play as planned and acquitted herself very well. A follow-up conducted six months later showed that she had remained well and no substitute symptoms had arisen.

Wolpe (1958) distinguishes between two types of hysteria. He describes the treatment of twenty-two hysterical patients, thirteen of whom had associated neurotic anxiety, and the remaining nine who had very little anxiety. Wolpe tended to use different methods in the treatment of these high and low anxiety patients. Hysterical patients with high anxiety were treated by Wolpe's conventional methods, such as desensitization and assertive training. The low anxiety hysterics were treated by special methods. These special methods included the use of hypnosis and abreaction.

As Wolpe does not provide separate recovery indices for different diagnostic categories, it is not possible to estimate the recovery rate for his hysterical patients. Lazarus (1963), in his report of 126 cases of severe neurosis, obtained a 71 per cent recovery rate in those twenty-seven patients who had hysterical symptoms. While there is a need for further information about the response to treatment of hysterical patients, numerous behaviour therapy techniques have already been shown to produce results in individual cases. The behaviour therapist who is required to treat an hysterical patient at least has the advantage of a variety of techniques at his disposal, ranging from avoidance conditioning and operant conditioning to desensitization, negative practice, and assertive training.

The relationship between hysterical disorders and the personality dimension of extraversion has already been described in Chapter 2 above. It is interesting to notice that in those three cases described above where information about the patient's personality was provided, they were described as being extraverted (Walton and Black's and the present authors' case), or psychopathic (Sears and Cohen). In at least one other case, that reported by Brady and Lind, although no formal investigation of the patient's personality was undertaken, his previous history suggests quite strongly that he was an extraverted person, possibly even psychopathic.

Hysterical disorders, like all neurotic disorders, are acquired by a learning process. In some of the patients described above and elsewhere, the hysterical symptoms appear to have developed as conditioned avoidance responses in the face of intense anxiety. Dollard and Miller (1950), for example, described two such patients in some detail. The first patient developed an hysterical paralysis of his right arm while in combat. The second patient, a married woman with a fear of sex and pregnancy, developed partial paralysis of the legs after her fourth pregnancy. In both of these cases, the onset of the neurosis resulted in removal from the anxiety-producing situation. In addition, both patients displayed little anxiety about their illness. The cases described by Brady and Lind, and by Walton and Black showed similar features.

Miller and Dollard argued that the symptom is acquired (learned) because it reduces the fear drive. 'Since the fear was not experienced as long as the symptom persisted but reappeared as soon as the symptom was interrupted it is apparent that the symptom reduced the fear.' Reduction of the fear drive reinforces the learned behaviour which, in these cases, is the hysterical disorder. While there is some merit in this analysis (which is, in general, shared by Walton and also by Metzner (1961)), it fails to account for some of the phenomena of hysteria.

The appearance of anxiety after the initial lifting of the hysterical symptoms has been noted by Miller and Dollard and also by Walton and Black and by Brady and Lind. Neither Sears and Cohen nor Malmo et al. report such observations, however. An important point, however, is the transitory nature of this anxiety. If the hysterical disorder is anxiety-reducing, in the sense intended by Miller and Dollard, we might ask why it does not persist after the completion of successful conditioning treatment. In the case histories described above (excluding some of the cases of Wolpe and

Lazarus) the conditioning process was aimed at changing the hysterical behaviour and not at the alleviation of anxiety. Nevertheless, the patients were successfully treated and had remained well when they were seen at follow-up.

A second difficulty with the Miller-Dollard analysis is that hysterical patients continue to experience anxiety even after the onset of the hysterical disorder (see Wolpe's cases, for example). This difference can perhaps be overcome by arguing that, in these patients, the hysterical disorder has not succeeded in reducing all the anxiety. A third shortcoming is their omission of any reference to the influence of personality on the onset of the illness. Why should the patient develop an hysterical disorder rather than any other form of neurotic illness, such as a phobia or compulsions?

Walton and Black are of the opinion that, in their aphonic patient at least, the hysterical disorder originated as an avoidance reaction to an anxiety-provoking situation and then persisted as a habit. The aphonia became virtually autonomous and hence the patient was fully recovered once the remaining hysterical habit had been altered. This view, coupled with the personality predisposition postulated above, may in fact provide a possible model for the analysis and treatment of hysterical conditions. An additional contribution to this process may be traced to the person's general psychological state at the time of the onset of the anxiety-producing situation. Some of the hysterical patients described by Grinker and Spiegel (1945) and by Miller and Dollard, for example, were in a state of extreme fatigue and physical weakness when the precipitating trauma occurred. A suggestion of this nature was in fact made by Pavlov (1941), who drew attention to the role of excessive stimulation in the hysterical process. A more direct connection can, however, be seen between the presence of fatigue and Eysenck's typological postulate concerning extraversion, hysteria, and reactive inhibition. Extraverts develop reactive inhibition quickly and dissipate it slowly, and tend to 'block' under stress (see next Chapter).

In view of the reasonably high degree of successes obtained with these patients (see Chapter 16) by Wolpe, Hussain and Lazarus (who both used Wolpean methods), the best course to adopt is as follows: ' . . . Hysterical reactions may accompany anxiety or occur on their own . . . In the former case their treatment is the treatment of anxiety, and in the latter, special procedures are employed' (Wolpe, 1958, p. 89). The special procedures, which in our opinion are to be recommended, have been described in the cases mentioned above, and can be conveniently summarized as consisting of either avoidance conditioning or operant conditioning. In addition, the adroit use of stimulant drugs, such as dexedrine and amphetamine, may be of considerable assistance. Apart from their general 'introverting action', stimulant drugs facilitate the development of conditioned responses (see Chapter 4, above).

Chapter 8

PSYCHOMOTOR DISTURBANCES

PSYCHOMOTOR disturbances such as tics, tremors, writer's cramp, and spasms are commonly grouped under the title of hysterical disorders. For present purposes, however, we will regard them as a group of disorders in their own right.

In an important review of psychomotor abnormalities, Yates (1960) examined the existing literature in terms of the following five postulates:

'1.   Performance in the test situation may be conceptualized as dependent upon the interaction of drive strength and task complexity.

2.   Neurotics are characterized by high drive.

3.   High drive may also be defined in terms of the strength of a stimulus. Thus, a strong stimulus will have high drive value; a weak stimulus a low drive value.

4.   Where the response required is simple, it will be facilitated by high drive.

5.   Where the response required has to be chosen from among others (i.e. discrimination is involved) it will be impeded in its appearance by high drive.'

With these postulates providing the theoretical framework, Yates analysed various generalizations concerning psychomotor behaviour and examined their experimental support. He concluded that the results support the hypothesis that neurotics are characterized by 'a high state of drive which facilitates the correct response in a simple situation, but which impedes the correct response in a complex situation.' In normal subjects an increase in stimulus intensity will produce increased speed and amplitude of response. 'Above a certain intensity, however, a stimulus ceases to facilitate the response and begins to inhibit it.' An increase in drive (induced by stress or anxiety) in normal subjects will also facilitate the speed and amplitude of simple responses but impede responses in a complex task.

Concerning the psychomotor performance of introverts and extraverts, Yates proposes that there are two major types of psychomotor response to be found within normal and neurotic groups and that these correspond to the types described by Davis, namely inert and overactive. Davis (1946*a*, *b*, 1949) conducted a series of experiments on the causes of pilot error, using a simulated cockpit and, in later work, an apparatus in which the subject moved a pointer to left or right of centre. Yates summarized Davis's findings in this way:

'Neurotics tend to make more errors of judgment compared with normals. Within the neurotic group, dysthymics tend to make errors of over-activity, hysterics errors of inertia. Similar tendencies are found within normal groups.'

Davis also reported that errors of inertia predominated over errors of overactivity in all subjects, provided the test is continued for a sufficiently long period. This finding is similar to that reported in an experiment by Eysenck (1960*i*), in which industrial apprentices were tested for reminiscence effects under two conditions of drive. The account which Eysenck provides of the development and action of reactive inhibition makes Davis's observations on late effects readily understandable. In brief, it may be stated in this way. Errors of inertia (typical of the high-inhibitory, extravert group) are produced by the rapid accumulation of reactive inhibition, and it follows then that if anybody, even a member of a low reactive inhibition (introvert) group, is made to practise long enough, the inhibition will be allowed to accumulate to the point where it produces errors of inertia. In other words, everybody will make errors of inertia eventually, but the extraverts will begin making them well before the introverts.

Venables (1955) reported an investigation into changes of motor responses with increase and decrease in task difficulties. His samples consisted of 210 industrial trainees, and twenty-two hospitalized neurotics. All the subjects were given three consecutive practice periods on a motor response task. The task consisted of moving a lever in response to light stimuli, and could be made easy or difficult. After the first, easy period of practice, the subjects were given a difficult period, followed again by an easy period. His major finding was that normal and neurotic extraverts showed increases in inertia when the task was made difficult, and that normal and neurotic introverts showed increases in overactivity with increasing difficulties. He also found a reversal of these trends when the stress condition was withdrawn.

Similar results to those obtained by Venables were reported by Rachman (1961). Thirty-six hospitalized neurotic patients were classified into hysteric and dysthymic groups and observed in a conflict-stress situation (see Fig. 19). Like Venables, he found that as the difficulty of the task was increased, the hysteric patients tended to respond inertly and the dysthymic patients to respond more actively. With a decrease in task difficulty, the hysterics tended to respond more actively and the dysthymics showed a decline in activity. Further information, from an entirely independent source, also supports the indentification between predominance of the inhibitory processes and hyperactivity in psychomotor tasks. Voronin et al. (1959) obtained a measure of overactivity in a conditioning experiment. Their twenty-five subjects were required to anticipate the presentation of various complex stimuli by pressing a button. Voronin et al. found that the errors made by subjects on complex tasks were of two types: over-activity (in which the subject pressed the button too quickly) and under-activity. These measures of activity were then correlated with adaptation on the G.S.R., the E.E.G. pattern, and other phenomena. Rapid adaptation on the G.S.R. was found to correlate with errors of underactivity, as did 'sleep inhibition' (based on E.E.G. recordings). The authors interpreted their results in terms of Pavlovian theory. Subjects who are predominantly inhibitory adapt to the G.S.R. quickly, develop sleep inhibition, and make errors of under-activity. Excitatory subjects show the reverse pattern— slow G.S.R. adaptation, little or no sleep inhibition, and overreactivity. Arising, as it does, from such an independent source, this experiment provides impressive substantiating evidence for the claim that extraverts make errors of under-activity and introverts make errors of overactivity. The importance of obtaining clear information about the role of personality factors in psychomotor disturbances is well demonstrated by

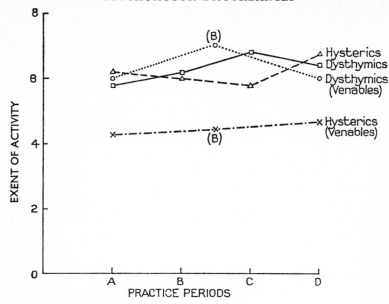

Fig. 19. Performance of hysteric and dysthymic patients in a conflict situation. With an increase in difficulty, the hysteric patients tend to respond inertly and the dysthymic patients to respond more actively. When the difficulty of the task is decreased, the hysterics respond more actively and the dysthymics less actively.

an examination of the treatment of writer's cramp by the methods of behaviour therapy.

Writer's cramp

The most extensive work on the subject of writer's cramp is that of Liversedge and Sylvester (1955) and Sylvester and Liversedge (1960). Over a period of six years, they examined fifty-six patients who were suffering from writer's cramp, and treated thirty-nine of these patients by various conditioning techniques. Twenty-nine of their cases were cured and only five of these were found to have relapsed when a follow-up was carried out, four and a half years after completion of treatment. If we exclude the patients who relapsed within four and a half years, the recovery rate obtained by Sylvester and Liversedge is still in the region of 60 per cent. In their reports, they present some striking photographic illustrations of the changes in hand-writing which were produced in the successfully treated patients.

In the majority of the cases, Liversedge and Sylvester carried out the treatment in three stages. In stage one, a metal plate with holes of diminishing diameter, from one inch to an eighth of an inch was used. 'The subject was required to hold a metal stylus in these holes, starting with the largest. The plate and stylus were connected up so that whenever the stylus touched the sides of the hole the patient received a painful electric shock in the other hand. This was immediately successful: after two or three sessions, patients who had started with a tremor violent enough to give continuous shocks when in the largest hole could keep the stylus for minutes quite still in the smallest one. The next step was to attack the tremor with the hand *moving*.'

The second phase of the treatment is described as follows. 'Strips of PVC tape were stuck on to a metal plate and the patient had to trace over these with a stylus; if the stylus came off the tape on to the metal, he got a shock. The tape was cut so as to require the basic movements involved in writing. Again about half an hour a day was spent on this practice. We found that usually patients could accomplish all movements, including writing letters on the tapes, by the end of six to eight days.'

Stage three is described as follows: 'A fountain pen was fitted with a spring contact such that whenever the patient had a thumb spasm (gripped the pen too hard), he received an electric shock in the other hand. This method was combined with Method 2 after the first dozen patients—i.e. stylus used on the plate was fitted with this spring contact. Writing with a fitted pen on paper was usually commenced before the end of the second week of treatment. In the majority of cases the patients themselves were able to adjust the apparatus and carry out the programme after the first five or six sessions, the experimeter merely interviewing them from time to time to guide them.' Sylvester and Liversedge also describe two other methods which were used in special cases. As these last two methods only feature to an insignificant extent in their report, we will not describe them here.

Sylvester and Liversedge, discussing the failures in their

patients, point out that most of their failures had greater anxiety than the successfully treated patients. They point out, however, that this anxiety may well be a result rather than a cause of the writer's cramp. Whatever the casual relationship between the anxiety and writer's cramp, it is noteworthy that, according to their experiences, the failures were found mostly in those patients who were excessively anxious.[1] It should be pointed out that the majority of the patients treated by these therapists were not psychologically abnormal in any general way, although some of the members of the group were neurotic.

Beech (1960) criticized the rationale and the method of treatment employed by Sylvester and Liversedge on several grounds. While some of his comments are of little weight, his work does emphasize the possibility that the anxiety level of the patient is an extremely important determinant of the outcome of avoidance conditioning treatment. Beech described the treatment of four patients and was able to achieve only partial improvement in one of them by means of avoidance conditioning. One patient failed to improve at all, and the other three patients improved only when the avoidance conditioning was entirely replaced by another method, or at least supplemented by some other form of treatment. The first patient, Mr. A. B., deteriorated when avoidance conditioning treatment was commenced and it was necessary to switch to a treatment based on negative practice. He responded to the negative practice procedure fairly quickly and within seven sessions, was able to write reasonably well. Beech points out that the quality as well as the quantity of writing was very much improved. This patient was highly neurotic and extravert according to his scores revealed on the Maudsley Personality Inventory. The second patient, Mr. C. B., was a neurotic introvert, and he too, deteriorated when avoidance conditioning was instituted. The patient made some temporary inprovement with negative practice procedures and also made some improvement with reciprocal inhibition methods. None of these techniques, however, was able to produce a lasting improvement in his condition. The third patient, Mr. E. F., was highly introverted and moderately neurotic. This patient showed quite a considerable

---

[1] This observation is in keeping with Yates' theoretical analysis described on p. 105 above: psychomotor performance may be impeded if the (anxiety) drive level becomes excessive.

improvement after avoidance conditioning treatment, but reported continuing sensations of fatigue and discomfort during the act of writing. Beech, therefore, decided to supplement the treatment with relaxation exercises. This method produced favourable results over a long period, and the patient was symptom-free when seen at follow-up, one year after the conclusion of the treatment. The fourth patient, Mr. G. H., was highly neurotic and moderately extraverted. After carrying out a preliminary experiment involving avoidance conditioning, Beech decided to treat this patient by systematic desensitization, because the indications were that he would deteriorate under the avoidance type of procedure. Although the treatment of this patient was not completed at the time when Beech wrote his paper, he had already made some significant improvement.

Beech's experiences with these four patients led him to underline the tentative conclusion of Sylvester and Liversedge, to the effect that patients with high anxiety levels do not respond favourably to avoidance conditioning. Beech concluded that 'where the general level of anxiety is high the evidence presented would indicate that avoidance conditioning might fail to produce positive results and may even worsen the condition . . . On the other hand, avoidance conditioning might successfully reduce the frequency and amplitude of the symptoms where the anxiety level is low.' He argues further that in those patients where the anxiety level is high, the most appropriate treatment would appear to be reciprocal inhibition.

Apart from the fact that Beech's conclusions are based on only four cases, as compared with Sylvester and Liversedge's thirty-nine patients, there is another difference in the sample which might be of some importance. Sylvester and Liversedge pointed out that most of their patients were not neurotic in any general sense, but were suffering from a specific disability, namely, writer's cramp. All four of Beech's patients, however, appeared to have general neurotic disorders accompanying their writer's cramp. Beech's information about the introversion-extraversion ratings of his four patients is interesting and invites speculation on the possible contribution made by these personality factors to both the development of the disorder and the reaction to treatment of extraverted and introverted subjects. It will be remembered that the first patient reported by Beech was a neurotic extravert and he responded best to treatment based on negative practice, whereas the patient who was a neurotic introvert responded most favourably to a desensitization procedure. Unfortunately, Sylvester and Liversedge did not obtain information about the personalities of their patients in a systematic fashion, and so it is not possible to examine the role of personality factors in their sample. In view of the relationships which have been demonstrated to exist between psychomotor behaviour and personality, it seems probable that we will benefit both in our understanding of the aetiology and of the treatment of writer's cramp by paying greater attention to personality factors in this group of patients. One suggestion which arises from Beech's four cases, for example, is the possibility that the form of writer's cramp is related to introversion-extraversion. The neurotic extravert patient described by Beech complained of cramp-like symptoms, whereas two of the neurotic introverted patients complained of excessive pressure applied to the pen. In our earlier description of the relationship between personality and psychomotor behaviour, it was pointed out that introverts react to stress by psychomotor overactivity, and it is conceivable that this psychomotor overactivity is manifested in writer's cramp as excessive pressure. Hysterical or neurotic extravert patients might be expected to produce psychomotor disorders involving inertia—the cramp complained of by Beech's extraverted patient might well be interpreted as a psychomotor inertia. These speculations must, of course, await proper investigation.

Returning to the relationship between anxiety level and response to treatment, it is interesting to notice that in Wolpe's 1958 series he reported two cases of writer's cramp. Both of the patients were suffering from other neurotic disorders in addition to the writer's cramp, so that the information which can be derived about writer's cramp is a little obscured. One patient, who suffered from social anxiety, voyeurism, and writer's cramp, was successfully treated by a combination of desensitization and assertive training. This patient had a high anxiety level, as measured by the Willoughby Neurotic Tendency Scale. The second patient, who complained of social anxiety and writer's cramp, was treated by the same combination of methods, and showed only a partial improvement. His social anxiety was considerably reduced but his writer's cramp remained unaffected. This patient had a low anxiety level, as measured by the Willoughby Neurotic Tendency Scale, and it is tempting to consider how this patient would have fared under treatment by avoidance conditioning. Two cases of writer's cramp were also successfully treated by one of the present authors, using a combination of negative practice and desensitization. Both patients were anxious and extraverted, but it was felt that, in both instances, the anxiety was probably the result rather than the cause of the writer's cramp.

Although a reasonable degree of success has been obtained by behaviour therapists in the treatment of writer's cramp, it is clear that there are a number of important problems which need investigation. In particular, the relationships between anxiety level and response to treatment require immediate attention. A second, and equally significant, area for investigation concerns the possible relationships which might exist between the aetiology and response to treatment of writer's cramp and the personality factors of introversion and extraversion. At present, the three main methods which are available to behaviour therapists are: avoidance conditioning, desensitization, negative practice. In view of our incomplete knowledge of the relationships mentioned above, it is difficult to suggest a clear and direct way of tackling the condition of writer's cramp. Bearing these inadequacies in mind, however, we would like to suggest that the first choice in treatment should be desensitization, in combination with negative practice, particularly in those cases where a high anxiety level is known to exist. Avoidance conditioning can be used as a third alternative, and may even be used as the first method of treatment, where the patient's anxiety level is low.

Tremors. Although it is unusual for people to seek psychological treatment simply and solely because of tremors, there is considerable evidence that these involuntary motor disturbances are more common in groups of neurotic people than in the general population. Much of the evidence on this subject has been accumulated by research workers who have used the Luria method. Luria's (1932) experiments demonstrated that tremors increase under conditions of stress or conflict. He showed, furthermore, that these involuntary tremors are more common in neurotic patients. These findings have now been confirmed by numerous workers in different countries (see Yates, 1960; Rachman 1961). Despite the variations in methodology and in sample selection which are found in these reports, the overall findings show a remarkable consistency. Although tremors frequently accompany neurotic states, they are seldom of direct clinical significance. A recent case treated by Yorkston (1963), however, provides an example of a patient whose main problem was that of involuntary motor disturbances of his hands. This patient, an adult male, developed excessive hand tremors after experiencing considerable anxiety on one occasion while attending a church service. After this unpleasant experience, he was unable to control the movements of his hands in social situations, and found that he was increasingly restricted by this disturbance. He avoided going out on social visits or attending church, and sought treatment for his condition. He was treated by systematic desensitization; various hierarchies concerning social situations were constructed, and he was exposed to these disturbing situations in increasing doses while under deep relaxation. The patient made a rapid and full recovery.

Spasms. Clark (1963*d*) described the successful treatment of a thirty-year-old woman whose main symptom was that she was troubled by a spasm of the jaw muscles or by the anxiety that a spasm was impending. It seemed probable that the spasm and the associated anxiety had been learned when the patient was about ten years old and had seen a frightening film, in which a patient with lockjaw had died under extremely unpleasant circumstances. The patient also suffered from a mild agoraphobia and the spasm was exacerbated when she was outside. Some subsidiary problems which this patient complained of included sexual difficulties and some social problems. In addition, she had difficulty in chewing hard foods, because of the fear that her jaw would lock when attempting to eat meat and so on. Her Maudsley Personality Inventory scores showed that she was neurotic and introverted. Reciprocal inhibition of the muscular spasm 'was induced by training the patient in progressive relaxation, along the lines suggested by Wolpe and Jacobson.' While under deep muscle relaxation, the patient was encouraged to think about and discuss various disturbing subjects. 'As soon as the patient felt a spasm about to come on or felt the anxiety associated with this, she was instructed to

smile broadly . . . She had to put her face in the set of a smile.'
Whenever she smiled, Clark emphasized the relaxation instructions and encouraged her to re-enter the state of drowsy deep
relaxation. This technique, with some additional refinements,
produced an almost complete inhibition of the spasm. The
patient's subsidiary problems were tackled in a variety of ways,
and they, too, had improved very considerably at the end of the
seventh session. Because of the woman's impending emigration,
treatment had to be stopped after the seventh session, and she
was instructed to write to the therapist if she encountered any
further difficulties. No communication had been received from
her fully one year after the end of treatment, and the presumption is that she has remained well.

Fits. Efron (1957) provides an intriguing description of a case
in which a patient's uncinate fits were inhibited by conditioning
methods. The patient, who had suffered from seizures for
twenty-six years, had always been able to arrest these seizures
by applying an unpleasant olfactory stimulus at the correct
time—i.e. at the onset of the aura. The study of this phenomenon (seizure arrest) has, according to Efron, been neglected,
and he accordingly attempted to produce a conditioned inhibition of the patient's fits. The unpleasant olfactory stimulus
acted as the unconditioned stimulus, and a bracelet as the
conditioned stimulus.

The patient was given the conditioning trials (which lasted
for 15-30 seconds) four times per hour. She was conditioned in
this manner for eight days (allowing for sleep and other rest
periods). In order to facilitate generalization of the treatment
procedure, the conditioning was carried out by a variety of
people in a variety of situations. After completing the conditioning trials, it was found that the conditioned stimulus
(the bracelet) could arrest the seizures as successfully as the
unconditioned stimulus (jasmine stimulus). Furthermore, the
patient was also able to inhibit the fits merely by visualizing the
bracelet. Efron checked the effects of the treatment by means
of metrazol injections. Prior to the treatment, 50 mg. metrazol
would have precipitated a seizure. After treatment, the patient
showed a marked decrease in sensitivity to the drug, and on
one occasion even the administration of 1350 mg. metrazol
failed to produce a fit.

The treatment process can be illustrated by reference to the usual conditioning diagram (see Fig. 20).

Efron points out that it is widely accepted that both E.E.G. patterns and fits can be conditioned, and argues that this case report is merely a therapeutic application of such knowledge. Efron's paper is lucid and feasible, and invites replication and development.[1]

1. UCS (jasmine) ————————————————→ arrest of fit
2. CS (bracelet)————→ UCS (jasmine) ————————→ UCR (no fit)
3. CS (bracelet)————→ CR (no fit)
4. CS[1] (image of bracelet) ——————————————→ CR (no fit)

Fig. 20. Treatment of a patient with uncinate fits by conditioning methods. (Adapted from Efron, *Brain*, 1957.)

Tics. Yates (1958) attempted to apply the constructs of learning theory to an experimental analysis of a tiqueur. Yates argued that some tics 'may be drive-reducing conditioned avoidance responses, originally evoked in a highly traumatic situation. In this situation, intense fear is aroused and a movement of withdrawal or aggression is made. If the movement produces or coincides with the cessation of the fear-inducing stimulus, it acquires strength through reinforcement.' Through stimulus generalization, the tic eventually comes to be elicited by a variety of stimuli, and acquires considerable habit strength. While he concentrated on this model, Yates was careful to point out that tics may also develop through a process of imitation, or as an avoidance response arising from irritating but non-traumatic stimulation, such as a tight collar. Nevertheless, the experimental treatment carried out by Yates should be applicable to any type of learned tic.

Yates was influenced in his choice of methods by the earlier work of Dunlap (1932) and others on the use of negative practice in the treatment of tics. If tics are regarded as learned responses, it should be possible to arrange conditions whereby the response can be extinguished or unlearned. All effortful activity generates a negative drive state known as reactive inhibition. Under conditions of massed practice, reactive inhibi-

[1]See the promising experiments of Forster and Chun (1964) and Forster *et al.* (1964).

tion builds up rapidly. If the aim of the experiment or treatment is to foster the extinction of a response, then massed practice provides a suitable learning technique. The frequent arousal and dissipation of reactive inhibition will also lead to the development of a conditioned inhibition or negative habit of not responding, i.e. not producing the tic.

Yates's patient was a twenty-five-year-old female of above average intelligence. She was extremely neurotic and slightly extraverted. She displayed four clearcut tics: a complex stomach contraction and breathing tic, a nasal expiration tic, a coughing tic, and an eye tic. These tics 'appeared to have started originally following two very traumatic experiences about ten years previously, when she felt she was being suffocated whilst undergoing anaesthesia; she said that she was terrified that she was going to die, and struggled madly. She could not bear the thought of an anaesthetic mask and could not tolerate any object being placed over her face.' In this case, the tic can reasonably be described as a conditioned avoidance response established in a traumatic situation, particularly as the patient said that she experienced relief when the tics occurred. Yates attempted to treat the four tics independently but concurrently. In the first experiment, Yates attempted to demonstrate that massed practice of the tic would lead to a significant decrement in the response. The patient was required to produce the tic voluntarily at the instruction of the therapist. She was given two treatment sessions per day, each consisting of five one-minute trials for each tic, with one-minute rest intervals between each trial. One hundred such sessions were conducted, each lasting 45 minutes. The results were consistent for all four tics and showed a significant decline in the strength of each of them.

Two comments can be made at this stage. Firstly, Yates's technique differs from that recommended by Dunlap, in one important respect at least, namely, Yates omitted the 'ideational instruction'. He did not, as Dunlap suggested, instruct the patient to say to herself (as she reproduced the tic voluntarily) that it was wrong. Secondly, although Yates described the treatment part of the experiment as consisting of massed practice, it can quite as easily, and perhaps more fairly, be considered as distributive practice. In the second part of the experiment, Yates tried some variations on the initial treatment programme.

Negative practice

In 1932, Dunlap described at some length his principle of negative practice, by which he meant the active, conscious practising of habits which the patient desired to get rid of. Dunlap recommended the use of negative practice for use in the treatment of stammering, tics, thumb-sucking, nail-biting, masturbation, homosexuality. When the method is used properly, it appears to give satisfactory and appropriate results; unfortunately, it has often been used in a perfunctory manner and under inappropriate conditions. The regrettable neglect of this method is partly explicable by the absence of explicit instructions for its application and the shortage of illustrative case histories. Lehner (1960) provides a valuable theoretical and practical discussion of negative practice as a therapeutic technique. He quotes Dunlap's view that 'what is repeated in negative practice of a motor habit is not the actual response involved in the habit, but a new response, in which only the behaviour pattern of the habitual response is repeated, with affective and ideational components quite different from those involved in the habit. This, of course, is quite in accord with the generalization, but the response in practice is not the response learned. This principle can be reversed to say that the response repeated in negative practice is not the response unlearned.' Lehner points out that the important part of Dunlap's theory, in so far as therapy is concerned, is what he referred to as the beta hypothesis. This states that repetition has 'no effect on the probable recurrence of a response except in so far as certain other factors operate through it,' (Lehner, 1960). According to the beta hypothesis, motivation plays a central role in changing behaviour, and may be directed towards either maintaining the habit or directed towards eliminating the habit. In therapeutic situations, Dunlap emphasized that the patient must desire to eliminate the habit and the therapist must reassure the patient as to the value of the technique. In the presence of negative motivational factors, the mere recurrence or repetition of the habit will not bring about extinction.

Lehner points out that negative practice has achieved an encouraging degree of success in a range of conditions (tics, stuttering, homosexuality, learning difficulties) but most of the evidence is inconclusive. Some additional examples of the

118

therapeutic application of negative practice are mentioned by Bandura (1961), Jones (1956), Williams (1959), Walton (1961). Case (1960). In most of these recent examples and in the tiqueurs described earlier in this Chapter, the instructions concerning ideational content have been omitted. In recent work, the stress has been laid on frequency of repetition and the importance of imitating the unwanted habit as closely as possible.

Lehner discusses two studies in which negative practice failed to bring about the elimination of the unwanted habit. These studies were carried out by Poindexter (1936) and by Peak *et al.* (1941). Poindexter was unable to bring about a reduction in typing errors made by a group of student beginners by the method of negative practice. Lehner comments that Poindexter was using the method of negative practice in an inappropriate manner, in that he apparently interpreted negative practice to mean a simple repetition of the error. Lehner argues that the beta hypothesis expressly states that 'repetition has *no* effect on the probable recurrence of a response except in so far as certain other factors operate through it.' Lehner's comment is not entirely satisfactory, however. Firstly, there are some cases now available in which repetition of the error without the conscious intent described by Dunlap has nevertheless produced satisfactory results. Secondly, and perhaps more important, the beta hypothesis as stated by Dunlap, is so vague and general as to make it extremely difficult, if not impossible, to specify precisely what these 'certain other factors' are supposed to be. Great care should be taken not to use the beta hypothesis as a means of explaining away all negative results. In the case of the second contradictory study, that of Peak *et al.*, an attempt was made to correct the spelling of twenty-four subjects by negative or positive practice. Peak *et al.* found that the negative practice group showed a slightly higher percentage of errors after practice than did the positive practice group. As Lehner points out, however, in this experiment the original cause of the error was still present when the subjects carried out their negative practice, and he correctly points out that when negative practice is carried out, it is important that the person should have available to him the correct alternative response.

Lehner has also provided an extremely useful summary of

the points which should be borne in mind by anyone who attempts to apply the technique of negative practice.

1. The patient should desire to eradicate the response and the therapist must ensure that this desire is maintained and encouraged through reassurance and direct instruction. 'The subject must undertake negative practice within the constantly maintained attitudinal framework of "This is wrong and I am not going to do it later".'

2. Any factors which might be maintaining the unwanted response (as a tension reliever, for example) must be eliminated, so that the response may be termed a habit residual. If the maintaining factors are not eliminated, it becomes extremely difficult to eliminate the habit.

3. The correct response must be available to the patient. For example, the poor speller must have the correct spelling of the word available when he misspells it.

4. In the practice sessions 'the patient must be cautioned and aided to reproduce a response as nearly like the voluntary response as possible. This may take the form of repeating responses which occur spontaneously in the sessions, or of reproducing characteristic responses upon the command of the therapist.' Lehner claims that if the patient simply practises a response which only distantly resembles the unwanted response, he may merely add a new habit to the one he already has. An example of this might be the development of facial grimacing in a stutterer.

Lehner's clear and simple recommendations will be of considerable assistance to research workers who are intent on examining the effectiveness of negative practice as a therapeutic method. Apart from the investigation of the general effectiveness of negative practice, two other, more specific problems appear to merit some study. What, if anything, is the role and importance of the 'conscious intent' aspect of negative practice? What, if anything, is the influence of personality factors on the effectiveness of negative practice? There are good grounds for believing that the techniques of negative practice will prove to be of greatest value in the treatment of extraverted patients.

It is interesting that the patient who failed to respond favourably to Yates's negative practice method was introverted, as measured by the Maudsley Personality Inventory. The patient who responded favourably to the negative practice technique was, on the other hand, extraverted. It could be predicted from Eysenck's typological postulates that the methods of negative practice, based as it is on the rapid build-up of reactive inhibition, would be more suitable for extraverted patients. Similarly, introverted patients should do better with therapeutic procedures based on direct conditioning. It is indeed tempting to regard the two cases described by Rafi (1961) as evidence in support of these typological postulates. Nevertheless, judgment about the validity of these predictions in the field of therapy and more particularly in the choice of treatment technique, must await further and large-scale investigations. An interesting aspect of the treatment of the female patient described by Rafi concerns the point at which the response is inhibited.

Walters and Demkow (1963) demonstrated, in an experiment on children, that the inhibition of a response is more effectively obtained if the response is interrupted early in the response sequence. That is, if one wishes to inhibit the response of, shall we say, scribbling on the wall, it is best to interrupt this activity right at the point of departure. In the case of scribbling on the wall, the most effective time to intervene would be as the child picks up the crayon and *not* once he has initiated the scribbling itself.

In Rafi's case, the re-conditioning of the foot-tapping tic was effected by inhibiting the response before it was actually carried out. The slightest movement of the patient's foot sounded the buzzer. In other words, he was inhibiting the tic response sequence right at the beginning and not after the actual tic had commenced. The wider implications concerning the timing of the introduction of the inhibitory stimulus have yet to be worked out, but there is little doubt that information of this kind may prove of considerable benefit in the field of aversion therapy, for example.

Walton (1961) reported the successful treatment of an eleven-year-old boy who had suffered from tics from the age of five. When the child was admitted to hospital his condition was quite serious. He displayed various major tics, some of which were of a violent character. 'If the symptoms occurred when he was in the car, their force would be sufficient to shake it . . . In hospital, the Sister noted that the tics were strong enough to move the bed . . . He would often be unable to eat a meal as he could not hold a glass or any cutlery . . . When he tried to use a knife and fork the food and cutlery often shot off the plate, ejected by the violent hand movements.' The boy received thirty-six treatment sessions in all, the first lasting for fifteen minutes. The practice of the major tic continued for twenty-nine sessions and the remaining seven sessions were devoted to the various other tics. The length of the session for the voluntary evocation of the tics was gradually increased to thirty-one minutes of uninterrupted massed practice. A gradual decline in the patient's ability to imitate his tic voluntarily was observed. This decline was accompanied by an improvement in his involuntary tics. Towards the end of his stay in hospital, his involuntary tics were observed to be very much improved, in that they were much less frequent and much less intense. When the child was followed up, a year after discharge, it was evident that he had maintained his clinical improvement and apart from one slight facial tic, was now normal. Walton reported that the boy's general adjustment had also improved following his treatment in hospital.

Barrett (1962) approached the problem of tics from an entirely different angle. She attempted to bring various multiple tics of a thirty-eight-year-old male patient under experimental control in a free operant conditioning situation. She demonstrated that it was possible to reduce the frequency of the response by making various environmental consequences contingent upon the production of the tic. The most effective method of reducing the rate of tics was by making the tic produce an interruption of pleasant music. The response rate was also reduced by 'tic-produced white noise and by continuous music.' The results of Barrett's experimental investigation may be summarized as follows: The rate of responding (tics) can be reduced by the removal of a positive stimulus or by the presentation of an aversive stimulus. The advantages offered by the operant method, such as that used by Barrett, are that the experimenter is enabled to obtain a precise and detailed record of all the tics produced and, in this way, to examine the effects of various types of manipulation on the tic behaviour. The direct therapeutic application of these methods is, at this stage, still a little obscure. There can be little doubt, however, that a considerable amount of important information about the nature of tics and the ways in which they can be reduced can be made available by using these experimental methods. It should then be possible to apply this knowledge in modifying and refining the methods of negative practice and conditioned inhibition which have been used by Yates and subsequent workers.

On the basis of this very limited number of cases, we can nonetheless set up four hypotheses concerning the treatment of tics.

(1) The repetitive, voluntary initation of a tic under prolonged periods of massed practice will produce a decline in the frequency of the tic.

(2) The introduction of prolonged rest periods after the completion of massed practice trials will facilitate this reduction in the frequency and intensity of the tic.

(3) Extraverted patients will respond more favourably to negative practice involving prolonged massed trials than will introverted patients.

(4) Introverted patients will respond more favourably to techniques based on positive conditioning than they will to massed extinction procedures.

In none of the cases reported so far has any evidence of symptom substitution been unearthed. Two problems of a practical nature which merit investigation are the following. Firstly, what, if anything, does conscious intention contribute to the elimination of the tic?[1] Secondly, in attempting to eliminate multiple tics or various tics within the same patient, should one concentrate on one tic at a time, or is it better to treat all the tics concurrently? In regard to the question of aetiology, Yates's hypotheses provides an extremely fruitful line of investigation, but as yet there is little direct evidence to support his views. According to Yates, tics are drive-reducing conditioned avoidance responses originally evoked in a highly traumatic situation. He also suggests that some tics might arise from simple imitation or as an avoidance response to some irritating but non-traumatic stimulation.

In addition to the suggestive clues which emerge from the description of the treatment of tiqueurs described above, the

[1] Anderson and Parmenter's (1941) success in treating a neurotic sheep by 'negative practice' suggests that, even if conscious intention facilitates the extinction process, it is not a *necessary* condition of practice.

overall theoretical explanation for the effects of negative practice make the association between extraversion and extinction processes (of which negative practice is merely one example) seem highly probable. A detailed discussion of the relationships between practice, rest, the extinction of habits, and the personality dimensions of introversion-extraversion is provided by Eysenck (1957). It is also worth recalling that two of the most important factors which determine the speed of extinction of a habit are: the effort expended in carrying out the response, and the degree to which the practice trials are massed. These generalizations have been found to apply under a wide range of conditions and tasks. Some of the evidence indicating that increases in the effort expended in carrying out the response are followed by greater speed of extinction is presented by Mowrer and Jones (1943) and by Solomon (1948). Evidence relating to the observation that massed practice trials produce extinction more quickly than distributive practice trials is presented by Porter (1939) and by Edmondson and Amsel (1954) among others. Another observation of direct relevance to the use of extinction procedures in therapy concerns the effects of drugs. The depressant drugs accelerate the rate of extinction (Kimble, 1961) and could presumably facilitate therapeutic procedures based on a process of extinction. The only example of the use of drugs in a patient treated by extinction procedures is that of Walton, described above.

Finally, Metzner (1961) has drawn attention to the fact that extinction can be brought about by a process of 'flooding'. He refers to two experiments in which extinction was brought about more rapidly by increasing the intensity or duration of the conditioned stimulus. He quotes an experiment of Bugelski's in which a strong avoidance response was extinguished in a single trial by flooding the animal with the conditioned stimulus while preventing it from making a response. This procedure is of obvious theoretical interest; it is difficult to see, however, how it can be adapted for use with patients, as it would give rise to serious practical and ethical objections.

Chapter 9

OBSESSIONAL-COMPULSIVE DISORDERS

METZNER (1963) has made an attempt to establish experimental analogues of obsessional and compulsive behaviour. For purposes of the present exposition, we will use his terms of reference in considering these conditions. He argues that there are three distinctive kinds of behaviour which typify obsessional-compulsive neuroses. These three kinds of behaviour, which may appear alone or in combination, are as follows. The first kind of behaviour is 'the occurrence of prolonged spells of brooding, doubting and speculation . . . ' The second type of behaviour is the occurrence of 'very strong temptations or impulses to do things, such as kill, confess, attack, or steal certain objects which are viewed with the utmost horror, disgust, shame, or anxiety by the patient experiencing them.' In the case of those impulses which are acted upon, we may describe the behaviour as compulsive, but where the impulses are not translated into action they are described as obsessional thoughts. The third distinctive type of obsessional behaviour is 'the elaborate and sometimes incredibly time-consuming rituals and ceremonial actions surrounding everyday activities, such as eating, going to the toilet, dressing and undressing, and sexual performance.'

Metzner draws attention to the interesting experiment conducted by Fonberg (1956), who demonstrated that dogs which are made neurotic in the classical Pavlovian way tend to re-adopt some earlier anxiety-reducing reaction which was successful in the past. If a learned response is successful in enabling the animal to avoid a painful stimulus, it may later re-appear when the animal is placed in a similar anxiety-provoking situation at a later time. In Fonberg's experiment, the animal was first trained to avoid the noxious stimulus (either an electric shock or a strong puff of air) by performing a specific response; for example, by lifting its foreleg. The animal was then subjected to a conflict situation and manifested the typical neurotic behaviour observed under these conditions. In addition, however, the avoidance response (e.g. lifting the leg) which had been learned in the first part of the experiment re-appeared. Fonberg also reported that those dogs which had been trained to avoid the painful puff of air were observed to engage in 'shaking-off' movements when they were placed in the conflict situation. In other words, when the animal is placed in a problem situation which is insoluble, he is unable to develop an appropriate response and re-adopts a response which is already part of his behavioural repertoire—a response from his habit hierarchy which has in the past, proved successful. This response is, of course, inappropriate in the conflict situation and may even give it a bizarre quality. The shaking-off movements exhibited by the dogs in the conflict situation were certainly of this character. It has, in other words, the 'senseless' quality of typical obsessional behaviour.

Metzner was able to formulate three types of experimental situation in which responses may get fixated and become compulsive in nature. (1) 'A positive approach response may get fixated when it also becomes an avoidance response,[1] so that the response which satisfies the approach response also reduces a learned anxiety.' Certain cases of compulsive masturbation can for example, be suitably analysed in these terms. (2) 'An instrumental avoidance response may get fixated by being punished, i.e. by becoming an unsuccessful avoidance response.' Numerous instances of this kind of development are provided by Maier (1949). (3) 'Avoidance behaviour may also be fixated by the delivery of "free" shocks, i.e. shocks which are not contingent upon any behaviour which the animal shows.'

The most extensive and intensive experimental investigations of compulsive behaviour were those carried out by Maier (1949). At least part of the explanation for the neglect of Maier's research work can be traced to his insistence that frustration

---

[1] See Martin (1963) for a detailed discussion of this phenomenon and related matters.

and frustration-instigated behaviour are different in quality from other forms of acquired behaviour. Maier's unfortunate views on this matter have probably interfered with the dissemination of his extremely interesting experimental findings. The recent work by Yates (1962) will, we hope, do something to remedy the situation.

Maier's experiments on stereotyped or fixated behaviour were carried out in a discrimination problem situation. The apparatus which is used consists of a Lashley jumping stand which comprises a small stand from which the rats jump in the direction of either of two windows which contain cards with differing designs on them (see Fig. 21). If the rat jumps towards the correct window, the card falls and the rat lands on a platform where it receives food. If, on the other hand, the rat jumps in the incorrect direction, it strikes the card which is rigidly fixed in position, and then falls into the net which is placed at the bottom of the stand containing the two windows. By using this situation, the animal can be taught a selective response of jumping towards windows which contain particular cards, e.g. a jump towards a card with a black circle is rewarded and a jump towards a card with a white circle is punished by a bump on the nose and a fall into the receiving net. A majority of rats trained under these conditions will learn to make a differential response towards the correct symbol or in the correct direction. These correct jumping responses are referred to as position habits or symbol habits, depending upon the type of response which the experimenter rewards. In addition to exposing the rats to this type of soluble problem, Maier also investigated the behaviour of rats when they were faced with an insoluble problem. In the case of the insoluble problems, the cards are presented in a random sequence. No response can be learned because the animal does not receive reward or punishment consistently when he makes either a jump in a particular direction or a jump towards a particular kind of symbol. When presented with this insoluble problem, most animals refuse to jump after a brief exposure to the experimental situation and it is then necessary to force the animal to jump by punishing it with a short blast of air or by delivering an electric shock. In other words, the rat is compelled to make a jumping response which is itself followed by punishment in a random sequence. When placed in this insoluble discrimination situation, a majority of the animals developed stereotyped and rigid jumping responses, or, to use Maier's terminology, they became fixated. A jumping response was considered to be fixated if the animal was unable to switch to a new response (when the situation was changed from insoluble to soluble) within 200 trials.

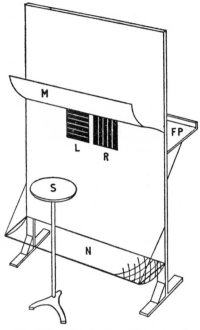

Fɪɢ. 21. The Lashley discrimination apparatus. (Adapted from K. Lashley, *Journal of Genetic Psychology* **37,** 1930.)

The compulsive quality of these fixated responses is attested to by several experiments which have been summarized by Yates. It has been demonstrated that the animals continue to display the stereotyped jumping responses even though they have learned the correct response. 'The rats with fixations do learn the correct response when the problem is made soluble, but are unable to exercise it except in certain favourable conditions' (Yates, 1962, p. 15).

Most of the criticisms which have been directed at Maier's work are concerned with his theoretical interpretation of the experimental findings. Maier has insisted throughout that the behaviour produced in the insoluble discrimination situation is different from 'learning' as that term is ordinarily employed by experimental psychologists. He argues further that fixated behaviour patterns do not conform to the ordinary phenomena of learning—that fixated behaviour, because it is instigated by frustration, is qualitatively different from other forms of acquired behaviour. According to Maier, fixated behaviour cannot be unlearned in the same way as other acquired responses, and the process of extinction does not apply to fixated responses. Various experimenters have, however, shown that fixated responses, produced in the manner described by Maier, are in fact subject to the ordinary processes of learning. The experiments of Wilcoxon (1952), Farber (1948), and Haslerud *et al.* (1954) are particularly relevant to this problem, and are described in some detail by Yates (1962), who quotes Wilcoxon's conclusion that: 'Fixations are not in any way symptomatic of abnormal condition. Rather they are strong habits which can be unlearned if the conditions are made appropriate.' Wolpe (1952) has also pointed out that the fixated jumping responses of Maier's rats can quite fairly be described as *adaptive*. The stimulus which compelled the rat to jump, it will be remembered, is of a noxious quality and by jumping, the rat is escaping from the pain engendered by the stimulus. Maier's (1956) rejoinder to these criticisms is not particularly convincing, and it is worth pointing out that the noxious stimulus was applied only to the rats participating in the insoluble problem situation. The mere fact that a noxious stimulus had to be employed in forcing these rats to jump indicates that the role of the trigger stimulus is crucial in any interpretation of Maier's findings. It is true, nevertheless, that many of the rats continue to display the fixated response even when the noxious trigger stimulus is withdrawn and in order to encompass Maier's experimental findings, it is necessary to resort to an explanation which combines the views of Wolpe and those of Farber, who stresses the role of the anxiety drive in developing and maintaining the stereotyped jumping response. The main interest of Maier's work is that he has been able to elicit techniques for developing compulsive and persistent habit patterns in his animal subjects. As a consequence of the work of Maier and of other research workers, it is now possible to list the factors which may produce compulsive behaviour.[1]

The conditions under which compulsive behaviour may develop are as follows: conflict, severe or persistent punishment, randomly ordered punishments, partial reinforcement. Some other variables which have been shown to contribute to the development of compulsive behaviour include (1) the duration of punishment (Knopfelmacher, 1953); (2) the order in which punishments and rewards are presented (Maier and Ellen, 1955); (3) the degree to which the animal is restricted (Berkson, et al. 1963) and (4) the amount of fear which the animal is experiencing (Berkson et al. 1963). Maier and his colleagues also investigated the persistence of the fixated responses and found that most of the techniques which they attempted were not successful in bringing about a cessation of the stereotype. The unsuccessful re-training procedures included a complete removal from the experimental situation for a period of at least four months, re-training on a symbol-reward problem, and other related techniques (see Yates, 1962). They were also unable to break the fixated responses by inducing metrazol convulsions or electro-shock convulsions, or by the administration of chlorpromazine.

Maier was able to develop only one technique whereby the fixated response could be broken and a new response substituted. This method he refers to as 'guidance', and it consists of preventing the rat from carrying out the fixated response by guiding it manually towards the correct window. After the animal has been guided in this way for approximately ten trials, it is then possible to re-train it on a simple discrimination problem. Once again, Maier insisted that this procedure was not a learning technique but something which was qualitatively different. Apart from the fact that this technique would be regarded as a forced choice method of learning by most psychologists, more recent experiments have shown that the fixated responses can be broken by other methods as well. Haslerud et al. (1954), for example, were able to stop the compulsive behaviour and substitute an alternative type of

[1] While some of these factors appear to be capable of producing compulsive behaviour in their own right, it is probable that most forms of fixated or compulsive behaviour develop as a result of a combination of these factors acting contemporaneously.

responding by soothing the animals for 30 seconds at the beginning of each response. This experiment is particularly interesting because of some similarities which can be drawn between the methods used by Haslerud *et al.* and some of the techniques used by behaviour therapists in the treatment of their obsessional patients (see Wolpe, 1958, for example). Knopfelmacher (1952) has also shown that if the fixated response is followed by severe punishment, it can in this way be eliminated. This experimental demonstration also has some similarity to techniques which have been used in the treatment of neurotic patients. The aversion treatment, described by Blakemore *et al.* (1963), in overcoming a patient's transvestite behaviour may be cited as an example. Furthermore, the result obtained by Berkson *et al.* (1963) is of obvious relevance for behaviour therapy. They demonstrated that the frequency of stereotyped or compulsive behaviour in chimpanzees was increased when their level of anxiety was elevated. It would follow from this that a reduction in the person's anxiety level might bring about a reduction in the frequency of the compulsive behaviour, and certainly some of the cases described by Wolpe and by Walton and Mather (1963) bear out this contention. One of the cases treated by Wolpe (described on p. 136 below) is a particularly clear example of how a reduction in the patient's anxiety level can bring about a reduction and total cessation of the obsessional and compulsive neurotic behaviour pattern.

So far, there have been no attempts to make a direct translation from Maier's technique of guidance in rats to the management and treatment of obsessional and compulsive disorders in human beings. Presumably, any such attempt would, like Maier's guidance technique, be carried out in two stages. In the first stage the patient would be prevented from carrying out his compulsive or obsessional behaviour by physical or other coercion, and his behaviour would be redirected in a more appropriate manner. After this restraint and redirection had been carried out on a number of occasions, the patient would then be retrained in order to ensure the adoption of a more adaptive and satisfactory alternate form of behaving. In the case of a patient who suffers from obsessional thoughts concerning illness, for example, it might be possible to interrupt such thoughts by the methods which have been described as 'thought stopping' (Wolpe, 1958), and then to substitute other more acceptable forms of thinking. This formulation is rather vague and crude, and it is to be hoped that a carefully planned and systematically conducted investigation of Maier's guidance technique will, at some stage, be undertaken.

Three aspects of obsessional and compulsive disorders which bear little resemblance to the behaviour observed by Maier in his experiments are as follows. First, more than a few of the obsessional-compulsive disturbances which are found to occur in human beings have a pleasurable aspect as well as an unpleasurable one. Obviously many of the sexual perversions are rewarding and satisfying, even though they might, at the same time, give rise to negative feelings such as shame and guilt. In considering these types of disorders, the best paradigm which is available seems to be that described by Metzner and quoted on p. 126 above. A second aspect of compulsive behaviour which deserves investigation is the slowness which forms so typical a part of the behaviour of obsessional neurotics and also the increasing expansion of the rituals which they are required to carry out. While none of the experiments which we have discussed so far has any direct bearing on this problem, at this stage it seems that the best way of regarding this aspect of obsessional neurotic behaviour is to consider it as an example of stimulus generalization. Thirdly, the ideational content or the obsessive content of the neurotic disorder cannot, of course, be directly investigated in animal studies. In a general way, we may expect that the frequency and intrusiveness of obsessional ideas is a function of the degree of anxiety which the patient is experiencing, In certain instances, however, the obsessional ideas, particularly ideas of remorse, may be a consequence rather than an antecedent of the compulsive act.

Wolpe (1958) has distinguished between anxiety-elevating obsessions and anxiety-reducing obsessions. In the case of anxiety-elevating disorders, it is the consequence of the thought or action which is disturbing and which causes the patient discomfort. Wolpe illustrates this type of disorder by reference to a patient who persistently felt the urge to strike people. As soon as he became aware of the impulse, he immediately felt a tremendous surge of anxiety and he was required to take appropriate restraining action. Taylor (1963) has described a very clear example of a patient suffering from an anxiety-elevating obsession, in which the anxiety which was experienced came as a consequence of the compulsive behaviour. Taylor argues that the distinguishing feature of obsessive-compulsive behaviour is that it arouses social punishment in the form of strong disapproval and derision. Although in many, if not most, instances socially undesirable habits do disappear as a result of social and other forms of punishment, the exceptions tend to be considered as evidence of obsessionality or compulsiveness. He argues that in those cases where social criticism fails to reduce the strength of the habit, this is attributable to the delay which intervenes between the execution of the act and the delivery of the aversive criticism. In these cases, the social disapproval contributes to the furtherance of the undesirable habit pattern rather than to its elimination. The reason for this is that the emotional disturbance produced by the disapproval increases the person's concern about his behaviour, without doing anything to reduce its habit strength. According to Taylor, the patient 'learns to condemn his own actions, and the subjective quality of the emotional experience that accompanies self-condemnation is guilt.' While this account has obvious merits Taylor's suggestion that all obsessive-compulsive disorders can be accounted for in this way is open to criticism. He states that since the emotional concomitants of the compulsive behaviour are a consequence of social criticism, which itself is a consequence of the compulsive action, then 'it is evident that any attempt to deal directly with the emotion must fail.' This implies that some of the techniques which are used in the treatment of anxiety states would be unsuitable for the management of obsessional patients, e.g. desensitization. There is, however, convincing evidence (both experimental and clinical) for believing that obsessional disorders are not only of the anxiety-elevating type, and contrary to Taylor's assertion, Wolpe does on occasion employ methods such as desensitization when dealing with obsessional patients.

In support of his argument, Taylor describes the successful treatment of an obsessional-compulsive patient by means of negative reinforcement. The patient, a forty-year-old woman, had been plucking out her eyebrows compulsively for a period of *thirty-one years*. 'She was instructed to arrest at its commencement each movement of her hand to her forehead for the purpose of plucking. Cure was essentially complete in ten days. Three months later the eyebrows were fully grown . . . and no substitute symptoms had developed.' The patient was actually instructed to use verbal self-inhibition whenever she saw her hand beginning to move toward her head for the purpose of plucking her eyebrows. Once this initial reaction was inhibited, a second part of the behavioural chain was inhibited in a similar fashion. After carrying out a few more exercises of this kind, the patient found that she was able to control the compulsive behaviour completely.

Another method developed by Taylor for treating obsessional thoughts is 'thought stopping'. In this method, the patient is asked to close his eyes and to verbalize a typical obsessive thought sequence. Suddenly the therapist shouts, 'Stop!'. This procedure is repeated several times and the therapist emphasizes how the introduction of this distracting stimulus interrupts the thought process. The patient is then instructed to intercept his own obsessive thoughts by giving himself the same instruction, sub-vocally. The procedure is then repeated many times in the consulting room and the patient is encouraged to practise the technique on his own, in a diligent fashion. Wolpe (1958) reports that he has obtained some remarkable successes with this method. In addition, he has also interrupted the thought sequence by using other disruptive stimuli such as a sharp buzzer noise.

The second, and perhaps more common type of obsessional-compulsive disorder occurs as a consequence of anxiety; the execution of the compulsive act diminishes the emotional arousal and in this way is self-reinforcing. Typical examples of anxiety-reducing obsessions are compulsive hand-washing and tidying. These anxiety-reducing rituals may well develop as a consequence of fortuituous associations between the ritualistic acts and a reduction in anxiety. In this connection, the work described by Metzner (1963) and by Skinner (1948) is pertinent.

Skinner's famous demonstration of the development of superstition in pigeons may be of some relevance in attempting to understand the extension and elaborations of obsessional and compulsive rituals. Skinner placed hungry birds in an experimental cage for a few minutes each day, and arranged an automatic presentation of food at regular, five-second intervals. In six out of eight cases, the birds developed clearly-defined response patterns of an irrelevant or 'superstitious' character. 'One bird was conditioned to turn counter-clockwise about the cage, making two or three turns between reinforcements. Another repeatedly thrust its head into one of the upper corners of the cage. A third developed a tossing response, as if placing its head beneath an invisible bar and lifting it repeatedly.' These ritualistic responses (which are sometimes reminiscent of tics) appear to develop because the bird happens to be executing some response as the food reward appears and as a result, it tends to repeat this response. In the early stages of the development of these rituals, short intervals between rewards are more effective because they do not permit extinction to occur. Once they are established, however, these ritualistic responses can be extremely resistant to extinction. In one case, 10,000 responses were recorded before extinction occurred. 'A few accidental connections between a ritual and a favourable consequence suffice to set up and maintain the behaviour, in spite of many unreinforced instances' (Skinner, 1948). Skinner also observed what he called a 'drift in topography' of response. For example, one pigeon began by displaying a sharp left turn of its head; this movement then became more energetic and incorporated other parts of the bird's body—'eventually the whole body of the bird turned in the same direction and a step or two would be taken.' It seems probable that in the case of neurotic rituals and obsessions, some adventitious acts or thoughts accidentally coincide with a reduction in anxiety or with the cessation of what Metzner describes as 'free shocks'. It is worth bearing in mind, however, that in Skinner's demonstration the adventitious responses were reinforced by *positive* food rewards. There is no reason for assuming that compulsive human behaviour may not also develop by the adventitious conjunction of an act and a positive reward.

Clinical observations leave very little doubt that large numbers of obsessional-compulsive neurotics perform their ritualistic activities in order to allay anxiety. The exhibitionist patient treated by Bond and Hutchison (1960) and described on p. 145 below is one such example. This patient was subject to recurrent fits of intense anxiety and tension from which he could experience relief only by exhibiting himself. As we have shown above, there is also a very close connection between the degree of anxiety which the person or animal is subjected to and the frequency and intensity with which the compulsive behaviour is carried out. It was argued that these observations would lead one to expect that a systematic reduction in anxiety should lead to a reduction and the eventual elimination of obsessional-compulsive behaviour in those patients who are suffering from what is here described as an anxiety-reducing condition. Wolpe (1958) has in fact described in some detail, the successful treatment of some obsessional patients by the method of systematic desensitization and by assertive training. One of the best examples of this type of treatment is the case reported by Wolpe (1963b) of an eighteen-year-old boy who complained of a severe hand-washing compulsion. The excessive hand-washing was provoked by the patient's fear of contamination by urine. After urinating, he would spend up to forty-five minutes 'in an elaborate ritual of cleaning up his genitalia which was followed up by two hours of hand-washing.' The therapist's analysis of the patient's history led him to the conclusion that the fear of urine contamination was the basis of the obsessional neurosis, and it was decided to desensitize the patient to stimuli of this character. Anxiety hierarchies dealing with situations in which urine featured were accordingly constructed and the patient was desensitized under deep relaxation. The boy made rapid progress under this regime and was eventually discharged very much improved. In a similar case treated by one of the present authors, a patient's hand-washing compulsion was found to be based on a fear of being contaminated by certain categories of people. Once this relationship had been established, the type of people who produced the anxiety in the patient were categorized and hierarchies were built up to deal with the emotional reactions of the patient. He was gradually and progressively desensitized to the anxiety produced by these people, while at the same time being instructed to use assertive training in all social situations and in particular with the people who were causing the disturbance. This patient also made considerable progress and was discharged after thirty-five interviews in a much improved condition.

The two other methods of behaviour therapy which have been used in treating obsessional-compulsive disorders are avoidance conditioning and negative practice or satiation. Wolpe (1958) obtained a successful result in the treatment of a patient with a food obsession by the method of avoidance conditioning. This patient, a thirty-six-year-old woman, had been dominated for sixteen years by a severe obsession concerning food to which she was irresistibly attracted. The patient was taught to obtain a clear imaginative picture of the desired food and when she signalled that the image was clear, a sharp electric shock was delivered to her left forearm. Ten such aversive stimuli were presented at each session and she made considerable progress within a few weeks. Avoidance conditioning, or aversion treatment, as it is often described, has, of course been widely used in the treatment of sexual disorders (see Chapter 10). Although negative practice or satiation would appear to be an appropriate method to use in the treatment of some obsessional-compulsive disorders, in practice it has been neglected. An example of the way in which it can be successfully used was recently obtained by Humphery and Rachman (1963). The patient was a four-year-old boy who persistently and compulsively indulged in chewing, biting, and tearing of various materials. For more than six months he had systematically torn and chewed all the curtains, sheets, and pillow-slips in his parents' home. In addition to the emotional reactions which his behaviour evoked, it was imposing a financial strain on the child's parents. After detailed consideration of the child's history and the parental environment, it was decided to attempt a treatment based on satiation. At each treatment session, the child was made to tear up large amounts of newspaper into smaller and smaller strips and then throw them into the waste-paper basket. At each treatment session he was required to do this for up to twenty minutes without pausing, despite the obvious appearance of fatigue. Within one week, the tearing and chewing behaviour in his home had declined and at the end of three weeks had disappeared entirely. Walton (1960) also used negative practice in combination with various other methods in treating a patient who complained of several compulsive activities. These included excessive hand-washing, kicking of stones, cigarette tapping, and so on. It is, however, difficult to estimate the contribution made by negative practice in the recovery of this patient, as he was concurrently receiving drugs and other types of treatment.

It will be apparent that there are a large number of techniques which may be considered in the treatment of obsessional-compulsive disorders. In summary form, they are: systematic psychomotor or vocal inhibition (thought stopping), assertive training, systematic desensitization, satiation or negative practice and avoidance conditioning. Furthermore, Maier's guidance method, which proved to be successful in overcoming compulsive behaviour in animals, offers another potentially useful technique if it can be successfully translated into the clinic.

An extremely important consideration which arises in the treatment of every patient is whether to concentrate on the motor manifestations of the compulsive behaviour or whether one should deal first and directly with the autonomic aspects of the neurotic behaviour. This problem arises in the treatment of compulsive behaviour and also in other disturbed motor reactions such as tics and cramps. It has been argued that 'motor reactions are frequently activated by their drive-reducing properties *vis-à-vis* the historically earlier conditioned autonomic responses; the extinction of the motor response without the simultaneous extinction of the conditioned autonomic response would only be a partial cure . . . behaviour therapy requires the extinction of all non-adaptive conditioned responses complained of by the patient, or causally related to these symptoms' (Eysenck, 1960*b*). This view is similar to that expounded by Wolpe who recommends the use of anxiety-allaying techniques (such as desensitization) in the treatment of what he calls 'anxiety-reducing obsessions'. The case example of one of Wolpe's patients which is described on p. 136 above illustrates the theory and practice of this attitude as does the animal experiment conducted by Haslerud *et al.* (1954) mentioned earlier. In addition, the failure of the conditioned avoidance method of Liversedge and Sylvester to cure *anxious* patients of their writer's cramp (Beech, 1960) also supports this view. The most direct evidence on this matter is that provided by Walton and Mather (1963) in their report on the treatment of six obsessional-compulsive patients. They found that the treatment of the motor aspects of the illness produced only temporary remissions—although they point out that in some cases the treatment of the autonomic reactions alone was likewise not sufficient to bring about a full recovery. In their first two cases, the 'removal of the basic conditioned autonomic drive was sufficient to remove also the motor reactions mediated by it.'

Taylor (1963), on the other hand, appears to argue that all compulsions are of the anxiety-elevating type and certainly in these cases it may be best to direct one's attention to eliminating motor activity itself. If the compulsive behaviour is of very long standing (as in the case treated by Taylor) and appears to bear no relation to anxiety, then success may be obtained by extinguishing or inhibiting the motor act. Theoretically, this procedure can also be recommended in those instances where the compulsive activity was generated by a drive state other than anxiety (see Skinner's experiment on superstitious behaviour). It seems likely, however, that this kind of compulsive behaviour is non-neurotic and will seldom be met in the clinic.

There are no figures available on the relative frequency of the anxiety-elevating and anxiety-reducing obsessional illnesses but on the basis of clinical impressions, we feel that the latter type is far more common. It would follow from this that the most important treatment techniques are those which reduce anxiety—desensitization, assertive training, and so on.

Chapter 10

SEXUAL DISORDERS

THE disorders of sexual behaviour which have been treated by behaviour therapy include impotence, frigidity, voyeurism, fetishism, exhibitionism, homosexuality, and transvestism.

Impotence

Wolpe (1958) reported the successful treatment of seven cases of impotence, using the methods of behaviour therapy, and Lazarus and Rachman (1960) give an account of a successful case treated by this method. The mean number of sessions taken to improve Wolpe's five apparently cured cases was 14·4. Seventy-five sessions were needed to produce the changes in the two much improved patients. The two latter patients were also diagnosed as suffering from inter-personal anxiety. None of the apparently cured patients had this symptom but two of them had phobias associated with their impotence. Another difference between the apparently cured and the much improved patients is to be found in their neurotic tendency scores (obtained by the Willoughby Scale). The mean score for the cured patients was much lower (26·5) than that for the improved patients (51·5). These differences suggest the possibility that impotence associated with high neuroticism scores and/or inter-personal anxiety may be more resistant to behaviour therapy.

The three methods of treatment used in these impotence cases were: desensitization, use of sexual responses, use of assertive responses. The desensitization method has been described in detail in Chapter 5 above. The second technique, the use of sexual responses, is based on theoretical grounds similar to those underlying desensitization. Sexual responses which can reciprocally inhibit anxiety in a manner similar to relaxation, are invoked in a graded and gradual programme.

Anxiety reactions are inhibited both during sexual activity and also for a period of time following such activity. Some examples of this reciprocal relationship have been presented by

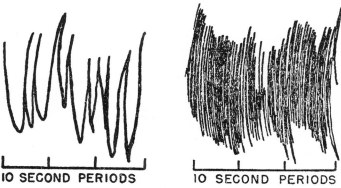

IO SECOND PERIODS   **IO SECOND PERIODS**

FIG. 22. Sexual activity and respiration. A comparison of the animal's (Nick) respiration (1) after orgasm (rate 20/min.) and (2) in the neurotic environment (210/min.). (From W. H. Gantt, *Psychosexuality in Animals.* New York: Grune and Stratton, 1949.)

Gantt (1949) who states flatly that 'sexual excitation has an inhibitory effect on the symptoms of anxiety.' An experimental animal, Nick, displayed intense anxiety in the neurotic environment (respiration: 210 per minute) but after achieving an orgasm, his respiratory rate decreased to 20 per minute. Figure 22 above illustrates the reduction in respiration produced by sexual activity. After sexual stimulation and orgasm, Nick remained calm and insensitive to the anxiety-producing stimuli for periods up to an hour. This is described by Gantt as a refractory period. He observed furthermore than *during* sexual stimulation the anxiety-producing cues were ineffective. This neurotic dog, Nick, was also observed to display less anxiety when placed in a paddock with a dog in oestrus (see Fig. 23). This reduction in anxiety lasted for several days but then gradually disappeared after the cessation of the bitch's oestrus period. Repeatedly exposing the neurotic animal to this sexual situation probably would have produced a permanent alleviation of anxiety.

The therapeutic use of sexual responses is particularly valuable when the sexual behaviour is only partially inhibited. 'The patient is told that he must on no account perform sexually unless he has an unmistakable, positive desire to do

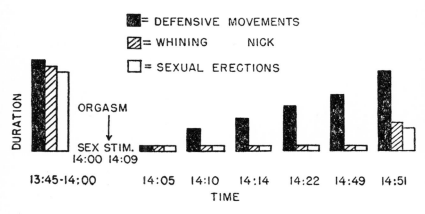

FIG. 23. Anxiety and sexual arousal. The animal's (Nick) anxiety reactions before, during and after sexual excitation. (From Gantt, *Psychosexuality in Animals*. New York: Grune and Stratton, 1949.)

so, for otherwise he may consolidate or even extend his sexual inhibition,' (Wolpe, 1958). The patient may be advised, for example, to engage several times in sexual activity (with the understanding of his partner) without attempting intercourse. With each repetition of relaxed sexual play in which no criterion is set, the patient's anxiety decreases. When a significant decrease in anxiety has been achieved, the patient is advised to attempt intercourse only if and when he feels *strongly* impelled to do so. Wolpe states that a patient instructed in this way experiences, 'increasingly strong erections and usually after a few sessions, coitus is accomplished and then gradually improves.' Sexual activity is ordinarily self-reinforcing and it is usual for these patients to obtain increasing satisfaction and general improvement with successive sexual experiences. This observation of patients' recoveries from neurotic sexual difficulties is paralleled by the observations of sexual behaviour in animals. Beach (1951) remarks on the increased sexual responsiveness observed in animals after a few successful experiences of copulation. 'The absence of sexual responsiveness may continue for months, but after one completed mating the male displays spontaneous courtship and copulation in all subsequent tests,' (Beach, 1951).

The therapeutic use of sexual responses is illustrated by a case drawn from Wolpe's series. The patient, a forty-year-old, unmarried male, had after many years of normal sexual activity, undergone a progressive decline in his sexual satisfaction. He had, for a period of four years, been complaining of premature ejaculations and failure to obtain an erection in sexual situations. His social adjustment was good, as was his occupational adjustment, and he had a low neuroticism score. Wolpe trained the patient in progressive relaxation, and explained to him the principle of reciprocal inhibition as applied to sexual situations. He was advised to explain his sexual difficulties to his current girl friend, and to obtain her co-operation in a gradual, therapeutic programme which was designed to resuscitate his sexual performance. After three failures, in which the patient failed to obtain an erection because he had attempted to go too quickly and had on these occasions experienced anxiety, he was advised to confine himself to preliminary love-play until such time as he felt a strong sexual urge and obtained a full erection. He was told that he was showing too much urgency about having successful intercourse and that he should, instead, concentrate on enjoying the preliminary love-play. The following week, the patient reported that he had twice been with his girl friend in the nude without intercourse being intended, and he had obtained several erections of varying quality. He was then told that if his erection was sufficiently good after manual handling, he could attempt coitus in the presence of a strong desire to do so. He achieved satisfactory sexual intercourse within the next two weeks, and after that continued to improve progressively. He eventually married his girl friend and, at follow-up eight months later, he reported that he was happily married and that their sexual activities were entirely satisfactory.

The third technique, the use of expressive responses, which Wolpe derived partly from Salter (1950), is useful in overcoming social inhibitions and anxieties. A patient is trained to use expressive, assertive behaviour, particularly in those social situations, or more usually with specific types of people, which provoke anxiety. The aim of this technique is to develop an inhibition of social anxiety by the use of expressive behaviour.

In all but one of the seven cases treated by Wolpe, the use of sexual responses was combined with one or both of these two associated procedures. In the case reported by Lazarus and Rachman, the methods of relaxation and systematic desensitization were used in the successful treatment of a thirty-two-year-old male patient.

This patient, a 32-year-old married man, complained that he had developed impotence during the previous three months. His impotence had first occurred during a period of considerable stress; he had been overworked and in a state of tension. 'Since then,' he said, 'I enter sex with a feeling of uncertainty and am frequently unsuccessful.' The patient was conditioned to become completely relaxed before the sexual act. After four interviews he had become proficient at relaxation and systematic desensitization was then completed in an additional four sessions. The desensitization consisted of his visualizing certain pre-coital scenes while under deep relaxation. He was followed up seventeen months later and there had been no recurrence of the disturbance.

In summary, the patient suffering from impotence is given the following instructions. Having obtained the co-operation and understanding of his sexual partner, he is instructed to attempt penetration only when he has a strong sexual desire, when there is very little or no anxiety present, and when the general circumstances are favourable. Until all these conditions are obtained, he is advised to build up to them in a gradual manner, by preliminary love-play and by various other methods which might develop strong sexual responses. Perhaps the most important instruction is that of refraining from attempting sexual intercourse when he is anxious, or when his sexual desire is low, or when the general circumstances are unfavourable or anxiety-provoking. Unsuccessful attempts, as has been mentioned earlier, may exacerbate the patient's condition.

In cases of premature ejaculation, there are two additional methods which may be of some value. The latency period of the ejaculation can be prolonged by preliminary love-play, particularly masturbation. Another technique which can prolong the ejaculation latency is to encourage the patient to attempt intercourse more than once on the same occasion.

From the case material which has been published to date, the indication is that behaviour therapy is of value in treating impotence. There is also reason to believe that the same general approach which is used in treating impotence could be applied equally to certain cases of frigidity.

Frigidity

Wolpe (1958) successfully treated a woman complaining of frigidity and inter-personal anxiety, by a combination of desensitization and the use of sexual responses. Lazarus (1963b) successfully treated nine out of sixteen 'recalcitrant cases of frigidity'. The mean number of sessions required to obtain improvement in these nine patients was 28. All of the patients in this series had received treatment prior to behaviour therapy. The method used by Lazarus in treating all these patients was systematic desensitization. Unfortunately, the follow-up information is somewhat scanty, but of the four patients who were seen more than a year after the completion of treatment, none had shown any sign of relapsing. It is interesting to note that all the women who responded successfully to the treatment had low extraversion scores and high neuroticism scores.

Exhibitionism

Bond and Hutchison (1960) obtained marked improvement in a patient with a severe and longstanding case of exhibitionism, by using the reciprocal inhibition technique. The patient was a 25-year-old married man of average intelligence. His first exposure occurred at the age of thirteen, following sexual play with a young girl. His exhibitionism continued through adolescence and it reached bizarre proportions by the time he reached adulthood. The attacks of exhibitionism were preceded by tension, dread, and sexual excitement. The attacks were often provoked by the perception of attractive young women.

The antecedent tension was constant and the patient often exposed several times a day. He had been convicted of indecent exposure on eleven occasions and had, as a result, spent a considerable amount of time in detention. The severity of his condition is best illustrated by the authors' account. 'A frequent practice was to hide, completely nude, in a small wooded area in the centre of the town where he then lived, and spring out and expose himself to the first woman who passed.' Various types of therapy had failed to relieve his condition. It was decided to attempt Wolpe's desensitization procedure, and the patient was accordingly trained to relax. A hierarchy of exposure-provoking stimuli was constructed, and the patient gradually desensitized over a period of thirty sessions. By the eighth interview, the patient evidenced distinct improvement. He was less tense, less prone to expose himself, and able to venture out unaccompanied. As the desensitization therapy continued, further evidence of progress appeared. His exhibitionist urges declined in frequency and strength, his sexual fantasies diminished, and he reported an improvement in his sexual relations with his wife.

Therapy had to be discontinued after twenty-nine sessions but the patient reported in the succeeding month that he had continued much improved. He then exposed himself in a feeble and uncharacteristic manner in a store. The patient was returned for treatment on a weekly basis and two months later no relapse had occurred.

Bond and Hutchison's view is that, 'Exposure either follows some environmental stress . . . or is provoked by an encounter with a female of specified age and physical appearance . . . The exposure can be thought of as an instrumental act designed to reduce an anxiety response triggered off by certain classes of stimuli, and desensitization therapy would constitute an appropriate form of treatment.'

This account, provided by Bond and Hutchison, conforms to a case treated by Wolpe (1958).[1] He obtained marked improvement in a 25-year-old patient with a history of exhibitionism dating back to childhood. This patient also suffered from social anxiety and had particular difficulty with authority relationships. The impulse to exhibit usually arose after frustration or when anxiety had been induced by his submission to authority. Treatment consisted of instigating assertive behaviour and desensitization to social situations which provoked

[1] We are indebted to Professor Wolpe for supplying us with supplementary information on this, and other, cases.

146

anxiety. Wolpe (1964) informed us that the treatment resulted in 'a tremendous general increase in well-being and heightened ability to deal adequately with social situations. Nevertheless, a small degree of autonomous tendency to exhibit, apparently purely sexually based, continued and only ceased when the patient married in 1956.'

Voyeurism

There is one case report of a voyeur who was markedly improved by behaviour therapy (Wolpe, 1958). In this case, as in some of the homosexuals discussed below, the sexual disorder disappeared as the patient's other symptoms improved. A 40-year-old male complained of writer's cramp and voyeurism. Clinical examination revealed the presence of deep and long-standing inter-personal anxiety, however. Assertive training and desensitization were initiated and a considerable improvement in the patient's social behaviour was obtained at the end of five months. The voyeuristic impulses had 'completely disappeared even though beyond some discussion of its relationship to frustration, no specific treatment was directed against it.'

Homosexuality

Freund (1960) remarks on the pessimism often expressed by therapists regarding the treatment of homosexuals, and argues that insofar as psychotherapy has any beneficial effect, this is attributable to a particular causal element. The causal element, he says, is, 'the encouragement of behaviour patterns which emphasize restraint or complete abstinence from homosexual behaviour and which involve heterosexual behaviour.' Freund accordingly devised a conditioning programme designed to inhibit homosexual and to stimulate heterosexual behaviour. He adapted and developed the aversion procedures commonly used in the treatment of alcoholism.

Freund's treatment consisted of the administration 'of an emetic mixture by subcutaneous injection.' While the noxious effects of the injection were being experienced, the patient was shown slides of dressed and undressed males. In the second phase of the treatment, the patient was shown films of nude and semi-nude females, approximately seven hours after the administration of testosterone.

Freund reports the result of this type of therapy on forty-seven patients. Follow-up studies three and five years after treatment indicated that 51 per cent of the patients showed no improvement; 14·9 per cent, temporary improvement; 25·5 per cent, permanently improved; the remaining 8·5 per cent were not adequately documented and hence were excluded from the final analysis. Freund concludes that his therapeutic results do not differ in quality and degree from those claimed by other methods. Such rule of thumb comparisons with other reports are, however, of little value because of the numerous variations in patient selection, evaluation of outcome, and other important but uncontrolled variables. It is a pity that Freund did not include in his otherwise valuable study a matched control group. Another important aspect of this treatment which would repay investigation is the effect, if any, of booster treatments such as that used by Raymond (1956) in his treatment of a fetichist. For example, would boosters reverse those cases which relapsed or, better still, prevent them from relapsing at all? An interesting innovation of Freund's is the inclusion of positive, adient stimulation which complements the aversion therapy.

An early attempt to use aversion conditioning was presented in a brief report by Max (1935). He claimed success in treating a homosexual with the use of faradic aversion conditioning. Unfortunately, it is impossible to assess the value of this report because of its brevity. Stevenson and Wolpe (1960) recently reported the successful treatment of two homosexuals, using non-specific behaviour therapy. They were able to produce marked improvements in both these cases with the use of assertive training, desensitization, and environmental manipulations. The importance of this study is that it illustrates how a sexual disorder may be treated in a non-specific manner by improving the patient's mental health generally.

A case which received a considerable amount of publicity was that described by James in 1962. The patient, a 40-year-old man, was admitted to hospital after a suicide attempt. He had been exclusively homosexual since the age of eighteen. The treatment employed by James was aversion therapy, using apomorphine. The treatment was administered at two-hourly intervals. During the treatment sessions the patient was shown photographs of nude men and listened to tape-recordings which described homosexual situations—while experiencing nausea from the injection. After this rigorous treatment programme, the patient was much improved and, a few months later, began to engage in successful heterosexual activity. He reported that he felt like a new man, and when he was followed-up, nearly a year after the completion of treatment, he reported that he had continued to improve and was able to enjoy normal heterosexual activity.

Thorpe, Schmidt and Castell (1964) recently produced a partial improvement in the case of a young homosexual. After they had failed to induce a change in behaviour by means of positive re-training, they introduced aversion training based on faradic shock. These combined procedures resulted in beneficial changes. Finally, McGuire and Vallance (1964) obtained improvements in 3 out of 6 homosexuals treated with a mild form of aversion conditioning.

Despite the considerable amount of literature on the subject, the nature and causation of homosexuality are still not clear. If we are to expect progress in the treatment of this disorder, more investigations like those of Freund will have to be conducted. These further studies should include control groups and should also explore the possibility of substituting faradic for chemical aversion procedures. In addition, further attempts should be made to treat homosexuals in the non-specific way used by Stevenson and Wolpe, in those cases where such a procedure appears to be appropriate.

Fetishism

After examining the literature, Raymond (1956) was able to find only three cases of fetishism in which treatment had produced successful results. Although this disorder has been extensively described, it remains extremely resistant to therapeutic modification. For this reason, Raymond's successful treatment of a fetishistic patient is of considerable interest and value.

A thirty-three-year-old married man was given treatment on probation after having been convicted of causing wilful damage to a perambulator. From the age of ten he had been attracted by prams and handbags. These objects aroused him sexually, and he obtained a release of tension by attacking them. The attacks on prams had resulted in several convictions, and he had spent periods in mental hospitals. He had not benefited from previous therapy, including psychoanalysis.

Raymond constructed a conditioned aversion[1] programme similar to that used in the treatment of alcoholism. The patient was shown a collection of handbags, prams, and coloured illustrations, 'after he had received an injection of apomorphine and just before nausea was produced.' Treatment was given two-hourly, day and night; no food was allowed, and he was kept awake with amphetamine. Treatment was suspended after one week and the patient went home temporarily. He returned eight days later and reported some progress. Treatment then continued for a further nine days. By this time he was showing strong aversion to the fetish objects. He was then seen at the out-patient clinic for a period of six months, after which a booster course of treatment was given in the hospital. Nineteen months later the patient 'still appeared to be doing well.' He no longer had fantasies concerning handbags and prams, his sexual relations with his wife had greatly improved, his probation officer reported very noticeable progress, and he had no further trouble with the law.

In a case seen by one of the present authors, faradic aversion therapy was attempted. The patient was a thirty-two-year-old bachelor who was sexually aroused by women's buttocks and bloomers. He had never had intercourse, but masturbated with fantasies concerning these fetish objects. The patient was given five aversion conditioning sessions. Three stimuli were used: the patient's photographs of women wearing bloomers, visual images of women with attractive buttocks, visual images of bloomers. The electric shocks were administered with an induction coil and finger electrodes. The patient was given ten to fifteen trials with each stimulus at each session. The strength of the shock was gradually increased after every four trials. During the first session the patient complained that the visual image of buttocks was constantly with him but by the fifth session he could obtain the images only with great difficulty. The time elapsing between the instruction to obtain an image and its appearance was found to increase significantly from session to session. After the final session the patient reported

---

[1] In most of the cases in which aversion treatment has been employed, the patients have been given nausea-producing drugs—see Raymond (1964) for a full account of the chemical aversion method.

feeling better, and said he no longer felt attracted by buttocks. He had ceased having his former fantasies and disposed of his numerous pornographic photographs. Unfortunately, it is impossible to draw any firm conclusions from this pilot investigation, since the therapeutic programme was not completed and the case was considerably complicated by several other abnormalities, including transvestite impulses. In addition, the patient was receiving other forms of treatment at the same time as the conditioned aversion sessions.

McGuire and Vallance (1964) recently reported the successful treatment of a fetishist using a similarly simple aversion technique, in which the shock was delivered to the patient's forearm instead. Ten of the 14 patients with sexual disorders who were treated in this way showed a good initial recovery. The long-term outcome in these cases should prove to be of particular interest in view of the simplicity of the method used.

Clark (1963a) reported on a case of fetishism treated by negative conditioning but in view of the nature of the case we feel that it is best described as a case of transvestism rather than fetishism; it is accordingly discussed in the following section.

Transvestism

Davies and Morgenstern (1960) reported an unsuccessful attempt to treat a transvestite patient by apomorphine aversion conditioning. It is impossible, however, to ascertain any possible effects of this therapy on the patient because of the marked organic syndrome involved. The patient had temporal lobe epilepsy and cerebral cysticercosis. The authors concluded that the transvestite behaviour could be curbed in the hospital but not at home. More recently, Morgenstern, Pearce and Davies (1963) reported that they had obtained successful outcomes in four of the six[1] transvestite patients whom they treated by the same method. In this report, Morgenstern et al. draw attention to some of the many complexities and difficulties encountered in this type of treatment (e.g. declining motivation, increased aggressiveness).

In 1961, Barker et al. reported the successful treatment of a transvestite, using apomorphine aversion conditioning, after

[1] One of the two failures reported in this paper refers to the brain-damaged patient mentioned in their earlier article.

the method described by Raymond in his treatment of a fetishist. Their patient had been engaging in transvestite behaviour since the age of eight. This behaviour had been constant for fourteen years, but cleared up during treatment. The patient was seen three months after the completion of treatment and was found to be progressing satisfactorily. Similarly, Glynn and Harper (1961) reported a case treated by the same method. This patient, who was twenty-seven years old, had been engaging in transvestite behaviour for thirteen years. The behaviour was curbed during treatment and when the patient was followed-up, seven months later, he showed no sign of relapsing and continued to progress.

Clark (1963a) described the successful treatment of a twenty-nine-year-old married man who was referred because of the embarrassment and anxiety produced by his habit of wearing a woman's girdle and stockings. 'The wearing of these garments gave the patient great sexual satisfaction, but did not exclude normal heterosexual activity. The patient's activities had begun some twelve years previously when he had masturbated wearing various female clothes.' The patient received intensive treatment in hospital over a ten-day period; the treatment consisted of apomorphine aversion conditioning which was administered twice daily. The patient was followed up at an out-patient clinic after three weeks, and declared himself cured. 'He has been back at work, enjoying a normal sex life, and is symptom-free over the past three months. He occasionally thinks wistfully of his erstwhile pleasures, but has never wanted to wear a girdle since treatment ended.'[1]

Cooper (1963) also obtained a successful result in a 25-year-old transvestite after treating him by a chemical aversion conditioning method. The patient's impotence was successfully treated (by Wolpe's methods) after he had ceased engaging in his perverted behaviour. This case-history contains many interesting features and provides a fine illustration of the way

[1] In a later communication, Clark (1963c) reported that this patient had relapsed. He discussed the possible reasons for the relapse and stated that he hoped to give the patient booster treatments. The most probable causes of this reversion were, according to Clark, the inadequate control of timing which is inherent in chemical aversion procedures or possibly, the effects of oscillation (See Chapter 17). The first possibility can be countered by using faradic stimulation, and the second by the planning of booster treatments.

in which a compulsive act can be acquired. The patient indulged in his transvestite activity when he was anxious (especially after sexual failures) and stimulated himself to emission. In this way, the perverted activity reduced both the sex drive and the anxiety drive—a combination which, according to Metzner's (1963) analysis, is conducive to the development of compulsive behaviour.

A very well-designed and administered treatment programme is that described by Blakemore et al. (1963). In designing the treatment planned for their patient, the therapist took into account the numerous criticisms which had been made of the use of apomorphine in aversion conditioning (see Eysenck, 1960b; Rachman, 1961b). The patient, aged thirty-three, was married and had one son aged two years of age. His earliest memory of transvestism was of an incident which occurred when he was four years old. He recollected deriving pleasure from wearing his grandmother's shoes. Thereafter 'he dressed frequently in his mother's and sister's clothes in secret, which was always a pleasurable experience. Whilst wearing a corset at the age of twelve, he experienced emission and afterwards found cross-dressing more satisfactory when accompanied by masturbation. Tranvestism occurred approximately fortnightly between the ages of twelve and eighteen years and was usually, but not invariably, accompanied by masturbation.' The transvestite behaviour continued until the completion of the behaviour therapy. Four years prior to entering the hospital for behaviour therapy he had married but this had not proved satisfactory, largely because of his perverse sexual behaviour. Prior to behaviour therapy, the patient had been in treatment for six years on and off, at two other hospitals which had provided supportive psychotherapy. He was of superior intelligence and had a high neuroticism score on the Maudsley Personality Inventory. Because the treatment plan was carefully thought out and constituted an innovation, we will describe it in detail. The treatment was carried out in an isolated room at the side of the ward. One half of the room was furnished with a chair, a full-length mirror, and an electric floor grid. The other half of the room contained the equipment necessary for producing the electrical stimulation and also a buzzer sounding device. 'The electric grid was made from the four foot by three foot rubber mat, the upper side of which had a corrugated surface. Tinned copper wire, 1/10th inch diameter copper, was laid and stapled lengthwise in the grooves of this mat at approximately half inch intervals. Alternate wires were connected to the two terminals of the electric current generator. This was a hand-operated generator which produced a current of approximately 100 volts a.c. when resistances of 10,000 ohms and upwards were introduced on to the grid's surface. It was found that two quick turns of the generator handle were sufficient to give a sharp and unpleasant shock to the feet and ankles of anyone standing on the grid.

'The procedure adopted in the treatment of this patient resembles in certain respects the paradigm involved in instrumental conditioning, in addition to the classical conditioning model employed in earlier studies (Kimble, 1961). Although the cross-dressing behaviour was followed by the onset of the noxious stimulus, as in the classical conditioning situation, the procedure to be described has much in common with escape learning in the absence of a warning signal, and in which the patient's subsequent behaviour was shaped by verbal instructions.

'The treatment was organized in such a way that the patient was seen on a daily basis, with him attending hospital from 9 a.m. until late afternoon each day, while spending the evening and sleeping at home. Throughout each day, treatment sessions were administered at thirty minute intervals, each session consisting of five trials. The number of trials per day varied between 65 and 75, until 400 trials had been given over a total of six days. The duration of this treatment was not continuous, however, for a weekend break of two days which the patient spent at home intervened between the fourth and fifth treatment days.

'At the beginning of each session the patient, dressed only in a dressing gown, was brought into the specially prepared room and told to stand on the grid behind the screen. On the chair beside him was his favourite outfit of female clothing, which he had been told to bring with him at his first attendance. These clothes had not been tampered with for the most part, with the exception that slits had been cut in the feet of nylon stockings and a metal plate fitted on to the soles of the black shoes, to act as a conductor. Each trial commenced with the instruction to start dressing, at which he removed his dressing gown and began to put on the female clothing. At some point during the course of dressing he received a signal to start undressing, irrespective of the number of garments he was wearing at that time. This signal was either a shock from the electric grid or the sound of a buzzer, and these were randomly ordered on a fifty per cent basis over the 400 trials. The shock or buzzer recurred at intervals, until he had completed his undressing. He was allowed a one-minute rest between each of the five trials which made up a treatment session.

'In order that the number of garments put on should not be constant from trial to trial, the time allowed from the start of dressing to the onset of the recurrent shock or buzzer was randomly varied between one and three minutes among the trials. It was possible, also, that the patient's undressing behaviour would become stereotyped if the interval between the successive shocks or soundings of the buzzer remained constant from trial to trial; therefore, while these intervals were kept constant within a trial, they were randomly varied between five, ten, and fifteen seconds among trials. The explanation of the procedure given to the patient before treatment commenced did not contain any reference to the randomization of the variables, and did not contain any instructions pertaining to the speed of undressing. At the start of each new trial the patient did not know, therefore, how long it would take before he received the signal to undress, whether this would be a shock or the buzzer, or the frequency with which these would recur during his undressing.

'Prior to the commencement of the treatment, it was predicted that towards the end of the treatment the patient's undressing behaviour might be characterized by a differential response to the shock and the buzzer. To check this prediction, his time taken to undress was recorded for each trial during the last day of treatment. During these 75 trials, the patient behaved in no way differently to the shock and buzzer, and there was no significant difference between the times taken to undress during repeated presentation of these two stimuli.'

After four days of this arduous and unpleasant treatment, the patient returned home for the weekend and it was obvious that his motivation had declined very considerably. It was thought possible that he would not return to complete the remaining treatment sessions. He did return, however, largely as a result of his experiences during the weekend when, he claimed, a reduction in the impulse to cross-dress had been noticed. The treatment was completed on his return and the follow-up, carried out six months after the completion of the last treatment session, indicated that the transvestite behaviour had ceased and that his sexual relationship with his wife had improved. He also stated that he was less anxious than he had been prior to the treatment.

Contrary to prediction, the therapists did not find a differential response to the buzzer and shock. During the last 75 of the 400 trials, they could detect no significant difference in his undressing behaviour with the shock or the buzzer.

A follow-up study (Blakemore *et ali.*, 1963*b*) of this patient, carried out 14 months after the completion of treatment, revealed that the patient had experienced one minor and atypical relapse. Some two months before the second follow-up investigation was carried out, the patient experienced a crisis. On the day prior to the birth of his second child[1] he became drunk whilst attending an office party, and while under the influence of alcohol, he made an appointment by telephone with a prostitute catering for transvestites. 'He kept the appointment and cross-dressed once, apparently obtaining some, but he maintains not complete, sexual relief. He then returned home, still under the influence of alcohol.' There had been no further relapses nor any desire to do so. He reported that he was strongly attracted to various females and that he experienced considerable satisfaction from sex play with his wife. This partial reversion to transvestite behaviour is reminiscent of the relapse reported by Bond and Hutchison in their case of an exhibitionist. Bond and Hutchison's patient also had a single relapse in which he indulged in atypical acts of exhibitionism.

Behaviour therapy of transvestism has, it is clear, recorded some important advances. Nevertheless, many problems of procedure remain to be refined and modified. One of the main difficulties which arises in the treatment of these patients by aversion techniques is that they tend, not surprisingly, to suffer a decline of motivation soon after the treatment has commenced. Morgenstern, Pearce and Davies describe in some

---

[1] Pearce (1964) has observed in his treatment of transvestism that the probability of a relapse is increased during periods of enforced abstinence from normal intercourse, e.g. during the wife's pregnancy.

detail the difficulties which may arise from this occurrence and also the way in which it can affect the relationship between the therapist and the patient. The case reported by Blakemore *et al.* is of particular significance because of the careful manner in which the treatment was carried out and also because of their use of faradic rather than chemical aversion. The substitution of faradic stimulation permits great control of the therapeutic situation and also allows the experimenters to make careful measurements of changes during therapy.

Discussion

Some disorders of sexual behaviour are produced by direct interference (e.g. painful intercourse) with the person's sexual activity, as seen in the case of A. G. described on page 68. Secondary disturbances of sexual behaviour may, however, arise in association with other neurotic habit patterns (Stevenson and Wolpe, 1960; Salter, 1950). This type of genesis was demonstrated in Gantt's (1949) experiments, in which he noted that the disturbing environment produced an 'inhibitory effect on the reaction of the animal to adequate sexual stimuli.' Some neurotic animals, when confronted with a bitch in oestrus *in a disturbing environment*, showed ejaculatio praecox and/or impotence. The inhibiting effect of strange or disturbing surroundings on the sexual behaviour of animals is also described by Beach (1951).

A paradoxical phenomenon was also observed in some of Gantt's experiments. On three occasions, the neurotic animal produced 'pathological sexual reactions to inadequate stimuli.' These adventitious sexual reactions (e.g. erections) were aroused by conditioned anxiety-producing stimuli such as a buzzer or light. Can anxiety-producing stimuli produce adventitious sexual reactions in human beings? Numerous sexual aberrations would seem to support this idea, notably exhibitionism and fetishism.

The research carried out on animals suggests a simple means of classifying deviant sexual behaviour. Sexual disorders may be regarded as comprising one *or both* of these two characteristics. The patient is unable to make an adequate sexual response to appropriate stimulation (e.g. impotence, frigidity). The patient responds sexually to inappropriate stimuli (e.g. fetishism). A combination of these features is seen in homosexuality.

Disorders of the first type require the therapist to eliminate the stimuli which are inhibiting the sexual behaviour, and also to encourage the development of an adequate response. In disorders of the second type, it is likely that the therapy will consist of some form of aversion treatment in which the patient will be taught to avoid or abhor the inappropriate stimuli. Disorders of the third type will probably require a combination of aversion treatment and also the stimulation of sexual activity in an appropriate direction.

The compulsive quality of certain sexual disorders (see Jaspers, 1962) can perhaps be accounted for by reference to Metzner's (1963) theoretical analysis of obsessional and compulsive behaviour. He proposed three experimental paradigms for this type of disorder, one of which appears to have a direct bearing on sexual compulsions. Metzner asserts that 'a positive approach response may get fixated when it also becomes an avoidance response, so that the response which satisfied the appetitive drive also reduced a learned anxiety.' This paradigm, Metzner proposes, can be used in the analysis of cases where 'some stimulus is an approach incentive and an anxiety-evoking conditioned stimulus for a learned avoidance response.' The example he uses is of some form of sexual behaviour. If sexual activity has been punished, then the sexual impulses can become anxiety-evoking stimuli. The sexual impulses also retain their appetitive quality, however, and a habit pattern which reduces both the anxiety and the sexual drive will tend to become fixated. Metzner quotes compulsive masturbation as an example of this kind of development—the masturbatory activity reduces both drives. The exhibitionist patient treated by Bond and Hutchison can profitably be viewed in these terms. The act of exposing himself to attractive women succeeded in reducing his feelings of tension and also gave him sexual relief. Similarly, Cooper's (1963) transvestite patient reduced his feelings of anxiety and also satisfied his sexual drive by self-stimulation while dressed in female clothing.

On the evidence available, it is fair to conclude that behaviour therapy may prove valuable in the treatment of sexual disorders. The most convincing advances so far have been in the treatment of impotence, frigidity, and transvestism. On voyeurism, fetishism, and exhibitionism, more clinical information is required. In cases of homosexuality, it seems that there is a need for more carefully designed methods and for information concerning the nature of this disorder. All the methods employed to date, ranging from aversion conditioning to assertive training have been justified, to some extent at least. It is probable that most cases require a combination of the available methods. We can confidently predict that these techniques will be refined with further experience and also that new procedures will be forthcoming. Some suggestions for developing the behaviour therapy methods can in fact already be offered on the basis of present knowledge. One possibility is the greater use of faradic as opposed to chemical aversion conditioning. This topic will be discussed in some detail in the next Chapter.

A second possibility is the use of Wolpe's anxiety relief technique in the treatment of voyeurism, exhibitionism, and fetishism. There is a hint present in the cases reviewed here that in many of these patients the abnormal sexual act is preceded or precipitated by an accumulation of tension. The anxiety-relief technique is designed to produce greater control of anxiety or tension and may, therefore, prove useful in such cases. Briefly, the technique is as follows. The patient is given a strong electric shock and told to say the word 'calm' when the pain and tension become unbearable. At this, the therapist switches off the current and the patient experiences considerable relief. This procedure is repeated ten to twenty times a session, with one-minute rest periods between trials. In this way the patient is given a degree of voluntary control over his feelings of tension and anxiety.

A refined version of this therapeutic approach is currently being investigated by Thorpe, Schmidt, Brown and Castell (1964). Their early results are promising and the long-term outcome of the successfully treated patients will be followed with considerable interest.

A third suggestion is provided by Freund in his treatment of homosexuality in which he emphasizes the necessity for stimulating and encouraging positive sexual behaviour in addition to eliminating the abnormal sexual activities. It may often prove unwise to concentrate on the negative aspects of the patient's behaviour, and hope or assume that adaptive sexual behaviour will automatically follow. Wolpe's use of sexual responses is an important method to be borne in mind for this purpose.

Chapter 11

AVOIDANCE CONDITIONING AND AVERSION TREATMENT

IN recent years aversion treatment has been used predominantly in the management of sexual disorders. Formerly, however, these forms of treatment were used almost exclusively in an attempt to cure alcoholics. For various reasons, the interest in aversion treatment was relatively short-lived. Aversion treatment, particularly chemical aversion, can be an unpleasant and arduous form of therapy and this fact, coupled with the often equivocal results obtain in the treatment of alcoholics, probably contributed to its decline in popularity. Franks (1960, 1963) has drawn attention to the poor quality of much of the early work on aversion treatment for alcoholics. 'Unfortunately, not all modern practice is sound . . . For example, some clinicians advocate giving the alcohol after the patient reaches the height of nausea. This, of course, is backward conditioning (since the unconditioned stimulus of the apomorphine or the emetine is preceding the conditioned stimulus of the alcohol) and backward conditioning, if it occurs at all, is at best very tenuous.' (Franks, 1963.) In any conditioning situation, the time-intervals which elapse between the presentation of the various stimuli and the response are of considerable importance and, as Franks has pointed out, aversion therapists were either ignorant of this fact, or tended to ignore it. He says that 'Under such circumstances, it is hardly surprising that reports of evaluation studies range from virtually zero success to virtually one hundred per cent success.' Furthermore, some of the drugs which have been used to induce nausea also act as central depressants. The effect of this type of drug would be to interfere with the acquisition of the conditioned response. An additional difficulty of some importance is the confusion regarding the nature of the unpleasant response which one is attempting to attach to the sight, smell, and taste of the alcohol. In some of the earlier studies, the therapists concentrated on the actual vomiting rather than on the feeling of nausea. As Raymond (1964) has shown, however, the act of vomiting is not the important event—it is the feeling of nausea which influences the acquisition of an avoidance reaction to alcohol. The difficulties involved in chemical techniques of aversion conditioning are multiplied by the existence of individual differences in reactivity to the various nausea-producing drugs. People differ in the speed and extent of their reaction to the various drugs and, furthermore, the same person may react differently to the same quantity of drug on different days or even at different times on the same day. Individual differences in reactivity, therefore, make the planning of a carefully controlled form of conditioning treatment extremely difficult.

Considering the mixed quality of a great deal of the work on the aversion treatment of alcoholics, we have decided to concentrate on the studies of Voegtlin, Lemere and their associates. (Readers with a particular interest in the treatment of alcoholism are recommended to refer to Franks (1960; 1963)). Although Voegtlin and his colleagues were not entirely successful in overcoming the very serious difficulties inherent in chemical aversion treatment, their work has some admirable qualities. Their persistence in maintaining follow-up contacts with more than 4,000 patients (some for periods exceeding ten years) is particularly praiseworthy.

Voegtlin and his colleagues (Voegtlin and Lemere, 1942; Lemere and Voegtlin, 1950) substituted emetine for apomorphine because of the hypnotic effects often produced by the latter drug. The patient is given a hypodermic injection of a mixture of emetine, ephedrine, and pilocarpine. At the same time, he is given an oral dose of emetine in order to bring him to the verge of nausea and vomiting, with both gastric mucosa and central nervous system in a hypersensitive state; the additional gastic irritation of a small drink of spirits then produces nausea after 30 to 60 seconds. Vomiting is usually delayed for another two minutes or so, or may not take place at all. These time-relations suggest that nausea, rather than vomiting, is the unconditioned response and that, in any case, we are probably dealing with delayed conditioning in some form. (The main purpose of the vomiting in this procedure is probably the elimination of the oral emetine and the alcohol, so as to avoid toxic action on the heart and the depression of the conditioning process.) There are other parts of the procedure which are emphasized by Voegtlin: the treatment room is quiet, bare, and darkened, with a spotlight on the row of bottles in front of the patient, thus ensuring prominence of the desired stimuli as CS. Soft drinks are given freely between sessions, so as to extinguish undesired conditioning to inappropriate CS. Under these conditions, over 4,000 patients were followed up for a year or more, of whom the following percentages succeeded in reaching the criterion of complete abstinence:

Abstinent for one to two years after treatment	60%
Abstinent for two to five years after treatment	51%
Abstinent for five to ten years after treatment	38%
Abstinent for ten to thirteen years after treatment	23%

Twenty-nine per cent of the original patients relapsed and were treated a second time. Of these, 39 per cent remained abstinent subsequently. At the time of writing, Lemere and Voegtlin (1950) quoted an overall abstinence rate of 51 per cent for all of their patients. Considering the probability of relapse in aversion therapy (See Chapter 17 below), this is an extremely encouraging figure, particularly as the procedure itself leaves much to be desired. There was no effort, for instance to take account of differential conditioning rates of extraverted and introverted patients (Vogel, 1962); more extraverted patients could, with advantage, have been given stimulant drugs to increase the rate of conditioning. The timing was far from perfect, CS and UCS being separated by a very sub-optimal interval, which, in addition, seems to have been rather variable. No attempt was made to decrease the occurrence of relapses by the use of partial reinforcement; 100 per cent reinforcement was used throughout. In spite of these criticisms, it must be said that the work of Voegtlin and his associates does present a genuine scientific attempt to make use of the principles of conditioning in treatment, and that, on the whole, their success has been quite remarkable. They must receive credit for having provided a base from which further research could have achieved an improved success rate.

With few exceptions, however (e.g. Thimann, 1949), the studies inspired by Voegtlin's claims are of a poor quality. Usually these studies contain variations from Voegtlin's procedure which are so serious and so counter to the laws of learning theory, that positive results would have been astonishing. Edlin's (1945) study is one example and Wallerstein's another (Wallerstein et al., 1957). Many other studies claimed to use conditioning treatment of one kind or another, but again, scant attention was paid to quite elementary principles of learning theory (cf. comments by Franks (1958)). The reader may like to consider the confusion of conditioned stimuli, unconditioned stimuli, conditioned and unconditioned reactions, together with their attendant trains of generalization gradients, adventitious conditioning, pseudo-conditioning, inhibition of reinforcement, sensitization, sensory preconditioning, and what not, offered by Oswald (1962) as a serious suggestion for work in this field, to realize that for all the attention that is being paid to them by practitioners in the field, the theoretical and experimental advances of learning and conditioning methodology might just as well not have taken place.

It is evident from our discussion of aversion treatment in sexual disorders (Chapter 10) that most of the recent work on this subject has been inspired by the earlier attempts to cure alcoholism in this manner. Some of the practitioners of this method are, in fact, engaged in the treatment of sexual disorders *and* alcoholism, as well as various forms of addiction (see Raymond (1964)). Although there is little doubt that some valuable recoveries have been obtained by chemical aversion techniques, there are, we feel, good reasons for advocating the substitution of faradic aversion treatment in most instances.[1] The advantages of faradic aversive stimulation appear to include the following points.

Faradic stimuli can be precisely controlled—the therapist can administer a stimulus of precise intensity for a precise duration of time at precisely the required moment. The use of inter-

[1]This view is encouraged by the recent work of McGuire and Vallance (1964) who obtained mild to considerable improvements in 70 per cent of 39 patients with varied behaviour disorders. These figures refer to the patients' progress one month after treatment.

mittent reinforcement is very much simpler to programme if one employs electrical stimuli rather than drugs. Faradic stimulation is less cumbersome and requires fewer personnel to administer it. It precludes the possibility of dangerous side-effects from drugs such as emetine. It also precludes the interference with the conditioning process induced by some of the drugs through their depressing qualities—e.g. the hypnotic effect of apomorphine is excluded. Finally, and perhaps most important of all, the bulk of the available laboratory evidence on avoidance conditioning (and there is a considerable amount of such evidence) concerns experiments in which the aversive stimulus was electric shock.

The effects of aversive stimulation on behaviour have, for a long time, constituted a serious and complicated theoretical problem for psychology. Much of the experimental evidence is conflicting and extremely difficult to reconcile. While there are still a large number of important problems which have yet to be resolved, some of the difficulties and ambiguities are now being clarified. An important contribution to our understanding of the effects of aversive stimulation on behaviour was recently made by Church (1963) and the present account is strongly influenced by Church's assessment. Summing up the position, Church writes: 'In comparison with a procedure involving no aversive stimulation, the effects of punishment are varied. If punishment reinstates a condition of original training, or if it elicts a response similar to the act which is being punished, then the procedure may produce response facilitation. Otherwise, punishment will produce response suppression.' If the aversive stimulation is not contingent upon the discriminative stimuli, 'the effect of punishment is simple . . . It always produces suppression.'

The effectiveness of aversive stimulation may depend on numerous factors, e.g. the severity of the stimulus, the effortfulness of the response, the amount and kind of previous training, the person's drive level, the time-relations between the administration of the stimulation and the occurrence of the response. We will now consider the role of some of these variables on the effectiveness of aversive stimulation. On the question of the timing of the onset of the aversive stimulus, it seems clear that if the punishment is made contingent on the appearance of the response, then the likelihood of the response being eliminated is increased. Response-contingent punishment produces greater suppression of the punished response and a longer-lasting inhibition. There seems little doubt that the presentation of aversive stimulation can produce almost total suppression of even the most essential forms of behaviour. For example, there are a few experiments in which the application of electrical (or other aversive) stimulation during eating has

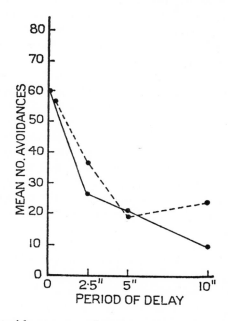

FIG. 24. Avoidance as a function of CS delay. The total number of avoidance responses, in two experiments, as a function of delay of CS-termination. (From Kamin, *Journal of Comparative and Physiological Psychology*, 1957.)

produced very serious feeding inhibitions (e.g. Lichtenstein, 1950; Masserman, 1943; Klee, 1944). One of the clearest demonstrations of the importance of temporal contiguity between the response and the application of the aversive stimulation is provided by the work of Kamin.

Kamin (1957) measured the speed of acquisition and the strength of conditioned avoidance responses in the rat. The animals were shocked in a shuttlebox and could avoid the shock by running to the other end of the experimental box as soon as the conditioned stimulus (a buzzer sound) was presented. Four groups of rats were trained with different periods of time elapsing between the onset of the conditioned stimulus (buzzer) and the delivery of the unconditioned stimulus (shock). Kamin found that the acquisition of the avoidance response was 'a negative monotonic function of delay of conditioned stimulus termination.' The strongest and quickest avoidance responding was obtained when the buzzer sound and the shock were presented simultaneously (see Fig. 24, above).

In a later experiment, Kamin (1959) investigated the effects of varying the time interval between a learned response and the administration of punishment. When the punishment was delivered without delay, the response was eliminated rather quickly. If, however, the punishment was delayed for long periods (30 seconds or more) then the response tended to persist (to resist extinction). The exact relationship between delay of punishment and the persistence of the response is shown in Figure 25 below. In this experiment, Kamin also obtained evidence of what Church describes as a generalized emotional effect of the shock. This generalized effect was also found to be influential in bringing about extinction of the response. The application of aversive stimulation gives rise to what has been called the anxiety drive, and stimuli which are associated with the aversive stimulus subsequently become capable of arousing that anxiety state even when they are presented in isolation. In other words, the mere presentation of stimuli which have been associated with an aversive stimulus may themselves serve to suppress the relevant behaviour. In general, however, the present position may be summed up in this way. 'The greater the interval between response and punishment, the less effective the punishment for the suppression of the response' (Church, 1963).

There is little doubt that the intensity of the noxious stimulus is a critical factor in determining its effect on behaviour. Within certain limits, an increase in the intensity of the aversive stimulus brings about greater suppression of the response. Church suggests that as the intensity of the stimulus is increased, the organism's behaviour goes through the following sequential changes: firstly, the animal detects the noxious stimulus; this is followed by temporary suppression of the response, then

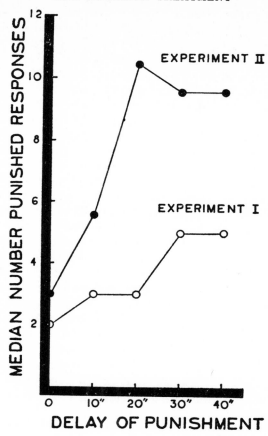

FIG. 25. Extinction and delay of punishment. Median number of extinction responses as a function of delay of punishment. (Results of an experiment by Kamin, *Journal of Comparative and Physiological Psychology*, 1959).

partial suppression and, finally, total suppression. If a mild noxious stimulus is used, the response is not weakened but the stimulus is used as an additional cue and may, in certain circumstances, even facilitate the response. When the intensity of the noxious stimulus is stepped up, the response is temporarily suppressed but is followed by a complete recovery. A further increase in the intensity of the stimulus results in suppression of the response followed by a recovery which is not entirely

167

complete, i.e. the response may reappear in an attenuated form. If the intensity of the stimulus is increased even further, the response is completely suppressed and never reappears. This last phenomenon, the total elimination of the behaviour, has been observed on numerous occasions and examples of this kind led Solomon and Wynne (1954) to postulate the occurrence of what amounts to an irreversible change. They argue that when traumatic conditioning occurs, the response may disappear totally and this process is described by them as 'partial irreversibility'. Clear instances of virtually total suppression of behaviour are provided by Masserman (1943) and Klee (1944), in which animals refused to eat for very long periods of time after thay had been punished in feeding situations. A variable which is closely related to the intensity of noxious stimuli but about which little is known at this time, concerns the effect of variations in the duration of the noxious stimulus.

Although they seldom state it specifically, most clinicians make the assumption that the chances of eliminating the patient's neurotic behaviour are greatly influenced by the length of the illness. In the case of aversion treatment at least, there is some evidence to support this assumption. Summing up the work on aversive stimulation and behaviour, Church states that the amount of suppression of a response which can be obtained by the administration of noxious stimulation is inversely related to the strength of that response. In other words, it is reasonable to predict that a patient with weak transvestite impulses will respond more favourably and more quickly to aversion treatment than a patient with powerful and persistent transvestite impulses. At the same time, it should be remembered that there is some evidence which indicates that if an organism has had prior exposures to (mild) punishment, this may confer on him some degree of immunity to punishments of slightly greater intensity. The work of Azrin (1961) and of Miller (1960) indicates that animals which have been given brief and/or moderate noxious stimulation develop a resistance to the effects of such stimulation. It follows, therefore, that if neurotic patients are subjected to brief, moderate noxious stimulation they may adapt to these conditions and the neurotic behaviour will not be fully suppressed.

There is also evidence that when animals are subjected to mild aversive stimulation, this procedure may, in certain circumstances, increase the strength of the relevant response. It appears that one of the ways in which this somewhat paradoxical effect may exert its influence is by providing the organism with an additional discriminative cue. In this connection, the work of Muenzinger (1934) provides some of the clearest examples of situations in which punishment facilitates the development of a particular response. Another instance in which the application of aversive stimulation may produce paradoxical effects is described by Gwinn (1949). He demonstrated that the punishment of acts which are motivated by fear will serve to increase the strength of these acts. This experiment, and others like it may have an important bearing on the application of aversion treatment in neurotic conditions. If the neurotic behaviour is motivated by fear, then it is conceivable that the use of aversion treatment may in some instances, bring about an intensification of the neurotic behaviour rather than its elimination. An example from the clinical literature which immediately comes to mind is that of writer's cramp. It will be recalled that Beech (1960) reported that the application of the Sylvester and Liversedge conditioned avoidance method (involving the application of electric shock) actually aggravated the cramps in three of the four anxious patients whom he treated. In view of the experimental and clinical evidence, it is conceivable that the presence of high levels of anxiety might contraindicate the use of aversion treatment—although it must be emphasized that at this stage the evidence on this matter is mostly indirect and rather tenuous.

In his review of the literature on this subject, Church pays particular attention to those instances in which the application of noxious stimulation produced a facilitation rather than a suppression of responses. He offers the following explanations for these paradoxical effects. He states that the following possibilities may be considered: 'It may be (a) that the punishment reinstated one of the conditions of training, (b) that the aversive stimulus elicited fear which facilitated the response, (c) that the aversive stimulus elicited skeletal acts compatible with the punished acts, or (d) that the response associated with the termination of the aversive stimulus was compatible with the punished act.' It was pointed out in Chapter 10 that aversive stimulation may serve to maintain or facilitate neurotic behaviour if it is associated with positive satisfaction. Martin

(1963) has published a useful review of the literature on this subject, and quotes numerous examples in which the combination of reward and punishment for the same act may ensure its continuance. Some obvious examples of this nature are provided in the literature on sexual disorders, e.g. sexual masochism. In similar vein, the experiments of Ullman (1951) have demonstated how the introduction of noxious stimulation may serve to sustain compulsive eating behaviour.

There is little doubt that there are still numerous serious gaps in our knowledge on the subject of aversion conditioning. And it is to be expected that further progress in the use of aversion treatment will depend on the use to which clinicians put the available experimental evidence. In our opinion, the substitution of faradic for chemical aversion methods will provide greater therapeutic control and an opportunity to develop reliable and significant techniques of aversive treatment. In the absence of sufficient clinical experimentation on this subject, we must attempt to translate the laboratory findings directly into the clinic. This, it must be remembered, is merely a starting point for systematic and careful *clinical* investigation of these techniques.

The experiments of Solomon and Wynne (1953) on traumatic avoidance learning in dogs provide some useful information about what may be expected to occur in aversion treatment with patients. One of the most interesting observations made by these experimenters was that the transition from escape responses to consistent avoidance responding is very sudden. In other words, once the experimental animals learned to anticipate (and thereby to avoid) the onset of the noxious stimulus, they quite quickly became adept at making the appropriate conditioned response. This abrupt change from merely escaping from the painful stimulus to anticipating and avoiding it, is clearly illustrated in Figure 26 below. After fifteen trials, during which the animal received the shock and then escaped, it learned to anticipate the appearance of the noxious stimulus and, from that point on, consistently succeeded in avoiding the unpleasantness. These findings of Solomon and Wynne have recently been confirmed by Turner and Solomon (1962), who carried out a series of experiments with human subjects. Their findings are consistent with those reported in the earlier experiments, and their subjects also displayed the sudden transition from mere escape responding to consistent avoidance responding. A typical result is presented in Figure 27 below, in which the subject received the noxious stimulus on seventeen trials and then switched to consistent avoidance responding. Turner and Solomon state that: 'The development of conditioned fear reactions with both visceral and skeletal components certainly presages the emergence of

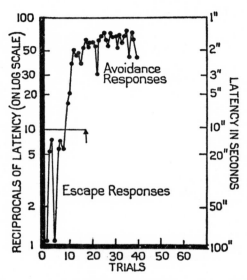

FIG. 26. Escape responses in a shuttle box. The performance curve for a typical dog subject in the shuttle-box situation. Note the long-latency escape responses and early achievement of the avoidance learning criterion. (From Solomon and Wynne, *Psychological Monographs*, 1953.)

avoidance responses. There is some evidence that the first avoidance response will not occur until a fear reaction has been conditioned to the conditioned stimulus.' On the basis of their experiments, Turner and Solomon suggest that the following procedure will ensure the development of consistent avoidance reactions. They state: 'We need conditioned fear reactions for the development of anticipatory avoidance responses. Short CS-UCS intervals should be best for this conditioning. But we also need more time in the presence of shock for relatively slow responses to be reinforced by CS and UCS termination.

We conclude, therefore, that the avoidance training of a highly emotional subject will proceed most rapidly if we start off with a short CS-UCS interval and then lengthen it, at the same time we start with an intense UCS level then lower it to produce long latency escape responses. When these procedures are combined, we should be able to produce rapid learning.' It remains to be seen, of course, whether this suggested pro-

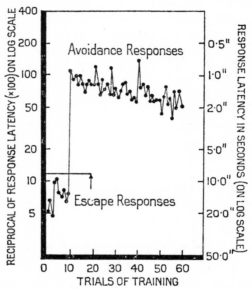

Fig. 27. The sudden transition to avoidance responding. The performance curve for a typical human subject. Note the long, variable escape-response latencies followed by a sudden transition to regular avoidance responding. (From Turner and Solomon, *Psychological Monographs*, 1962.)

gramme of Turner and Solomon's will in fact produce successful outcomes in aversion therapy.

Another variation in technique which would certainly repay investigation is the possibility of using other forms of aversive stimulation, such as unpleasant auditory stimuli. A small beginning in this direction has already been made by Barrett (1962) and by Blakemore (1963). In both of these reports, a limited amount of success was obtained in suppressing unwanted responses by making the administration of an unpleasant loud noise contingent on the appearance of the undesired response. In social situations, the use of aversive stimulation usually involves 'the removal or discontinuation of positive reinforcement rather than some kind of primary aversive stimulation' (Ferster, 1958). The usual social punishments are, as Ferster points out, disapproval, criticism, fines, or incarceration. And indeed the withdrawal of positive rewards has already been used, to a limited extent, in therapeutic situations (e.g. Wolf et al., 1964; Williams, 1959; Ayllon, 1963).

Before concluding this discussion of the possibilities of aversion treatment, it is worth drawing attention to some of the practical difficulties which have already been encountered or which may be expected to occur when this method is fully developed. It has already been observed experimentally that the administration of aversive stimulation can give rise to an increase in aggressive behaviour (see Martin, 1963, for example). There is also some clinical evidence of increased aggressiveness and hostility on the part of the patient during the conduct of aversion treatment (Morgenstern and Pearce, 1963). It may prove necessary to develop special methods for handling this increased aggression if and when it occurs. A second difficulty which may be anticipated is that concerning the anxiety level of the patient. As we have already suggested, there is a possibility that highly anxious patients may respond unfavourably to aversion treatment. Finally, as we will discuss in a later Chapter, there is reason to believe that the application of aversion treatment may give rise to a larger number of relapses than other methods of behaviour therapy unless provision is made for the administration of booster treatments at regular intervals.

Apart from suggestions which have already been made in this discussion, we would like to draw attention to two particulars which might prove to be of some value. In the first place, there is a strong case for including the use of stimulant drugs during the progress of the aversion treatment, as there is considerable evidence that these drugs facilitate the acquisition of conditioned responses (Eysenck, 1960a). Secondly, Turner and Solomon (1962) found in their experiments that the nature of the instruction given to their subjects was of considerable importance in determining the speed of avoidance conditioning. The better and fuller the explanation given, the quicker the learning. This suggests that in addition to giving the prospective patients a full and frank account of the nature of the treatment to be administered, he should also be given specific instruction about the kind of avoidance reactions which he will be required to learn. Finally, we wish to emphasize that the primary aim remains that of developing a scientific, controlled, and reliable method of employing aversive stimulation for the elimination of neurotic behaviour patterns.

Chapter 12

MODIFICATION OF THE BEHAVIOUR
OF PSYCHOTIC PATIENTS

I T follows from the dimensional analysis described in Chapter
2 that a person suffering from a psychotic illness can simultaneously display neurotic habit patterns. Neurotic behaviour is
acquired by a learning process, and the onset of a psychotic
illness does not eradicate the person's conditionability, although
the psychosis can, of course, modify both the opportunities for
learning and even the process of learning (see for example,
Rachman, 1963*b*). The theme of this book is that neurotic
behaviour is learned and can, therefore, be 'unlearned'.
Theoretically, if a psychotic patient also displays neurotic habit
patterns it should be possible to eliminate such behaviour by
learning therapy. In many, perhaps most, psychotic patients
the procedures of behaviour therapy cannot be applied because
of the patient's inaccessibility and lack of co-operation. Some
attempts are now being made to treat the neurotic behaviour
of psychotic patients, and the indications are that at least some
patients can be helped by behaviour therapy.

Cowden and Ford (1962) attempted to treat two long-term,
paranoid schizophrenic patients by desensitization therapy.
These patients were chosen because of their 'well-structured
and encapsulated phobic reactions'—from the account given
by the authors, however, one of the patients appears to have
been obsessional rather than phobic.

The first patient had been hospitalized for six years and had
not shown any significant improvement despite the variety of
treatments which he had received. Cowden and Ford decided
to treat his 'clear-cut phobic reaction of being unable to talk to

other people without becoming extremely panicky and frightened.' The patient learned the relaxation techniques quickly and appeared to visualize the hierarchy scenes quite vividly. The hierarchy was composed of items involving conversation, and ranged from talking about a movie to discussing his future with his parents. Altogether, eighteen treatment sessions were given over a period of four months. Halfway through the hierarchy, the patient, the ward staff, and acquaintances reported that the patient was more relaxed, friendly, and talkative. In general, the desensitization treatment brought about a significant improvement in his behaviour, particularly in his ability to speak to other people.

A second patient, who had been in hospital for seven years, had shown some slight, transient improvement in response to electro-convulsive therapy. At the time of the present treatment, this patient's primary difficulty seemed to revolve around his compulsive need to check that he had left nothing behind when he left a room. Cowden and Ford decided that 'his symptom was a marked obsessional reaction which appeared to be amenable to hierarchy development and gradual desensitization.' and they proceeded accordingly. The patient received fifty-six treatment sessions and showed some limited improvement. Although he was able to leave the room and walk out of the ward in the presence of the therapist, this improvement did not generalize to other people or to other situations. Cowden and Ford are unable to account for this failure of the desensitization treatment to generalize to real-life situations. These two cases indicate, however, that it is possible, in certain cases, to subject psychotic patients to the methods of behaviour therapy.

Walton (1960) attempted to treat a catatonic schizophrenic's phobia of women by a mixture of methods derived from learning theory. Walton's description of these methods, as consisting of reciprocal inhibition therapy, is a little misleading. Closer examination of his report shows that he actually used a combination of assertive training, psycho-drama, and negative practice.

The patient was initially required to read lists of words which included a few words with feminine and sexual connotations. He then graduated to meaningful sentences which included words of this kind. Finally, he was required to use these words in mock social situations, in the presence of males only, and then females as well. During these mock-ups, the patient was made to assume various roles, both masculine and feminine. A gradual decrease in tension was observed during the various stages of the treatment, and eventually he was adjudged to be much improved and, consequently, discharged (the manifestations of his psychotic illness had also subsided). At the first follow-up, one year later, he was found to have improved even further and had engaged in satisfactory heterosexual activities. Unfortunately, he relapsed soon after this follow-up and was re-admitted because of his inability to cope in social situations. After further treatment he again improved and was discharged.

Walton's suggestion that the elimination of this patient's phobia then transferred to and improved his psychotic illness must be regarded with reserve. The patient had shown similar improvements on earlier admissions to the hospital, and had also received numerous forms of treatment in addition to behaviour therapy. It should be pointed out, however, that no other treatment was being carried out during the period of the behaviour therapy—at least no other treatment is mentioned. It should also be remembered that the spontaneous remission rate in catatonic schizophrenia has been estimated to be fairly high (Hastings, 1958).

Walton, Cowden and Ford, have demonstrated that at least some psychotic patients are amenable to behaviour therapy, and that their neurotic behaviour can be beneficially modified. Cowden and Ford also point out that, in some cases, the psychotic patient could return to society if his *neurotic* behaviour were curbed. Most behaviour therapists do not accept patients for treatment if they are diagnosed as psychotic, but Cowden and Ford have indicated the need for further explorations in this field. Pending further information, however, it seems advisable to restrict the application of these methods to an experimental rather than a treatment basis when dealing with psychotic patients. Above all, it is necessary to keep such investigations in perspective and to define one's aims very carefully.

Operant conditioning

The application of operant conditioning methods to psychotic patients is an extremely interesting and significant development. While numerous studies have shown that it is possible to condition the verbal behaviour of psychotic patients (e.g. Salzinger, 1959; Beech and Adler, 1963), the greatest therapeutic possibilities seem to stem from research on other aspects of psychotic behaviour. Therapy of a primarily verbal nature appears, at present, to be faced by serious obstacles (see Cowden and Ford, 1961; King, Armitage and Tilton, 1960; Rosenthal, 1962). Operant conditioning of the non-verbal behaviour of psychotic patients, on the other hand, has already produced some remarkable results, and we will confine ourselves largely to a discussion of these investigations.

The work of Lindsley

We have already mentioned Lindsley's (1956, 1960, 1961a, b) protracted studies of the operant behaviour of a substantial number of chronic psychotic patients. Lindsley's experiments were conducted in an indestructible room which contained only one chair and a manipulandum panel on the wall. The panel contained a lever and a small aperture through which rewards were automatically presented (see Fig. 28). All recordings were made automatically, and the experimenter (in an adjoining room) observed the patient's behaviour through an aperture or a one-way screen. By using this basic situation imaginatively, Lindsley was able to investigate 'motivations ranging from food to social altruism, and discriminations ranging from simple visual to time estimation and complicated concept formation.'

Lindsley found that nearly 90 per cent of the chronic patients were unable to respond normally to his simple conditioning situation. What he describes as their 'extreme degree of behavioural debilitation' is indeed a striking characteristic of these patients. When the patients could be induced to make the correct conditioning responses, they tended to produce low response rates: far lower than one observes even in children. Furthermore, their operant response rates were exceedingly inconsistent. The records produced by normal people are relatively even, whereas the psychotics displayed numerous pauses during the conditioning sessions. Despite careful attempts to isolate the reason for these breaks in responding, Lindsley was unable to trace any extrinsic stimuli which might

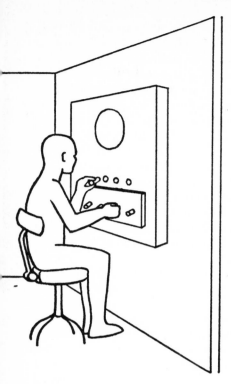

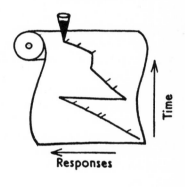

COUNTERS

00969 RESPONSES
00011 REINFORCEMENTS

RECORDER

FIG. 28. An apparatus for the free operant conditioning of psychotic patients, using small objects (candy, coins, cigarettes) as reinforcing stimuli. The experimental room is indestructible and is designed to observe the behaviour of even extremely disturbed patients. (Adapted from Lindsley: *Psychiatric Research Reports*, 1956; *Dis. Nervous System*, 1960.)

have caused these interruptions. Another feature of their behaviour was that many of the chronic patients tended to develop highly stereotyped ways of responding. Having developed a particular way of acting in the conditioning situation, they persisted in this manner despite attempts to change their behaviour by selective reinforcements.

On the basis of his experiments, Lindsley summarized the characteristics of vocal, hallucinatory symptoms, and possibly these findings can be generalized to many other psychotic symptoms as well. He says that vocal hallucinatory symptoms have the following functional properties: (1) a high degree of competition with non-symptomatic behaviour (i.e. when the patient is hallucinating this tends to interrupt any other on-going normal behaviour);[1] (2) the psychotic symptoms can be elicited by 'hidden stimuli of incomplete topography in the appropriate modality'; (3) an abnormally long after-reaction was observed to follow the elicitation of psychotic behaviour; (4) psychotic symptoms appear to be relatively independent of environmental stimulation.

The endogenous quality of the psychotic symptoms was carefully measured, and Lindsley was able to exclude a wide selection of extrinsic stimuli. He found that the onset of these psychotic symptoms in the conditioning situation was not related to temperature, humidity, home visits, or changes in the hospital social environment. Psychotic symptoms appear to have an internal rhythm of their own.

Lindsley has also investigated the effect of various forms of therapy on individual psychotic patients. In a study reported in 1960, he described the effect of insulin treatment on a chronic schizophrenic patient. No effects of the injection of insulin could be detected until the appearance of the first insulin coma. Following the patient's recovery from the coma, a marked increase in responsiveness was noted. This increased responsiveness was found after each of the eleven occasions on which the patient was put into a coma, but his responsiveness returned to the pre-therapy level as soon as the insulin treatment was stopped. In the same report, Lindsley described the effect of 50 mg. t.i.d. of iproniazid (Marsilid) on another psychotic patient. This drug was administered for four weeks without any observable effect. When the dosage was increased to 100 mg. t.i.d. a slight increase in responsiveness was observed, and continued for a few days. This increase, however, was of no greater amplitude than previously recorded increases which had occurred spontaneously. The conclusion drawn from this study was that Marsilid had a slight, transient effect which was of a lesser magnitude than spontaneously occurring improve-

[1]This finding has been disputed—Hamilton (1962) for example, has pointed out that psychotic patients who have been given industrial training may continue to display bizarre symptoms (such as conversing with Moses) while they are busily engaged in their work.

ments.[1] The greatest increase in responsiveness was observed after one of the patients had undergone 'psychotherapy'. The psychotherapy was carried out by a nurse who did little more than speak to the patient in a sympathetic and understanding manner, several times a week. These therapeutic sessions produced a substantial increase in responsiveness which disappeared when the psychotherapy was stopped. The improvements produced by the psychotherapy exceeded in magnitude any spontaneous improvements observed in this patient.

Rehabilitation procedures

Working along the same lines, King *et al.* (1960) attempted to develop therapeutic procedures which might be applied to extremely withdrawn, chronic schizophrenic patients. The rationale underlying their experimental treatment was as follows. Attempts at rehabilitation should commence with the responses which the patient has available. As verbal ability is either absent or inappropriate in many of these patients, it was decided that the therapy would begin from simple motor activity and gradually be built up into more complex motor activity and, eventually, verbal behaviour.

King *et al.* carried out their experiment on forty-eight chronic schizophrenic patients. These patients were divided into four matched groups, each containing twelve subjects. The four groups were treated in the following ways: group 1 was given operant therapy, group 2 was given verbal therapy, group 3 was given recreational therapy, and group 4 was given no therapy at all. All of the forty-eight patients were transferred to a special ward of which they were the sole occupants.

The twelve patients comprising the operant therapy group were seen three times a week for a period of fifteen weeks, and each therapeutic session lasted for approximately half an hour. The therapeutic procedure was carried out in three phases. In the first phase the patients were conditioned to produce simple operant responses and a gradual transition was then made to a situation in which they made complex operant responses. In

[1]The effects of chlorpromazine and of dexedrine were found to be unpredictable and caused increased responsiveness in some patients and decreases in others.

the final phase they were trained to co-operate in operant problem-solving behaviour. During the first phase of treatment, the patients were seen individually and trained to make operant responses for rewards of candy, cigarettes, and coloured slides. The required responses were of a simple, lever-pulling variety, similar to those used by Lindsley in his experiments (see Fig. 29 above). In the second phase of the treatment, more complex psychomotor and verbal responses were incorporated into the training procedure, in accordance with the patient's progress. In the final phase, the patients were required to communicate with other patients and to enter into co-operative relationships in order to solve the problems and hence receive the rewards. The effects of the therapy were measured in a variety of ways, including questionnaires and ratings, and also by the amount of verbalization produced by the patient outside the therapeutic situation.

King *et al.* summarized their results in the following way. 'The operant-interpersonal method was more effective than all the control methods in promoting clinical improvement, based both on ward observation and interview assessments.' Comparisons on the following variables also yielded differences in favour of the operant-interpersonal method: level of verbalization, motivation to leave the ward, resistance to therapy, more interest in occupational therapy, decreased enuresis, and transfers to better wards. The patients undergoing verbal therapy actually became worse in some ways (e.g. verbal withdrawal). A further evaluation carried out six months after the completion of the treatment experiment, showed that the operant group was significantly better than the control groups.

Isaacs, Thomas and Goldiamond (1960) have described attempts to restore speech in chronic schizophrenic patients who were mute. They present two case histories of patients who were subjected to operant training in an attempt to reshape their verbal behaviour. The first patient had been mute for fourteen years at the time of the experiment. He had been attending group therapy sessions with other chronic schizophrenic patients who were, however, able to speak. He made no progress in the group therapy, and appeared to be indifferent to the various rewards which were offered to him. At one session, however, the experimenter accidentally dropped a packet of chewing gum. He noticed that the patient's eyes moved towards the gum and then resumed their usual position. The experimenter decided to try and use the eye movement responses as the foundation stone on which to reshape the patient's behaviour. In addition to continuing in the group sessions, the patient was also seen individually three times per week. The authors describe the procedure which they adopted in this way. 'A stick of gum was held before the patient's face, and the experimenter waited until his eyes moved towards it. When this response occurred, the experimenter as a consequence gave him the gum. By the end of the second week, response probability in the presence of the gum was increased to such an extent that the patient's eyes moved towards the gum as soon as it was held up. The experimenter now held the gum before the subject, waiting until he noticed movement in the subject's lips before giving it to him. Towards the end of the second session of the third week, a lip movement spontaneously occurred, which the experimenter promptly reinforced. By the end of this week, both lip and eye movements occurred when the gum was held up. The experimenter then withheld giving the gum until he made a spontaneous vocalization, at which time the experimenter gave him the gum. By the end of this week, holding up the gum readily occasioned eye movement toward it, lip movement, and a vocalization presenting a croak.

'Then the experimenter held up the gum and said, "Say gum, gum," repeating these words each time the patient vocalized. Giving the patient the gum was made contingent on vocalizations increasingly approximating "gum". At the sixth session (at the end of sixth week) when the experimenter said, "Gum, gum," the subject suddenly said, "Gum, please." This response was accompanied by a reinstatement of other responses of this class, that is, the subject answered questions regarding his name and age.' Thereafter the patient responded to questions from the experimenter, but did not reply to anyone else. The next stage was to bring about a generalization of the verbal responses. Accordingly, various other people were introduced into the sessions, and he started speaking to these people as well. In addition, various other ward staff were encouraged to obey the patient when he made explicit spoken requests.

The second patient described by the authors had been mute for fourteen years. He was treated in a way similar to that described for the first patient, and also made some progress, in that verbal behaviour was resuscitated. They found it impossible to get this verbal behaviour to generalize to a wide range of situations however.

In 1958, Robertson attempted to shape the behaviour of three mute, catatonic patients, but was unsuccessful. He ascribes the failure of this attempt to the fact that it was difficult to find a suitable reward for which these patients would work. Consequently, his attention was directed towards the effects of different kinds of rewards in modifying verbal behaviour of schizophrenic patients (Robertson, 1961). After studying twenty-four shizophrenic patients, he concluded that these individuals responded positively to different kinds of rewards—some patients responded to praise, and others responded to concrete rewards. Furthermore, those patients who responded to praise tended not to respond to concrete rewards and *vice versa*. He also noted that the effects of rewards were greatest when the patient was instructed both as to the response required and the reward to be obtained.

Recently, Kennedy (1964) obtained marked improvements in the behaviour of two out of three chronic schizophrenic patients by means of operant conditioning. In all three cases the emphasis was on verbal re-conditioning.

The work of Ayllon

The work on reshaping of verbal behaviour in psychotic patients is, of course, an attempt to modify the *psychotic* behaviour of these patients, and not an attempt to diminish or eliminate the neurotic components of the psychotic patients' behaviour. This difference is important, for the reasons already given above—it is important to define one's aims clearly in advance of planning any treatment or behaviour changes. Over the past five years, Ayllon and his colleagues have been conducting a series of extremely interesting and imaginative research programmes. They have studied various behaviour problems presented by hospitalized psychotic patients, including hoarding, seclusiveness, destructiveness. In addition to curbing these unwanted response patterns, Ayllon has also succeeded in reshaping positive responses such as eating, dressing, bathing, etc.

They found that approximately half of the ward population

had a history of some difficulty in their eating behaviour. Many of these patients refused to eat except with the assistance of the ward staff. Techniques which had been used by the ward staff to get these patients to eat included spoon-feeding, tube-feeding, intravenous feeding, and electro-shock. Ayllon's preliminary analysis of the behaviour of these patients suggested that their feeding difficulties were being maintained because of the social reinforcement which this behaviour produced. He states that 'social reinforcement in such forms as coaxing, persuading, and feeding the patient tend to shape the patients into eating problems so that they are conditioned to eat only with assistance,' (Ayllon and Haughton, 1962). The first thing that Ayllon did was to discontinue the practice of spoon-feeding, coaxing, and persuading the patients to eat. At meal-times, a time interval of thirty minutes was allowed for the patients to be admitted to the dining room. If they did not arrive at the dining room within this specified period, the door was locked and they were not allowed to enter. A full illustration of the procedures which were used is given in the case histories described below. With surprisingly few difficulties, the eating problems of the vast majority of these schizophrenic patients were eliminated.

Ayllon (1960) described a typical case of a near-mute, catatonic patient whose eating problems were eliminated by a programme of this nature. For sixteen years this patient would not eat unless a nurse led her to the dining room, gave her a tray, cutlery, and food, and seated her at the table, urging her to eat and occasionally spoon-feeding her. A day-to-day analysis of her behaviour suggested that her feeding difficulty was being maintained by the social attention which she received as a result of her awkward eating pattern. At first, the nurses were instructed not to take the patient to the dining room but to help her as much as before if she did enter the dining room. For four days the patient merely sat in a chair during meal times and consequently missed all her meals on these days. By the seventh week, she was going to the dining room entirely unaided. The next phase of the programme consisted of shaping her behaviour in the dining room. The nurses were instructed not to get the patient's tray for her once she entered the dining room. When the patient did pick up her tray, however, she was rewarded by having a piece of candy and one edible item placed on her tray. After further shaping along these lines, the patient eventually started feeding herself entirely and also coming to the dining room on time. Another behaviour problem which they have succeeded in treating successfully is hoarding. Ayllon and Michael (1959) report on three interesting cases of this nature.

A recently reported case of Ayllon's (1963), concerns a schizophrenic patient who had been hospitalized for nine years. Ayllon treated three aspects of her behaviour which constituted problems—stealing food, hoarding towels, wearing excessive clothing. Each of these behaviour patterns was modified separately under different operant training conditions. In addition to eating her own food, this patient stole from the dining room and also from other patients. She was grossly overweight and had weighed more than 250 pounds for many years. An initial recording period lasting nearly a month showed that the patient stole food during two-thirds of all meals. The treatment consisted of isolating the patient in a corner of the dining room and allowing no other patients to sit at the same table with her. Then the nurses were instructed to remove the patient from the dining room when she picked up any unauthorized food. In effect, this meant that the patient missed a meal whenever she attempted to steal food. The withdrawal of positive reinforcement (i.e. a meal), was made 'dependent upon the patient's stealing.' The stealing was eliminated in two weeks (see Fig. 29). It will be seen from the Figure that there were only three slight relapses after the stealing had been stopped at the end of two weeks. In addition, the patient's weight showed a considerable decline and it eventually stabilized at 180 pounds (see Fig. 30).

An assessment of the patient's hoarding behaviour showed that she had between twenty and thirty towels in her room at any one time, despite the fact that the nurses were continually recovering their towels from her room. Ayllon decided to treat this problem by a procedure of stimulus satiation. The nurses were instructed to take a towel to the patient whenever she was in her room and simply hand it to her without any comment. During the first week she was given an average of seven towels daily, and by the third week this number was increased to sixty. When the number of towels in the patient's room reached 625, they had developed into an aversive stimulus. The

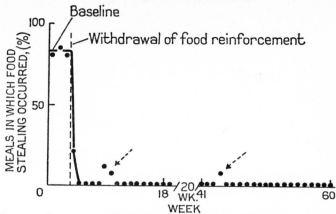

FIG. 29. A response, food stealing, is eliminated when it results in the withdrawal of food reinforcement. The dotted arrows indicate the rare occasions when food stealing occurred. For purposes of presentation a segment, comprising 20 weeks, during which no stealing occurred, is not included. (From Ayllon, *Behaviour Research and Therapy*, 1963.)

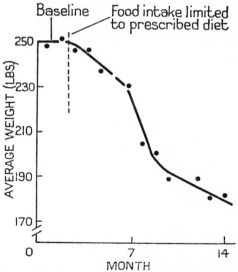

FIG. 30. The effective control of food stealing results in a notable reduction in body weight. As the patient's food intake is limited to the prescribed diet, her weight decreases gradually. (From Ayllon, *Behaviour Research and Therapy*, 1963.)

187

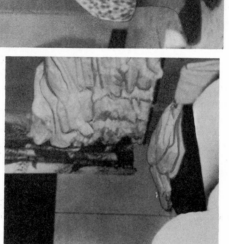

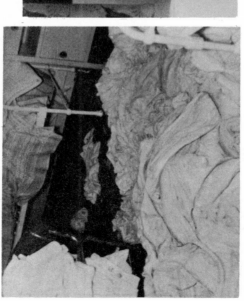

(a) The treatment of towel-hoarding by the method of satiation. This picture illustrates the early stage of satiation treatment. As the patient received the towels she folded them neatly and stacked them around her bed.

(b) The patient's room just before she started to rid herself of the towels. Notice that there are still a few stacks of folded towels in the background.

(c) Treatment of the patient's bizarre dressing habits. This picture illustrates the patient's appearance at the start of the treatment programme. She was wearing approximately two dozen pairs of stockings, bandages on her wrists and several dresses.

(d) The same patient eating in the dining room during the early stage of treatment.

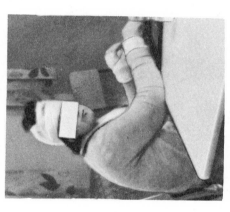

(e) Her appearance after she started to discard a few items of clothing.

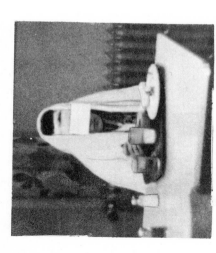

(f) The patient during the final stages of the operant conditioning procedure.

Figs. 31. (a-f). Progress in the treatment of a psychotic patient by operant conditioning methods. (From Ayllon, *Behav. Res. & Ther.*, 1963.)

patient proceeded to get rid of the towels herself, until she had virtually none left in her room. The progress of the satiation treatment is illustrated in Figure 31. The photographs reproduced on page 188 illustrate the state of chaos which existed in her room at the height of the satiation treatment. When the treatment began, the patient would smile at the nurse and say, 'Oh, thank you, you've found it for me.' As the number of towels in her room increased, she began to tell the nurses that she didn't need more towels. By the third week she was offering to take them out of her room, and by the fourth, fifth, and sixth weeks she was imploring them to take them away. The patient's behaviour was closely observed during the following year and she showed no sign of reverting to the hoarding behaviour. Furthermore, no symptom substitution occurred.

The third part of the treatment programme was directed at getting the patient to wear a normal amount of clothing. On being admitted to the hospital, she was observed to be wearing an excessive amount of clothing which Ayllon describes as including 'several sweaters, shawls, dresses, undergarments, and stockings . . . the clothing also included sheets and towels wrapped around her body and a turban-like headdress made of several towels . . . The patient also carried two to three cups in one hand, while holding a bundle of miscellaneous clothing and a large purse in the other.' (See photograph on page 188). Ayllon decided to tackle this problem by making the patient's entry to the dining room dependent upon her meeting a specified weight. She was weighed before entering the dining room before each meal and if her weight exceeded the specified amount she was not permitted to take that particular meal. Initially she was given an allowance of twenty-three pounds over her current body weight. As she began slowly and gradually to shed superfluous clothing, the extra weight allowance was gradually decreased. At the conclusion of the experiment, her clothes weighed three pounds, instead of the previous twenty-three. The quantified progress of this treatment is illustrated in Figure 30 and the photographs presented on page 189 give adequate testimony to the remarkable all-round improvement produced in this woman.

It will be clear, particularly from the case report of Ayllon described above, that in order to carry out this kind of operant retraining and rehabilitation with psychotic patients, it is necessary to have a very carefully run and strictly supervised ward. This implies the complete co-operation of all staff members.

We may summarize the work on psychotic patients in this way. The neurotic behaviour of accessible, co-operative patients can, in certain instances, be treated by the conventional methods of behaviour therapy. In addition, certain behaviour problems of psychotic patients can be modified by operant training procedures. Even allowing for the limitations imposed by the psychotic illness itself, some encouraging new possibilities arise out of this research work. The imaginative application of learning theory will, we hope, make a significant contribution to the rehabilitation of psychotic patients.

Chapter 13

CHILDREN'S DISORDERS—I

PROGRESS in the investigation and treatment of behaviour disorders in adults has not been accompanied by a similar rate of advance in child psychology. With the exception of the problems of enuresis and to a lesser extent, phobias, there has been little systematic research conducted in this field by learning theorists. On purely historical grounds, this uneven development is a little surprising. The first experimental demonstration of the genesis of neurotic behaviour in a human being was carried out by Watson (1920) on a young boy, Albert. Watson produced a phobia in Albert by presenting a disturbing loud noise when a white rat was brought into the boy's presence. After a few repetitions of this association, Albert developed a phobia for small white furry objects (see page 81 above). In addition to Watson's classical demonstration, the first attempt at treatment based on learning principles was also carried out on a child. In 1924, Mary Cover Jones used deconditioning methods to eliminate a rabbit phobia in a three-year-old boy, Peter. The techniques she employed were a precursor of some of the new methods used by contemporary behaviour therapy. In particular, Wolpe's (1958) systematic desensitization method has an affinity to Jones' early study. The next significant advance in the application of learning theory to children's disorders was Mowrer and Mowrer's (1938) work on the conditioning treatment of enuresis. This disorder has continued to receive the attention of behaviour therapists but in general, the progress made in the treatment of adults since 1948 has not been reflected in child psychology and psychiatry.

The reason for this discrepancy can probably be ascribed to an important difference in the nature of behaviour disturbances in children and adults. Many behaviour problems in children (especially in the early years) are associated with inadequate or inappropriate responses. These deficits usually centre around the activities of eating, sleeping, elimination, and speaking. In most instances the problem arises because (in a learning theory sense) the child has failed to develop an adequate way of responding (e.g. enuresis, aphemia, anorexia, dyslexia). In adults, most problems seem to be concerned with unadaptive behaviour, and the purpose of therapy is generally directed at eliminating the unwanted responses (e.g. phobias, anxiety states, compulsions, perversions). Most often the aim in therapy with adults is to break down a behaviour pattern, whereas in treating children the therapist usually has to build up an adequate behaviour pattern.

The recent infiltration of operant conditioning procedures into clinical psychology seems to provide a tool for building up deficient responses in children. Lindsley (1956, 1960) followed up the proposals of Skinner (1959) and Skinner, Solomon and Lindsley (1954) and has already produced extremely interesting analyses of the behaviour of acute schizophrenic patients. The clinical application of this technique in child psychology is foreshadowed by the work of Ferster (1961), Lovaas (1961a, b), Baer (1963), Spradlin (1961), and Bijou (1961) among others. The established methods of behaviour therapy, such as Wolpe's (1958) reciprocal inhibition technique and the extinction procedures used by H. G. Jones (1960b) and Yates (1958) have already been successfully used on child patients and are described first.[1]

Desensitization, conditioned inhibition, negative practice

In his book, Wolpe (1958) describes the treatment of eighty-eight patients. Of these, two were children. An eleven-year-old boy, suffering from interpersonal anxiety and tic-like movements, was treated by desensitization and was markedly im-

[1]With the exception of some cases which are described for purposes of illustration, the present account of children's disorders considers only published findings. Observations arising from ongoing studies have not been included.

proved after eight treatment sessions. The second case, a fourteen-year-old stammerer, relapsed under stress after showing considerable improvement in the first few months of treatment. Further treatment was only able to counteract the relapse to a limited degree. The methods used in this case consisted of relaxation and breathing exercises.   In a later series of thirty-nine cases treated by desensitization, Wolpe (1961) describes two further child patients. An eleven-year-old boy was successfully treated for his fear of authority figures in six sessions, while another stammerer (aged thirteen) failed to respond. This boy, being unable to obtain vivid visual images, was unable to comply with the requirements of desensitization therapy. While the lack of success with two cases of stuttering is not conclusive, there are grounds for believing that some of the methods used in treating this condition in adults may prove more successful. The work of Case (1960) on negative practice, Meyer and Mair (1963) on speech rhythms, Sheehan (1951) and Sheehan and Voas (1957) on non-reinforcement, and of Cherry and Sayers (1960) on shadowing are among the most promising.

White (1959) described the successful treatment of a five-year-old girl who suffered from anorexia. The child's feeding difficulties started at the age of three, and worsened after the death of her father when she was five years old. She had been deeply attached to her father and was extremely disturbed by his illness and death. Her father had fed her from an early age. Attempts made by her mother, relations, doctors, and nurses to feed her were mainly unsuccessful. 'The immediate problem,' writes White, 'was formulated in terms of simple conditioning, with father as the conditioned stimulus upon which the conditioned response of eating had come to depend.' The reinforcement was 'supplied by the satisfaction of hunger as well as by anxiety-reduction through sitting on the father's knee and being fed by him.'

The method of treatment was based on this analysis and bears a strong resemblance to M. C. Jones' (1924) treatment of Peter. 'The first step,' says White, 'was to provide a substitute for the father and to arrange a series of experiences that might gradually approximate those obtaining before the father's death.' Initially, the psychologist attempted to replace the conditioned stimulus provided by the father. When this was accomplished, generalization to selected relatives was under-taken (aunts, uncles, and mother). This general plan of treat-ment (with some additions during the course of therapy) was followed for seven months. Some marked improvements were evident after only three to four weeks, and when treatment concluded at the end of seven months, the girl was very much improved. This improvement has been maintained over a three-year follow-up period. White's formulation of the problem in 'terms of simple conditioning' is not entirely satisfactory. His description of the child's eating as a conditioned response is questionable, and the analysis fails to account for the onset of the feeding difficulties prior to the father's death. It may be more useful to re-set the treatment programme in terms of an operant conditioning process in which the psychologist 'shaped' and expanded the range of the child's eating behaviour. While a clear theoretical explanation would be valuable, the successful outcome of this difficult case is encouraging.

Walton (1961) described how an eleven-year-old boy who suffered from a complex of severe tics was successfully treated by negative practice and conditioned inhibition methods (see Chapter 121). A follow-up conducted a year later showed that the improvements had been maintained and that the boy's general adjustment had been highly satisfactory. The essence of the treatment is that the repeated evocation of the tics produces an inhibitory effect which eventually 'exhausts' these movements. Williams (1959) treated temper tantrums in a 21-month-old child by a process of experimental extinction. The child displayed tantrum behaviour whenever he was put to bed in the evening. Williams argues that this unadaptive behaviour was being maintained, or reinforced, by the parental attention which it produced. The parents were instructed to refrain from re-entering the bedroom after the child had been placed in bed, and to record the duration of each tantrum. The duration of the tantrums gradually decreased, and in less than two weeks, had almost ceased. Spontaneous recovery of the tantrum pattern was later observed when one evening the maternal grandmother entered the bedroom before the child had stopped crying. The tantrum behaviour was reinstated for another few days, but persistent non-reinforcement (i.e. failure to re-enter the bedroom) brought the disturbance to an end after nine days. A two-year follow-up of this case revealed no further behaviour difficulties. Boardman (1962) reported the successful treatment of a rebellious and defiant child by manipulating the home environment in such a way as to inhibit his anti-social, unacceptable behaviour, and Zimmerman and Zimmerman (1962) succeeded in improving the classroom behaviour of two in-patients by similar manipulations of rewards and non-rewards.

Enuresis

The first systematic investigation of therapy derived from learning theory was Mowrer and Mowrer's (1938) famous study of enuresis. Despite its efficiency, this method was neglected for many years. Serious interest in this so-called 'bell-and-pad method' has revived in the past five years, and a comprehensive evaluation of the available evidence (see Table 5) was carried out by Gwynne Jones (1960a), who concluded that 'if widely adopted, the specific conditioning method of

TABLE 5

The effect of conditioning treatment of enuresis. (From H. G. Jones in *Behaviour Therapy and the Neuroses,* ed. H. J. Eysenck, Pergamon Press, 1960a.)

Author	No. of Cases	Age Range	Per cent cured	Per cent markedly improved	Per cent failures
Mowrer and Mowrer	30	3–13	100	100	0
Davidson and Douglass	20	5–15 (+2 adults)	75	25	0
Crosby	{ 35	3½–10½	88	3	9
	23	11–28	83	5	12
Sieger	106	3–15 (+4 adults)	89	7	4
Geppert	42	5–10	74	16	10
Baller and Shalcock	55	Median 9.5	70	30	30
Wickes	100	5–17	50	24	26
Gillison and Skinner	100	3½–21	88	5	7
Freyman	15	5–14	33	40	27
Murray	33	—	75	9	16
Martin and Kubly	118	3½–18½	56	18	26
Lowe	{ 322	5–10	88	12	12
	276	10–16	88	12	12
	171	16+	85	15	15

treatment is capable of significantly reducing the incidence of *enuresis nocturna* at the later ages if childhood.'

This view is borne out by the recent work of Lovibond (1962, 1963*a*, *b*), who carried out a well-planned and executed investigation. He showed that the Mowrer, Crosby, and his own Twin-Signal technique of conditioning were all highly effective in arresting enuresis. The mean number of trials required to arrest the enuresis was 13·5, but the relapse rate for all three methods was unsatisfactorily high. Consequently, Lovibond tried some variations of the method, in an attempt to increase the stability of the newly-learned ability. He eventually developed a refined Twin-Signal method used on an intermittent reinforcement schedule. None of the fourteen subjects had experienced a relapse at the time of Lovibond's writing[1] (i.e. from one to nine months after treatment). This result is already an improvement on the earlier procedures, and deserves further field trials. Lovibond's work recommends itself for two reasons. His developments of the technique promise improved results, and his theoretical analysis is more convincing than either Mowrer's or Crosby's. The conditioning paradigms proposed by Mowrer and Crosby are both subject to criticism (Jones, 1960*a*; Lovibond, 1962) and Lovibond's re-formulation of the problem, in terms of conditioned avoidance training, seems able to accommodate all the available information. 'Reflex contraction of the detrusor and relaxation of the sphincter are followed by the noxious stimulus, electric shock or loud noise. After a number of such conjunctions the stimuli arising from sphincter relaxation becomes the conditioned stimuli for the avoidance response of sphincter contraction. In other words, the conditioned stimulus is not bladder distension but the pattern of stimuli arising from the response of sphincter relaxation and urination. When conditioning reaches the stage where the first indication of the stimulation gives rise to the antagonistic response of sphincter contraction, the child does not wet the bed and the noxious stimulus is avoided' (Lovibond, 1961).

[1]In a recent communication, Lovibond (1964) reported the following relapse rates at 12-month follow-up: (a) Twin signal intermittent reinforcement (n = 16) 19 per cent. (b) Twin signal continuous reinforcement (n = 34) 44 per cent. (c) Mowrer-type continuous reinforcement (n = 34) 35 per cent.

This analysis and its implications provided the basis for the design of a modified conditioning technique. Two essential considerations which determined the form of the new Twin-Signal were:

(i) the critical function of the unconditioned stimulus is to produce a sudden relaxation of the detrusor and contraction of the sphincter;

(ii) the child's response must 'turn off' or permit escape from the unconditioned stimulus, thus facilitating the formation of a conditioned avoidance response.

The Twin-Signal apparatus consists of a pad electrode, a strong auditory stimulus (240 volt signal similar to a car hooter, suitably attenuated), and a mild buzzer. When the pad is wet, the strong stimulus sounds for one second. After a minute of silence, the buzzer sounds—in order to summon the attendant.

During the acquisition (training) period, the apparatus is switched off for 50 per cent of the trials (intermittent reinforcement). The presentation or non-presentation of the unreinforced stimulus is randomly determined so that the child may experience 'runs' of hooter and no-hooter, e.g. wet—hooter, wet—hooter, wet—hooter, wet—no hooter, wet—no hooter, and so on. The purpose of this intermittent patterning is to enhance the stability of the developing habit of continence (Lovibond, 1963b).

Does the conditioning treatment of enuresis produce substitute symptoms or unfavourable emotional changes in the child? This notion appears to be unsupported by the evidence (Jones, 1960a). The only change noted by Lovibond (1963a), for example, was that his enuretic group displayed improved self-evaluation after successful treatment.[1] In a recent large-scale study reported by Young (1963), no symptom substitutions were observed after careful attention had been paid to this possibility (see also Jones, 1960a; Yates, 1960a).

Young discussed the significance of dividing enuretics into primary[2] and secondary types and in so doing raised a problem

[1]Similar findings have been reported by Morgan and Witmer (1939), Mowrer and Mowrer (1938), Davidson and Douglass (1950), Geppert (1953), Behrle et al. (1956), Baller and Shalcock (1956), Gillison and Skinner (1958), Wickes (1958).

[2]Primary enuretics are children who fail to develop continence, and secondary enuretics are children who relapse after a period of adequate control.

of some importance to learning theorists. It is, of course, well-known that if an organism is subjected to stress, some of its acquired behaviour patterns may be disrupted or entirely suppressed (see Chapter 1). In the case of enuresis, however, we are not yet in a position to specify precisely what type of stress will produce a loss of continence in which children. On theoretical grounds, it is argued that relapses of various kinds will be more frequent in extraverted people (see Chapter 17), and also that they should acquire the habit of continence more slowly than introverts (delinquents, for example, have a higher incidence of enuresis). In regard to the type of stress which may provoke a relapse, Young found that the main causes of secondary enuresis were the birth of a sibling and/or a change of school. Eysenck's (1963c) prediction that relapses are more frequent in extraverts receives some support from Young's study, in which he found that children who obtained high extraversion scores on the Junior Maudsley Personality Inventory had a higher relapse rate than the low scorers. Another finding which is in accord with the postulated relationship between conditioning and personality (see Eysenck, 1963a) is the increased rate of conditioning (arrest of the enuresis) obtained with the aid of a stimulant drug.

The three outstanding problems remaining in this field are as follows: What types of stress produce secondary enuresis? How can the relapse rate (after conditioning treatment) be reduced? Can the conditioning treatment of enuresis be facilitated with the addition of stimulant drugs, and what effect will this have on the relapse rate? Although we now have some information which has a bearing on these problems, further careful research will be needed before the conditioning treatment of enuresis can be developed into the firm, precise technique which it should be. The aim of behaviour therapy should be to provide the means for the successful treatment of *all* enuretic children, excluding, of course, those children whose enuresis is physical in origin.

Chapter 14

CHILDREN'S DISORDERS—II

APART from enuresis, the only other disorder which has been subjected to systematic consideration is phobia. The theory of phobias, described in Chapter 5 above, is an expansion of earlier theories which were designed to account for children's phobias, and it can be applied with equal pertinence to the disorder in children. The essence of the theory is that stimuli which make an impact on the child when a fear reaction is evoked, acquire the ability to evoke fear on subsequent occasions. A phobia is a persistent, unadaptive and exaggerated fear reaction which is produced by conditioned stimuli.

Normal and abnormal fears

During infancy, children's fears develop in response to pain and to 'any intense, sudden, unexpected, or novel stimulus for which the organism appears to be unprepared' (Jersild, 1950). With increasing age, the child's range of fears widens. He can recall past events and anticipate future dangers; he can also respond to imaginative impulses and images, such as ghosts and bogymen. As the child graduates to more complex fears, however, he also learns to cope with the earlier sources of fear—he is less likely to fear sudden noises, for example.

Jersild and Holmes (1935a) described the fear responses of children at different ages. They demonstrated an overall change from *immediate, tangible* fears to *anticipatory, less tangible*[1]

[1]This difference in this source and nature of the stimulus has sometimes been used to discriminate between *fear* and *anxiety*. Fear is a response to a tangible source of danger; anxiety is a response to an intangible danger.

fears with increasing maturity. Most two-year-old children, for example, respond fearfully to loud noises and to events associated with noise (see Fig. 32). Only a minority of six-year-old children show this response. On the other hand, six-year-old children are inclined to fear imaginary situations or objects far more frequently than two-year-olds.

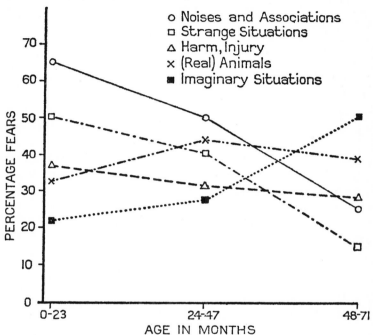

FIG. 32. The relative frequency of fear responses of children of different ages. (From Jersild and Holmes, *Children's Fears. Child Development Monograph*, 1935*a*).

Two important sources of fear which do not vary noticeably with age are: real animals and the possibility of harm or bodily injury. Both of these sources of stimulation are potentially painful, and children are likely to receive intermittent reminders of this fact. For this reason, they do not decrease during the early years. As the child's physical strength increases[1] and he gains experience, he should overcome the fear

[1]Macfarlane *et al.* (1954) report a correlation of 0·63 between fear and physical timidity in three-year-old boys.

of most animals. Most noises cease to elicit fear because of general adaptation, and the majority of fearful *associations* with noise disappear through a process of stimulus discrimination and extinction. The hissing of steam or the roar of a motorcycle receive reinforcement of a noxious kind and will retain the power to provoke fear. The proportional increase in fears concerning imaginary situations and objects can best be

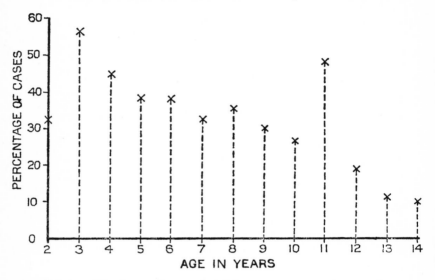

FIG. 33. The fears of normal children: percentage frequencies by age. (Adapted from MacFarlane *et al.*, *A Developmental Study of the Behaviour Problems of Normal Children*. University of California Press, 1954.)

accounted for by the fact that the conditions which eliminate fears are difficult to 'arrange' if the feared situation cannot be manipulated in ordinary circumstances. It is difficult to reduce a child's fear of a bogyman who is intangible and who cannot easily be recalled or re-created. The fear of *new situations* is gradually eroded by the very nature of the child's day-to-day experiences. Frequent exposures to a new situation will usually be followed by positive rewards or simply the absence of unpleasant stimulation. Consequently, the fear of new situations will tend to extinguish 'spontaneously'. It should be possible, by extending this type of analysis, to predict which sort of fear stimuli will persist and which ones will disappear spontaneously during the various periods of childhood.

Macfarlane *et al.* (1954), in their survey of some 200 normal children, found in fact that a second peak occurs at about eleven years of age (see Fig. 33). Their findings for the *younger* age groups are strikingly similar to those reported by Jersild and Holmes. In particular, they confirmed these observations: (i) the fears of young normal children are extensive; (ii) these fears undergo a steady natural decline; (iii) the quality of the fears changes from tangible to intangible with increasing age. Lapouse and Monk (1959) reported findings similar to (ii) and (iii) above, in slightly older groups.

The decline of fears with increasing age is demonstrated by the experimental findings of Holmes (1935). She exposed more than fifty children (ages two to six years) to numerous experimental situations of a provocative nature. The percentage of children in whom fear responses were elicited by the presence of a strange person decreased from 31 per cent in the two-year-old group to 22 per cent in the three-year-old group, 7 per cent in the four-year-old group, and 0 per cent the five-year-old group (see Table 6). Other examples include the fear of being placed in a dark room (declines from 47 per cent of two-year-olds to 0 per cent of five-year-olds), and the fear of being left alone (12 per cent of two-year-olds to 0 per cent of five-year-olds). As far as tangible fears are concerned, the most striking trend is the sharp decrease in the number of fearful children

TABLE 6

Percentage of children showing fear in experimental situations. (From Holmes, 1935, Child Development Monograph, No. 20.)

		Percentage showing fear		
		2-3 yrs.	3-4 yrs.	4-5 yrs.	5-6 yrs.
I	Being left alone	12	15	7	0
II	Falling boards	24	9	0	0
III	Dark room	46	51	35	0
IV	Strange person	31	22	7	0
V	High boards	35	35	7	0
VI	Loud sound	22	20	14	0
VII	Snake	34	55	43	30
VIII	Large dog	61	43	43	12
	Totals	32	30	18	5·2

found in the five-year-old group (and also the decrease in the number of fear-provoking situations). As we have seen, however, older children do acquire other, less tangible fears after they have overcome these more direct stimuli.

The development of fears is, of course, influenced by the child's history and the setting in which the noxious stimulation occurs. For example, children are less likely to develop fears when in the company of trusted, reassuring adults than when they are alone (Jones, 1925). Again, they are less likely to develop fears in the presence of unafraid children than in the presence of frightened children. The social facilitation or inhibition of fear was also noted by John (1941) in a study on the effects of air raids on children's behaviour. It was found that the fear (or lack of fear) displayed by the mother was an important determinant of the child's fears. It is well-known that there is 'a good deal of correspondence between frequency of fears of children of the same family'—the correlations between fears displays by siblings range from 0·65 to 0·74 (May, 1950). Similarly, Hagman (1932) found a correlation of 0·667 between the gross numbers of fears exhibited by children and their mothers. The probability of a child acquiring fears (by social learning) is directly influenced by the fears which he observes in his parents, siblings, and peers.

Prevention. An important demonstration of the extinction of fear responses in non-clinical circumstances was provided by Slater (1939). Forty children (aged 2-3 years) were observed during their first four weeks of attendance at nursery school. During the first week, the majority of children displayed signs of uneasiness and apprehension. By the end of the fourth week, all but three of the children had adapted to the new situation successfully (see Fig. 34). Apart from providing an instructive study of the process of spontaneous remission, Slater's results indicate the necessity for providing children with a gradual and gentle introduction to nursery school. Many nursery schools prevent the development of school phobias and related problems by careful planning of the child's early days. The Holmes experiment (1935) showed that at least 30 per cent of two-year-old children display fear in the presence of a strange person. Consequently, it is safer to introduce the child to the teacher and allow him to warm to this stranger in the presence

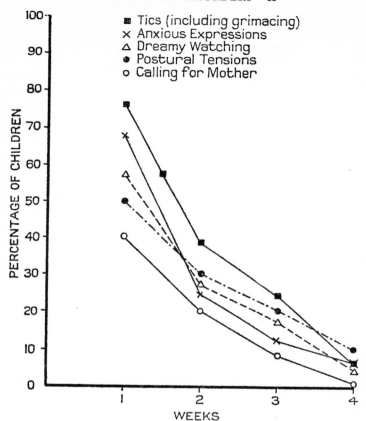

FIG. 34. The extinction of childrens' fear responses in nursery school. (Adapted from Slater, *Society Res. Child Develpm. Monograph*, 1939.)

of the mother or some other known and trusted person. Allowing the child to become acquainted with the new (school) *situation* in the presence of a trusted person is also advisable. For example, a headmistress of a London nursery school encourages the parents to bring the child on visits to the school even before he has reached the starting age. By this and other similar means, it has been possible virtually to eliminate school phobias in the infant and primary sections, and also to ensure a simpler and happier introduction to the long business of schooling. The first day of a new school year is no longer dreaded by the staff, and very few children now show signs of distress on this occasion (crying has all but disappeared, for example). In a different setting, the graded and gradual desensitization of a child's fears (or expected fears) is also practised with apparent success. The children's section of at least one London dental hospital uses this method, in an endeavour to prevent fear and avoidance reactions developing in a situation of objective discomfort and pain. No actual treatment is commenced on the child's first visit. If he is comfortable in the chair, a dental inspection is conducted and his teeth are charted. Depending on the child's reactions, treatment may begin on the second or even on the fifth visit. If he is anxious on the first visit, the full inspection is postponed until he is adequately desensitized.

The value of adequate preparation and careful handling in the prevention of fear and anxiety is also attested to by Prugh's (1953) study on the effects of hospitalization. Those children who were prepared for the experience and given fear-reducing care in hospital made better adjustments to the experience of hospitalization and showed less disturbances after returning home.

Treatment. The most common method used by parents in attempting to quell their children's fears is rational explanation (Jersild, 1950). This method is relatively useless unless supplementary means are used.[1] Jersild describes the effective methods of overcoming children's fears.

(i) Social imitation of adults and/or other children who display fearlessness in the noxious situation;
(ii) Reconditioning;
(iii) Acquiring experience and skill in handling the feared situation.

Social imitation has not received serious attention from therapists, despite the considerable experimental evidence which indicates the powerful effects of this process on children's behaviour. Most of the recent research on imitation has been directed at the problem of aggression. For example, Bandura and

[1] In a study by Hagman (1932), mothers reported that explanation *and* gradual exposure to the feared situation was the most effective combination.

Walters (1963), Bandura *et al.* (1963*a*, *b*) and Walters *et al.* (1962) have produced convincing evidence that vicarious participation in aggressive activity increases the child's aggressive behaviour. Bandura (1963) points out that the probable effect of providing a child with an aggressive model (or simply encouraging aggressive 'working out') will be to produce more aggressive behaviour. He calls into question the validity of psychotherapeutic theories which consider that the child is some sort of reservoir of aggression which needs occasional 'tapping'. Bandura argues that 'in contrast to this "drainage" view, social learning theory would predict that the provision of agressive models and the inadvertent positive reinforcement of aggression, which inevitably occurs during the encouragement of cathartic expressions, are exceedingly effective procedures for enhancing aggressive response tendencies.'

The therapeutic application of social imitation received passing mention in the early work of M. C. Jones (1925) and Jersild (1950). An experiment which highlights the potential value of social imitation was reported by Chittenden in 1942. He found that the aggressive behaviour displayed in frustrating situations could be reduced if the child was given constructive alternative ways of behaving. It is likely that therapeutic imitation will prove to be a valuable method of treating excessive fears, aggression, and other disturbances of childhood. It is worth remembering that imitation may in certain instances, provide a quicker way of approaching clinical problems. Bandura (1962) for example, points out that, in learning to drive a motor car, the method of imitation is far less tedious and time-consuming than the methods of operant conditioning. Any attempt to acquire this skill by conditioning each separate unit of motor control would indeed be exhausting and unrealistic. It is true that social imitation lends itself more readily to the learning of whole chunks of behaviour, but there is no intrinsic reason which prevents the conditioning of large segments of behaviour rather than the minute, specific actions. Ayllon's skilful conditioning of the behaviour of psychotic patients (see Chapter 12) provides adequate proof of the range of applicability of conditioning methods.

The last two methods, *reconditioning* and *acquiring experience*, can legitimately be subsumed under the label 'desensitization'. The power of these methods can be illustrated by two experiments (Holmes, 1935).

It was observed that fourteen out of twenty nursery school children were afraid to enter a dark room to retrieve a ball. The children were then exposed to the situation in gradually increasing doses. After a few practice sessions, thirteen of the initially frightened children went into the room without hesitation and recovered the ball. The second experiment concerned two children who were afraid of walking along an elevated plank. After a series of graded exercises had been successfully completed, they were able to walk the plank fearlessly.

The effectiveness of reconditioning was also demonstrated by Jones in 1924. She compared the effect of six different methods of overcoming the fears of a large group of children in temporary care. Only reconditioning and social imitation produced 'unqualified success'. The conclusions drawn from these experiments are supported by case history material, animal experiments (Wolpe, 1952; Kimble and Kendall, 1953), and controlled therapeutic experiments with adults.

The therapeutic experiments of Lazowik and Lang (1960) and of Lazarus (1961) both dealt with the effects of the desensitization technique. In both experiments, matched groups of adults with excessive fears were investigated. The results of these experiments indicated that the groups treated by desensitization improved significantly more than the control groups.

Various experimenters have attempted to treat experimentally-induced neuroses in animals. It has shown that improvements can be obtained with a selection of methods. The most systematic study of desensitization, however, was that conducted by Wolpe (1958), who obtained encouraging results. These experiments were in fact an important influence in the development of his methods of behaviour therapy.

Most of the case reports available to date which deal with the treatment of children's phobias involve the use of Wolpe's 'inhibitory therapy'. He defines the principle of reciprocal inhibition psychotherapy: 'If a response antagonistic to anxiety can be made to occur in the presence of anxiety-evoking stimuli so that it is accompanied by a complete or partial suppression of the anxiety responses, the bond between these stimuli and the anxiety responses will be weakened.'

The method may be illustrated by referring to some case reports which we summarize briefly here.

'A three-year-old boy, Peter, evinced fear of white rats, rabbits, fur, cotton wool, and other stimuli along this continuum.' He was treated by Jones (1924), using deconditioning methods. It was decided to work on the rabbit phobia, as this seemed to be a focus on Peter's fears. Peter was gradually introduced to contacts with a rabbit during his daily play period. He was placed in a play group with three fearless children and the rabbit was brought into the room for short periods each day. Peter's toleration of the rabbit was gradually improved. The progressive steps observed in the process included: "rabbit in cage 12 feet away tolerated . . . in case 4 feet away tolerated . . . close by in cage tolerated . . . free in room tolerated . . . eventually, fondling rabbit affectionately." Another measure employed by Jones involved the use of feeding responses. "Through the presence of the pleasant stimulus (food) whenever the rabbit was shown, the fear was eliminated gradually in favour of a positive response." '

Using these techniques, Jones overcame not only Peter's fear of rabbits but all the associated fears. The follow-up of this case showed no resurgence of the phobia. An analogous method was recently used by one of the present authors.

A nine-year-old boy (R.R.) was referred for treatment of a bee phobia. The phobia, which was intense and interfered with many of his activities (e.g. playing in the garden), had been present for three years. Although the boy could not remember ever having received a bee sting, he knew of several people who had been stung and/or displayed excessive fear of bees. After a full investigation had elucidated the nature of his fear, a hierarchy of anxiety-provoking situations was constructed. The techniques chosen for generating conditioned inhibition were social approval, encouragement, and feeding responses.

The desensitization began with exposure of small photographs of bees and then went through the following phases: large photographs, coloured photographs, dead bee in bottle at far end of room, dead bee in bottle brought gradually closer, dead bee out of bottle, dead bee on coat, gradually increasing manipulation of dead bee, introduction of several dead bees, playing imaginative games with dead bees. In addition to these desensitization sessions, the parents were encouraged to take R.R. on brief, controlled visits to a natural history museum. The boy made gradual and systematic progress and after eight sessions he and his mother both reported a considerable improvement. His mother stated that he was 'very much improved. He no longer has a physical reaction; he used to go white, sweaty, cold and trembling and his legs were like jelly. He can play alone in the garden quite comfortably.' A three-month follow-up showed no recurrence of the phobia.

The third case, reported by Lazarus (1960), deals with an eight-year-old boy who developed a fear of moving vehicles two years after having been involved in a motor accident. Initially the therapist rewarded the boy whenever he made a positive comment concerning vehicles, by giving him a piece of his favourite chocolate. By the third interview the boy was able to talk freely about all types of moving vehicles. Next, a series of 'accidents' with toy motor-cars was demonstrated. The boy, John, was given chocolate after each accident. Later John was seated in a stationary vehicle and slow progress (with chocolate feeding reinforcements used at each point) was made until John was able to enjoy motor travel without any anxiety.

In the same paper, Lazarus recounts the successful treatment of a case of separation anxiety and a case of dog phobia, and mentions fifteen other successfully treated cases. Additional case reports are provided by Landreth (1958), Bentler (1963), and by Lazarus and Abramovitz (1962).

Reciprocal inhibition. The success of reciprocal inhibition therapy depends on the appropriate choice and skilful manipulation of the inhibitory response. The inhibiting response which has been most commonly used in the treatment of adult phobics is relaxation. For obvious reasons, it is not possible to use relaxation with many children, especially very young ones.

The three inhibiting responses which seem to be the most promising alternatives are: affection, feeding, and social reassurance. Affection and comforting are among the methods frequently used by parents in assuaging their children's fears. Therapists can advise the parents in order to foster the effective application of affection as a direct inhibitor of anxiety. The treatment of an infant with a bath phobia, reported by Bentler (1963), is an illustration of this procedure. The effectiveness of social reassurance is demonstrated by the studies of Mary Cover

Jones (1924*a*, 1925) and, indirectly, by the work of Jersild (1950), Hagman (1932), and John (1941). A less obvious inhibitor of anxiety (and one which is rarely used by parents) is feeding.

Anxiety and feeding responses can be mutually inhibitory. Some of the evidence which supports this statement is presented by Metzner (1961), Wolpe (1958), Massermann (1943), Gantt (1944), Lichtenstein (1950), and Farber (1948). Massermann and Lichtenstein reported experiments in which animals were shocked while feeding. The effect of the shock was to inhibit feeding—often for long periods. In the case of the dog described by Lichtenstein, the feeding inhibition lasted for several months. Conversely, Gantt, Wolpe, and Farber were able to suppress anxiety and associated responses in their experimental animals by the careful introduction of food.

Clinically, feeding was one of the very first 'inhibitors' used by Jones (1924) in her treatment of Peter's rabbit phobia. More recently, Lazarus published an account of the successful treatment of a phobic child by means of feeding responses (see page 210 above). The use of feeding responses has, of course, to be carefully controlled. If the process of desensitizing is accelerated unduly, there is a danger that the anxiety evoked may inhibit the child's eating.

Conclusions

Mention has been made of Mary Cover Jones' (1924*a*, 1925) classic studies, in which she described her attempt to develop techniques for eliminating children's fears. The significance of this early work is only now becoming recognized. She gave an account of several methods of treatment, five of which appear to be promising, practical, and in accord with present-day learning theory. They are the methods of:

1. Direct conditioning;
2. Social imitation (see Bandura and Walters, 1963);
3. Systematic distraction;
4. Feeding responses;
5. Affectional responses.

The fruitfulness of the behaviour theory approach to phobias is well demonstrated if we add to Jones' list the new methods which have been, or could be used in overcoming children's phobias.[1]

6. Systematic desensitization (Wolpe);
7. Assertive responses (Wolpe);
8. Relaxation responses (Wolpe);
9. 'Pleasant' responses in the life situation—with drug enhancement (Wolpe).

In a suggestive article by Jersild and Holmes (1935), further possible methods for treatment of children's fears are discussed. From their survey of parents' experiences in dealing with children's fears, Jersild and Holmes suggest these techniques (among others): prompting the child to acquire skills which will enable him to cope with the feared situation; progressive contact with and participation in, the feared situation; verbal explanation and reassurance; practical demonstration of fearlessness.

Some of these techniques are already employed by prevailing therapies without receiving explicit acknowledgement. All these methods certainly provide therapists with a formidable range to begin with. What is now required is careful, thorough investigation of these methods and, above all, a major project to establish the degree and permanence of improvements which may be obtained by these techniques.

In the meantime, active therapists may consider conducting their own investigations of these methods when faced with children suffering from phobic conditions. Obviously, the choice of the method will depend to a considerable extent on the nature of the phobia. It is worth remembering also that these methods are not mutually exclusive and it is probable that in many cases a combination of these techniques may offer the most promising approach.

School phobia

A fairly common childhood phobia is school phobia. For this reason, and also because a good deal has been written on the subject, we have chosen to re-examine school phobia in learning theory terms.

The first point to emerge from an examination of the

---

[1] Naturally, many of these methods are equally applicable in the treatment of adults' phobias.

literature on this subject is that most writers regard the term 'school phobia' as a misnomer. It is argued that the child does not really fear the *school* but that his persistent refusal to attend is a manifestation of some other, deeper disturbance. Eisenberg (1958) described twenty-six cases of school refusal, and concluded that 'Systematic study of these children reveals that almost without exception, the basic fear is not of attending school but of leaving mother or, less commonly, father.' No details of the study beyond the clinical descriptions are provided, and this precludes an independent, external assessment of Eisenberg's rating system. Similarly, Waldfogel *et al.* (1957) insist that school phobia 'is invariably found to originate in the child's fear of being separated from his mother.' The clinical impressions of Klein (1945), however, led him to affirm the essentially sexual nature of the complaint. He offered a psycho-analytic view, which suffers from the weakness of Freud's original proposals (Wolpe and Rachman, 1959) and there is no serious evidence for the view that in school phobias 'an increase in sexual longing reactivates the oedipal or pre-oedipal fear of sexual injury of the mother' (Klein, 1945). Like Eisenberg, Waldfogel *et al.* and Kanner (1960), Klein supports the position that the school phobic-child is not basically frightened of school.

None of the major proponents of this view give adequate details for supporting their clinical impressions on this matter. It seems unlikely that a systematic examination of the child's school adjustment was conducted for, as we will indicate below, there are more than a dozen possible sources of school phobia in the school itself. Unless all these possibilities are firmly excluded in each case, a diagnosis of separation anxiety seems justified only on (dubious) theoretical grounds—that is, Jimmy Brown cannot be school-phobic because there is no such disorder. In one of the few studies to provide at least some basis for an *external* judgment, Hersov (1960*a, b*) was able to detect separation anxiety in only 36 per cent of his cases of school refusal. Twenty-two per cent of his cases were confirmed as *school* phobias. Even more convincing evidence of the role of the school situation, in the development of school phobias, is provided by Chazan's recent study (1962).

It was found, for example, that many of the children with this condition were experiencing severe educational difficulties.

The scholastic progress of twenty-four school-phobic children was assessed by several attainment tests and a school report. Four children were shown to be slightly backward, and another thirteen (mean I.Q. 98·7) were 'very backward, i.e. they were experiencing great difficulty with their work, and were in need of special educational treatment.'

It cannot be concluded from the evidence and arguments presented that school phobias, in their original and precise sense, do not occur. In fact, it is probably more reasonable and safer to begin one's enquiry with the belief that children who refuse to commence attending school, or who refuse to continue such an attendance, are displaying an avoidance reaction to a noxious or potentially noxious school situation. In other words, one should begin by regarding a school refusal at its face value—the child is attempting to avoid attendance at *school*. Secondly, the presence or absence of anxiety concerning school should be assessed; this assessment should include a full analysis of all aspects of the child's experience of school. Some possible sources of anxiety at school are the child's relations with his teachers and schoolmates; his intellectual ability and educational attainments; parental pressures and ambitions; examination stresses; specific learning disabilities; the size and routine of a new school; loss of close friends; experience(s) of educational failure; specific experience(s) of a disturbing nature (see Table 7).

Lapouse and Monk (1959) found that 38 per cent of 482 normal children experienced worry and fear about their school marks, and 20 per cent experienced fears about school examinations. Fears about examinations were more common in the older children.

If the clinical investigations (including a school visit) fail to reveal possible sources of anxiety at school, then one must avoid using the term 'school phobia'. An alternative possibility is that the child is suffering from separation phobia or, as it is more commonly known, separation anxiety. Some obvious tests can be applied in these cases: will the child attend school if he is accompanied by his mother/father? Is the child unable to go on excursions without his mother/father? Does the child get disturbed if left alone at home? If these behaviour patterns are present in a child who refuses to attend school, then it is preferable to call this condition *separation anxiety in a school situation.* It is necessary to specify the 'school situation' in this description if the refusal to attend school is the reason for referral and is in fact a prominent feature of the child's disorder.

As we have noted, some writers avoid using the term 'school phobia' because their theoretical orientation demands that the manifest phobic object is merely a symbol of some other, more important, fear. Even if one accepts the questionable view that

TABLE 7

School worries of sixth-grade children. (Adapted from Jersild *et al.*, *Journal of Experimental Education,* 1941.)

	% (often or sometimes)
Failing a test	90
Being late for school	66
Scolded by teacher	68
Left back in school	56
Poor in spelling	55
Asked to answer questions	50
Poor in reading	44
Poor report card	76
Reprimanded by pupils	46
No doing as well as other pupils	67
Giving report in class	44
Poor in arithmetic	67
Poor at drawing	45

the manifest phobic object is merely symbolic, this is insufficient reason for displaying such a fastidious attitude to the term 'school phobia'. On similar grounds, objections could be made to the use of terms like agoraphobia, claustrophobia, and so on. It is suggested, therefore, that the term 'school phobia' be retained and employed to describe a persistent refusal to attend school which can be attributed primarily to anxiety regarding some aspect(s) of the school situation. In those cases where school refusal is based upon, or closely related to, a fear of separation, the description 'separation anxiety in a school situation' should be used in preference. A distinction of this type is important because of its implications for therapy. Separation anxiety and school phobias require different treatment plans.

Personality factors. A great deal has been written about the personality of school-phobic children (and their mothers).

Regrettably, most of the literature consists of generalizations which are seldom supported by adequate evidence. For example, very few of these generalizations are drawn from investigations with control groups of similar children who are not school-phobic. Even the inclusion of a satisfactory control group does not, unfortunately, prevent over-generalized conclusions. Hersov (1960), for example, states that children who refuse to attend school 'are passive, dependent and over-protected, but exhibit a high standard of work and behaviour at school.' In fact, only 52 per cent of his group of school phobics were rated as being passive and dependent. Moreover, 28 per cent of his group of truants and 28 per cent of his control subjects were similarly rated. The statement that all school phobics exhibit a high standard of work at school has been corrected by Chazan (1962).

Studies (such as Hersov's) which attempt to tease out the personality differences between traunters and school phobics are likely to prove fruitful. Levitt (1963) has suggested that children's disorders which have elements of anti-social or asocial conduct may be more resistant to therapeutic changes than disorders with 'identifiable behaviour symptoms' (e.g. enuresis, phobias). Truancy and school phobias present a potentially valuable testing ground because they are both concerned with the child's reactions to school—truancy is an 'extravert reaction' and school phobia an 'introvert reaction' (see page 22 above).

Treatment. Lippman (1957) asserts that 'treatment of this condition has not been very satisfactory except when the child has been analysed.'

In one of the most successful series of cases (Talbot, 1957), the treatment was carried out primarily by social case-workers. Of the twenty-four children treated for this condition, twenty showed marked improvements. Most of these children were treated by social case-workers, and in spite of their dynamic orientation, they used a behaviour therapy type of treatment programme. After interviews with the child, the parents, and the school personnel had prepared the way, the child was gradually re-integrated into the school. Talbot's 'temporary plans' are reminiscent of the familiar anxiety-hierarchy used in behaviour therapy. When the child was ready, the following 'temporary plans' were worked through: 'Mother sits in the classroom, father remains in the car; child helps in the school office; child sits near a friend; child remains in school a brief period each day, gradually increasing the time' (Talbot, 1957). This outline programme seems more suitable for the treatment of cases of separation anxiety in a school situation, but could, with some modifications, be employed in the management of sheer school phobias.

Chazan (1962) also reports success in excess of 80 per cent. Twenty-nine out of thirty-three school phobia cases were successfully treated within five months. Five major measures were used (often in combination). Unfortunately, Chazan does not include an analysis of the relation between the type of treatment provided and the outcome of the case. Sixteen of the thirty-three cases received individual psychotherapy (details not provided), nineteen cases were moved to another school, nine cases received remedial education, nine received group therapy, and five were given sedatives. When a change of school was carried out, the child was generally placed in a smaller, more protected, special school. Two of the children recovered spontaneously. In Waldfogel's report (1959), the spontaneous remission rate was more marked. Seven out of sixteen cases received no treatment but showed improvement (i.e. 42 per cent). The recovery rate in this report was extremely good—eighteen out of twenty cases were successfully treated (90 per cent). Eisenberg (1958) similarly reports a high recovery rate of 80 per cent in a group of twenty-six cases. Hersov (1960a, b) reported 58 per cent successes in fifty cases.

Is it possible that there is a large spontaneous remission effect here? In other words, do these children recover irrespective of the treatment applied? The answer to this remarkable possibility must await a properly controlled investigation, which includes a group of school-phobic children who receive no treatment whatever during the specified period. One coincidence (?) is worth noting, *en passant*. According to Chazan, the peak age for the occurrence of school phobias is eleven. The peak age for general fears in older children (as shown by the Macfarlane survey—see Figure 33 above) is also eleven years of age. The Macfarlane data indicate, in addition, that there is a sharp decline in fears after eleven years of age.

Most writers agree, however divergent their theoretical positions or brand of psychotherapy, that a gradual re-introduction to the school situation is, at very least helpful. In Talbot's (1957) successful series of cases, the 'temporary plans' appear to have provided the basis for treatment. Waldfogel *et al.* (1957) also employed the method of gradual re-integration ('temporary compromises') as part of their treatment programme; even Lippmann (1957) was 'impressed by these devices used to lessen the child's anxiety.' Eisenberg (1958) recommends that 'if necessary, he may be permitted to begin by spending his day in the principal's or counsellor's office or by having his mother with him, but he must at any event be in the school building.' Chazan (1962) also reports the use of this method in some cases.

The most useful outline plan for treating school phobias would appear to be that proposed by Chazan. Depending on the information revealed by a thorough psychological and psychometric investigation, various procedures can be followed. Remedial education can be provided when necessary, a change of class or school can be arranged, and individual therapy can be applied. The co-operation of the parents and the school is, of course, of great importance. The type of individual therapy programme to be instituted will naturally be determined by the exact nature of the disturbance. In most cases, it is to be expected that some form of graduated desensitization programme will be called for.

The learning theory analysis of school phobias and the recommendations for treatment which flow from such an analysis are well illustrated in the case of Leslie, a thirteen-year-old boy. This patient had been unable to attend school for an entire school year and his condition had deteriorated to the point where he was unable to venture very far from his residence without experiencing some anxiety. He strongly resisted attempts to bring him to the outpatient department of the hospital, and after a domiciliary visit had been paid, it was decided that he required in-patient care. Because of his resistance to leaving home, even his transfer to hospital had to be carefully planned. His mother and grandparents hid all the door-keys a few hours before the ambulance arrived to convey the boy to the hospital. The patient's father had left the home when Leslie was still quite young, and the maternal grandparents had taken over a great deal of the care and management of the patient and his younger brother. The grandparents, particularly the grand-mother, were over-solicitous and tended to protect and restrict both children. During his primary school career, Leslie had been reasonably successful at his studies and was popular with his schoolmates. When he was transferred to secondary school, a fairly serious tooth infection prevented him from attending the new school on the first day of term. When he went to school on the first occasion, on the fifth day of the new term, he was enthusiastic about attending. During the morning of his first day at the new school he sustained an injury to the mouth while playing rugby and lost two front teeth. This accident caused him a considerable amount of pain which lasted throughout the luncheon period but disappeared by two o'clock in the afternoon. He stated, in retrospect, that even though the pain had diminished by the time he had gone to the canteen for lunch, he had nevertheless felt rather uncomfortable during the meal. In the classes which followed the lunch period, he felt increasingly uncomfortable, but nevertheless remained at school. The next school day was a Monday and Leslie pre-pared himself for school but then started feeling anxious and lied to his mother that he had a stomach ache. In this way he avoided going to school on that particular day, and on the three succeeding days. By this time, his mother and grand-parents were beginning to suspect that he was not really suffering from any stomach ailment but that he was avoiding school for other reasons. Several attempts, of varying degrees of determination, were then made to get Leslie to return to school, but none of them was successful. After the passage of several months, he was eventually referred to the hospital for psychiatric evaluation and assistance.

Soon after his admission to the hospital, it was decided to attempt to re-train Leslie to go to his own school from the hospital premises. For two weeks, a graded re-entry into the actual school situation was carried out by Dr. P. Graham. A small measure of progress was achieved during these two weeks, but with Dr. Graham's departure from the hospital, Leslie's treatment was suspended for two weeks. A more concerted form of behaviour therapy was then undertaken by one of the present authors in conjunction with J. Humphery.

After considering the history of the complaint, it was decided to combine desensitization treatment with a programme of graded re-entry into the actual school situation. Leslie was given instruction in progressive relaxation and also taught how to obtain vivid images of the anxiety-provoking situation. An anxiety hierarchy was constructed, which ranged from playing in the school grounds (least disturbing item) to being struck by a master in the classroom (most disturbing item). The patient's mother and grandparents were seen and advised by the therapists and by a psychiatric social worker.

When treatment was resumed Leslie toured the school with the therapist and the headmaster for an hour in the morning. Leslie reported his anxiety level as being in the range of 60 per cent. On the second day Leslie was again accompanied to school by the therapist, who conducted the patient around the school grounds and then left him in the school grounds on his own for a half an hour. The patient's anxiety level was 70 per cent on this occasion. In the afternoon, the boy was given his first session in relaxation. On the third day Leslie was again accompanied to the school, where he remained for nearly two hours, speaking to his friends and watching his class from outside the school building. On this occasion, his anxiety level rose to 85 per cent. In the afternoon he was given one hour's training in progressive relaxation and a desensitization hierarchy was completed. On the fourth day, Leslie was accompanied to the school, where he spoke to one of his favourite teachers and to some of his friends while standing in the corridor outside his actual classroom. He was allowed to remain in the corridor by himself for twenty minutes. He later returned to the hospital unaccompanied. His anxiety level on this day was 60 per cent. In the afternoon he received a further session of relaxation and desensitization. On the fifth day, Leslie was again accompanied to the school, where he sat in a classroom with the therapist and two friends during the recess. Later on, he sat outside a classroom, reading a textbook, for a further hour, and then returned to the hospital on his own. In the afternoon, he was given another session of relaxation and desensitization.

On the sixth day of treatment, Leslie was again accompanied to school, and this time he was left in a classroom with one friend. When the first lesson began, he remained in a corner of the room, standing up and following the lesson in his textbook. He then went to the gymnasium for games, but while he was putting on his games clothes, he experienced some anxiety and returned to the hospital in mid-morning. He was given two desensitization sessions on this day, and a fair degree of progress was noted by this stage in the desensitization programme. On the seventh day, Leslie was taken to school and left in the corridor outside the science laboratory. He remained at the doorway of the classroom for two periods, went for a walk around the block, returned to stand outside the classroom for a further five minutes, and then returned to the hospital on his own. As usual, he was given desensitization treatment in the afternoon. On the following day, Leslie went to school on his own, succeeded in getting changed in the gymnasium, and joined in the games with the other children. He then sat in the classroom during a music lesson and met the therapist at the school at mid-morning. The customary desensitization treatment was carried out during the afternoon. By this time, the anxiety levels which Leslie reported during the desensitization sessions had all fallen from the upper sixties to between 20 and 30 per cent. On the next day, Leslie attended school on his own in the morning and stayed for all but the last period of the morning. He returned to the hospital for lunch and then went back to school for the remaining periods of that afternoon. The next day, Leslie attended three of the four morning periods, returned to the hospital for lunch, and went back to school for three more periods in the afternoon

This therapeutic regime, which combined desensitization under relaxation with a gradual and supported re-entry into the actual school situation, was continued for a further two weeks, with Leslie making smooth and rapid progress on each day.

On the fourteenth day of this treatment, Leslie succeeded in attending all the periods for that entire day, only returning to the hospital for his lunch. On the fifteenth day, he attended all the school periods and also managed to eat lunch at school. He continued to attend school successfully from the hospital for the next ten days, until the school closed for the summer holidays. The desensitization treatment was continued at the hospital for a further week, and a full re-assessment of Leslie's condition was undertaken. It was agreed by all the people who examined him and the hospital ward staff that he had made a striking improvement. This change was confirmed by Leslie himself, who expressed considerable confidence and optimism about his recovery, as did his mother and grandparents. They expressed amazement and considerable satisfaction at Leslie's rapid progress. The boy was then discharged, and arrangements were made for him to be re-admitted to the hospital for booster treatment, one week before school re-opened. During this period he was given booster treatments of desensitization under relaxation. When school re-opened he faltered on the second day and returned to the hospital before lunch-time. He was accompanied to school on the next two days of the new term and his return to school has proceeded uneventfully. At the time of his discharge, one week after starting school again, he was undoubtedly very much improved and enjoying school. Two months later he was still well.[1]

We may summarize the development and treatment of this patient's school phobia as follows. The school phobia arose as a result of a painful experience which occurred during the potentially stressful transition from the primary school to a large secondary school. The anxiety which his unpleasant accident aroused, led the patient to indulge in avoidance behaviour which was successful in keeping him away from the anxiety-provoking situation. The habit of not attending school was reinforced by the solicitude of his mother and grandparents, until it had become extremely difficult for the child to return to school without professional assistance. The method of treatment, which was based on this analysis of the boy's disorder, was aimed at eliminating his neurotic behaviour by deliberately conditioning an inhibition of the anxiety which had become attached to the school situation.

---

[1]This patient experienced another relapse and after considerable additional treatment was able to return to school. He has now been attending satisfactorily for three months.

Chapter 15

CHILDREN'S DISORDERS—III

Operant conditioning

'OPERANT behaviour usually affects the environment and generates stimuli which "feed back" to the organism. Some feedback may have the effects identified by the layman as reward and punishment. Any consequence of behaviour which is rewarding or, more technically, *reinforcing*, increases the probability of further responding' (Skinner, 1959). After nearly three decades of persistent laboratory investigations (mostly with animals), Skinner and his colleagues are now exploring the application of operant conditioning in diverse areas of human behaviour. The topics which they have probed include the effects of drugs (Dews, 1956), attention (Holland, 1957), learning (Spiker, 1960), psychotic behaviour (Lindsley, 1956), motor behaviour (Verplank, 1956), verbal behaviour (Skinner, 1957; Krasner, 1958; Salzinger, 1959), therapy and the effects of therapy (Lindsley, 1961; King, *et al.* 1960), psychological functioning in retarded children (Orlando and Bijou, 1961; Spradlin, 1961; Ellis, 1962), personality (Staats *et al.*, 1962; Brady *et al.*, 1962), co-operative behaviour (Azrin and Lindsley, 1956).

As an introduction to the research on clinical problems in child psychology, it is necessary to mention again the work of Lindsley, King and Brady on adult psychopathology. Lindsley's (1956, 1960, 1961*a*, *b*, 1962*a*, *b*, 1963) observations of the operant behaviour of chronic schizophrenic patients (see Chapter 12 above) have already yielded important findings and have prepared the path for detailed functional analyses of schizophrenic behaviour. Lindsley's method can be used as a sensitive evaluative device and can also elucidate the characteristics of psychotic and neurotic behaviour. Further advantages which this method offers to the experimentally-minded clinician include the possibility of tight control of experimental variables, freedom from verbal instructions, exclusion of variables associated with the clinician himself, the possibility of controlled investigations of a single case, the possibility of therapeutic control. An 'unseen' advantage is provided, of course, by the substantial body of evidence concerning learning in human beings and operant conditioning in particular (for example, the effects of intermittent reinforcement). Each of the advantages listed here is of direct interest to child psychologists—evaluative procedures, analysis of disturbed behaviour, non-verbal instructions, control of variables, exclusion of 'clinician variables', therapeutic control, single-case studies. This technique also provides the child psychologist with a suitable environment for response-building in cases of behavioural deficit, such as mutism and anorexia, for example.

The possibilities of response-building are illustrated by the study of King et al. (1960), who shaped the behaviour of adult schizophrenics (of extreme pathology) in a Lindsley-type situation. They were able to develop the patients' initial lever-pulling response into relatively complex problem-solving and social behaviour. In this and other studies (King, 1956; King et al., 1957), attempts were made to relate operant behaviour to clinical status.

While there have been few reports of behaviour disorders in children treated by operant methods, the fine case-study described by Brady and Lind (1961) is worth noting. They cured an adult suffering from hysterical blindness by means of operant conditioning (see page 97 above). An interesting combination of reward and punishment was employed by Barrett (1962) in her treatment of an adult patient suffering from a multiple tic. As mentioned earlier, there are few reports of children being treated by operant methods for specific clinical problems (Wolf et al. 1964; Davison, 1964). The work of Flanagan et al. (1958), Baer (1963), Spradlin (1962), Salzinger et al. (1962b), and Ferster and de Meyer (1961), however, has a direct bearing on such problems.

Flanagan et al. (1958) attempted to bring the stuttering of three patients under operant control. Their preliminary analysis is encouraging as they were able to produce total suppression of the stutter in one patient and partial suppression in the other two patients. The suppression of the stutter, which was achieved by aversive control, lasted slightly longer than the period of aversive stimulation. This stimulation was similar to that used by Barrett (1962) in her study of a patient with multiple tics, and consisted of a loud, one-second blast of noise which was triggered off by the occurrence of a stutter. Spradlin (1961) conducted a pilot study to explore the possibility of modifying the behaviour of severely retarded children by operant conditioning techniques. Spradlin was able to train three children in such difficult tasks as detour, verbal and alternation behaviour. Spradlin's study also provides valuable information about procedures for adapting the children to the experimental room and the role of different types of reinforcers. Salzinger et al. (1962b) applied conditioning methods 'to the vocalizations of a four-year-old boy who had never learned to say any words at all and who had initially been hospitalized for autism'. In daily sessions over nine months, it was possible to increase his vocalizations and 'shape' at least a dozen words.

Ferster (1961) and Ferster and de Meyer (1961) have made a study of the performance of autistic children in an operant behaviour environment. Ferster and de Meyer conducted a prolonged investigation of the development of performance in two autistic children, age 8 and 9½ years, respectively. The experimental environment consisted of vending machines, a pin-ball machine, gramophone, kaleidoscope, and a trained pigeon. The experimenters were able to shape the behaviour of the children in relation to all these objects, and obtained information about the effectiveness of different training schedules and different reinforcers. 'Both subjects emitted more of the experimentally developed behaviour with continual exposure to the automatic equipment. Conversely, they spent less time in tantrums of inactivity while in the experimental room.' This finding recalls Lindsley's observations on adult psychotics, in which he noted an inverse relationship between operant performance and psychotic episodes.

This important study by Ferster and de Meyer shows that the behaviour of autistic children can be brought under experimental control. The next step is to develop situations and techniques of this type which can be used to induce *therapeutic* control[1] and, in a general sense, to find ways of developing the behavioural repertoire of children with deficit disorders. Salzinger, Spradlin, and Ferster and de Meyer have clearly demonstrated that such a programme is conceivable, even with the most severe cases. Ferster and de Meyer have also demonstrated that a range of reinforcers (candy, food, music) can be used effectively, that both fixed and variable schedules of reinforcement are effective, and that certain objects (e.g. coins) can generate a variety of other reinforcers in the manner of a generalized reinforcer. They are careful to point out, however, that their study was not designed for therapeutic purposes, and that it 'cannot be assumed that performances developed in the experimental room will have general effects elsewhere.' They suggest that social reinforcers may prove valuable in developing extra-experimental performance. These two topics, social reinforcement and the spread of experimental changes in behaviour, are likely to occupy the centre of the stage for some time, and are discussed below.

The application of operant methods to clinical problems has been explored in a limited manner at the Institute of Psychiatry, London. To date, attempts have been made to use operant methods in cases of reading disabilities, speech problems, encopresis, and in the analysis of the behaviour of a child suspected of experiencing auditory hallucinations. The remedial reading method was partly derived from the work of Staats and Staats (1962) on the teaching of reading to very young children. The procedure (Rachman, 1962) is, briefly, as follows. The child is rewarded for correctly-read words on a fixed ratio of 1 : 6.[2] The correct pronunciation of each word is signalled on a small panel consisting of six lights; when the sixth light is reached, a buzzer sounds and a sweet is automatically delivered. Words which are incorrectly pronounced are analysed phonically by the psychologist, who then demon-

---

[1]Wolf *et al.* (1964) recently reported considerable success in rehabilitating a severely disturbed autistic child of 3½ years of age. They succeeded in re-shaping his tantrums, feeding behaviour and speech. In a preliminary report, Baer *et al.* (1964) described several instances in which the disordered behaviour of normal children (e.g. excessive crying) was improved by these methods.

[2]This ratio is steadily increased, from about the third session, up to approximately 1 : 50. Later on, a variable ratio of reinforcements is substituted.

strates the correct pronunciation. The child is then required to say the word correctly. The wrongly pronounced words are placed on a subsidiary list for re-presentation at the end of the lesson. Naturally, the choice of reading material and rewards are tailored to the needs of the individual child. This remedial technique, like all operant methods, is extremely flexible. Provided that the requirements of the *learning process* are met, the particulars of the training technique can be freely manipulated.

One child, M.R., aged 9½ years, was unable to read more than half of the letters of the alphabet despite four years of ordinary schooling and several attempts at remedial coaching. He quickly warmed to the operant situation and in the first twenty sessions (each lasting twenty minutes) spread over five weeks, he learned 235 new words. The operant training was continued for another twenty-two sessions until his psychiatric discharge (he was initially referred for treatment of a general behaviour disorder). At the completion of training he had learned more then 500 new words and had read two elementary books. Another child, C.E., aged 9 years and 3 months, was unable to identify many of the letters of the alphabet when training commenced. After seven months of remedial teaching (for twenty minutes, twice a week) he was able to read books at an eight-year-old level. His Schonell GWRT scores increased from 0 to 24 (reading age, 7 years 5 months) during this period. Obviously it is not yet possible to assess the effectiveness of operant methods in remedial reading, speech training, and so on, but the preliminary results are not discouraging. Clinicians who are interested in the application of conditioning methods to problems of reading (and speech) are recommended to read the lucid analysis offered by Staats and Staats (1962b), and the experiments on the conditioning of continuous speech in young children (Salzinger et al., 1962).

Lindsley (1960) has described some attempts to evaluate the effects of therapy by means of operant procedures. The exploratory investigations carried out at the Institute of Psychiatry (Maudsley Hospital) were strongly influenced by Lindsley's work, and a few examples of these studies are given, in order to illustrate the general aim and procedures involved.

A five-year-old boy (S.M.) was admitted to the hospital because of his uncontrollable, aggressive, and hyperactive behaviour at home. According to Eysenck's theory (1957), there is a connection between extraverted behaviour and excessive cortical inhibition. In view of S.M.'s disturbed behaviour and the possibility of minimal brain damage, it was argued that his behaviour should deteriorate after excessive activity and improve after a rest period. In order to test this hypothesis, the boy was put on an operant training programme

FIG. 35. A simple operant conditioning situation for use with children.

and a baseline performance was established. The test situation was similar to Lindsley's operant lever-pulling situation in conception, but was less well constructed and controlled. The patient was trained to move a lever while in a relatively bare and isolated room (see Figs. 28 and 35). In the early stages he was rewarded (with sweets) on a small fixed ratio which was gradually expanded until he was responding regularly from day to day on a fixed ratio of 1 : 50. After more than two weeks of training, his response rate stabilized at between 100 and 150 responses per five-minute session. On the afternoon of 11th June, he was made to lie in his bed for one hour and was then tested. He showed a sharp increase in responsiveness (see

Fig. 36). On the 14th June, he was made to rest in the middle of the morning, after which he showed only a slight improvement in responsiveness. On the 17th June, he was rested for an hour in the afternoon and actually fell asleep. His test performance after sleeping showed a dramatic improvement of 500 responses (see Fig. 36). On the 18th June, S.M. was tested as soon as he awoke in the morning. His score at 7 a.m. was again

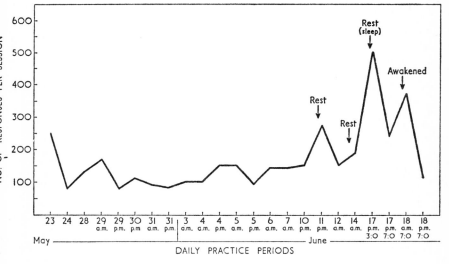

FIG. 36. The operant performances of a hyperactive child. Note the improved performances observed after rest periods, particularly sleep.

extremely high. When he was re-tested just before going to bed in the evening at 7 p.m., his response rate was low once more —110 responses.

Lindsley (1960) reported that the effects of dexedrine and of chlorpromazine on adult psychotic patients were generally found to be transient and slight. In the few children whom we have studied to date, similar results were obtained. The case of R.B., an eleven-year-old boy, illustrates the transient effects of amphetamine and of librium on his response rate. He was given amphetamine (5 mg., b.d.) from the 30th May until the 11th June and, as can be seen in Figure 37 below the, effects were short-lived. The administration of librium (5 mg., b.d.) was followed by increased responsiveness for four days only. Like Lindsley, we have found that some drugs (e.g. dexedrine) may increase the response rate of some patients and reduce that of others. It seems likely that these individual differences in reactivity are related to personality differences such as introversion-extraversion.

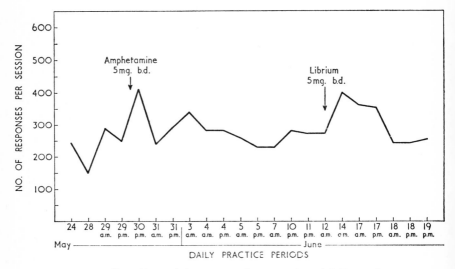

FIG. 37. The effect of drugs on a hyperactive child's performance in the operant conditioning situation. The effect of both drugs are transient.

Varying degrees of success have been obtained with operant methods in speech training (Salzinger, 1962; Robertson, 1958; Isaacs, Thomas and Goldiamond, 1960; Ferster and de Meyer, 1961). In the case of a five-year-old autistic child seen at the Maudsley Hospital, the attempt to condition speech responses was abandoned after a few sessions as it proved impossible to control the child's behaviour sufficiently to introduce the planned programme. A second case has met with a measure of success so far. This child suffered a fairly sudden deterioration at the age of twelve years and became virtually mute. The cause and nature of the illness is not clear, but an operant speech training programme was able to restore some communicative speech.

Operant training methods were successfully applied in the treatment of three out of four encopretic children (Neale, 1963). The general approach was to ignore all failures (soiling) and to give a prompt reward for successes (defaecation in the lavatory). The case of G.M. illustrates the method used.

This nine-year-old boy had been encopretic for nearly eighteen months. After six months of weekly out-patient treatment had failed to produce improvements, either in his encopresis or in his aggressive behaviour, G.M. was admitted to hospital. Six months after admission, his general behaviour was somewhat improved but the encopresis persisted.

Treatment was aimed at developing a normal pattern of defaecation in the lavatory and, at the same time, attempts were made to withdraw all rewards (e.g. attention) or punishments when the incorrect, soiling response occurred. The procedure was carefully explained to the child by a trusted nurse who ensured that G.M. did not regard the training as coercive or punitive. He was encouraged to go to the toilet at four specified times during the day and to report his successes. These were immediately rewarded by praise and a desired sweet, and also recorded in a special book in the boy's presence. If the boy failed to defaecate within five minutes of entering the lavatory, he was told not to persist. When soiling occurred he was given a clean pair of pants without comment.

As the training progressed, the four times daily routine was stopped and he was told to go to the lavatory whenever he felt the sensation of rectal fullness (which had returned by this stage). Successes in the lavatory continued to be rewarded. 'The response to treatment was rapid and complete in that he had become continent of faeces by day and night . . . the slow improvement in other aspects of his behaviour continued unchecked and he was discharged three months after completion of bowel training . . . after three months back in his own home there has been no relapse in bowel habits or in general behaviour' (Neale, 1963).

Descriptions of the successful conditioning treatment of two adult patients with eating difficulties have recently been brought to the attention of the present authors. Both of these patients were rewarded for appropriate eating behaviour and 'punished' by the withdrawal of rewards when they exhibited the disturbed eating pattern. The patient treated by Erwin

(1963) was suffering from longstanding anorexia, and Meyer's (1963) case complained of psychogenic vomiting.

In the substantial body of information on operant conditioning, there are four topics which seem to have particular relevance for clinicians dealing with children. These selected topics are social reinforcement, intermittent reinforcement, the generalization of responses, and the shaping process.

Social reinforcement

The important role of social reinforcement in child development is emphasized by some of the findings on operant conditioning. In this context, social reinforcement may be regarded as an event mediated by a person which has the effect of increasing the strength of the behaviour which immediately preceded it. By definition, then, most reinforcers would be social in nature. Ferster (1958) provides a detailed discussion of the nature and significance of social reinforcement in terms of operant conditioning, and Rheingold *et al.* (1959), and Weisberg (1963) have shown its effectiveness in altering the vocal behaviour of infants. The experimenters reinforced the babies' vocalizations by smiling and talking and these social rewards increased the infants' rate of vocalization.

The exploratory studies reported by Ayllon (1960) and Ayllon and Michael (1959) indicate some of the possible applications of social reinforcers in handling disturbed patients. Although their reports deal with adult psychiatric patients, some of their techniques have a direct bearing on the care and management of both normal and disturbed children. Ayllon (1960) describes, for example, how they were able to overcome an eating difficulty in a catatonic schizophrenic patient by operant training methods. The ward staff withheld attention when the patient displayed unadaptive eating behaviour (e.g. they ceased fetching her when she failed to walk to the dining-room), and reinforced satisfactory eating actions (e.g. placing candy on her tray when she served herself). These exploratory investigations are significant, because they demonstrate the possibility of transferring laboratory findings into the ward, the clinic, or the home. They also demonstrate that social reinforcers can be controlled and measured (albeit loosely so far) in extra-laboratory settings.

Experiments on the operation of social reinforcement in children have been reported by Gewirtz and Baer (1958a, b) and by Gewirtz, Baer and Roth (1958). They examined two variables affecting social reinforcement: brief social deprivation and the social availability of an adult. Their results showed that the 'frequency of attention-seeking responses was greater under Low Availability than under High Availability', and that the 'frequency of behaviours for approval was reliably increased by the Deprivation condition' (Gewirtz, Baer and Roth, 1958). The studies of imitative behaviour discussed by Bandura and Walters (1963) are closely related to these findings. For example, the transmission of social behaviour by imitation is facilitated by providing models of high prestige (Bandura, 1961). Individual differences in susceptibility to social influences have also received some attention. Dependent children are more easily influenced by social reinforcers than independent children (Jacubczak and Walters, 1959), and children with a history of failures are more likely to display social imitation and to respond to social reinforcement (Lesser and Abelson, 1959). Research along these avenues will eventually become incorporated in clinical work and child care. A promising start in this direction was recently reported by Baer, Harris and Wolf (1964).

Baer (1961a, b) and Ferster (1958) have in fact already started the process of integration. Baer (1961) emphasizes the 'reinforcement history' of the child, and indicates how the analysis of individual children may be used in designing techniques for promoting their development. He also outlines some methods which can be used to present social reinforcers In addition to the pointers derived from the research discussed above on imitation, prestige, deprivation, and availability, Baer describes some gadget-like aids. One of these 'gadgets' is a mechanized puppet which appeals to children, and which permits the experimenter to introduce and control simple and uniform social reinforcers. Lovaas (1961b) used the puppet to manipulate the eating habits of nursery school children and further investigations are being conducted.

The broad guide which emerges from the available evidence is that social reinforcers should be presented intermittently, and preferably by an adult of high prestige The use of social reinforcers in eliminating undesirable behaviour should follow a pattern of non-reinforcement rather than aversive conditioning. At the risk of over-simplifying, we may state it in this way: an undesirable response is more likely to be eliminated if it is met by no reaction at all than if it is met with a negative or punishing reaction.

Intermittent reinforcement

It has been found, in numerous experiments on animals and on humans, that intermittent (partial) reinforcement produces greater resistance to the extinction of the response than does continuous reinforcement (Jenkins and Stanley, 1950; Lewis, 1960; Fort, 1961). This effect may be illustrated by two recent examples from the literature. Spradlin (1962) investigated the effects of different reinforcement schedules on the operant behaviour of twenty severely retarded children. The children were divided into four equivalent groups and were trained on a Lindsley-type task, with candy acting as the reinforcer. As predicted, the group which received 100 per cent reinforcement (i.e. a reward for every correct response) showed faster extinction rates than the other groups of children who received intermittent rewards. Similarly, Lovibond (1961) found that the unsatisfactory relapse rate which occurs in the conditioning treatment of enuresis could be offset by the introduction of intermittent reinforcement. In other words, the high extinction rates (relapses) could be countered by altering the reinforcement schedule. In a different context, Salzinger et al. (1962) showed that it was possible to condition continuous speech in young children and that the stability and rate of such speech was enhanced by an intermittent reinforcement schedule.

Long et al. (1958) published extensive findings on the intermittent reinforcement of operant behaviour in over 200 children. Their monograph details the effects of various rewards and schedules of reinforcement on children's behaviour in a Lindsley-type operant environment, and provides a wealth of important details for child psychologists who propose to use this technique. For example, they show that small fixed-ratios rapidly produce satiation and cessation of response, while very large fixed-ratios make experimental control difficult to obtain. They suggest that an introductory session of small fixed-ratios should then proceed gradually to ratios of up to 1 : 100. Additional technical suggestions of this nature are provided in two further papers by Long (1959, 1962).

The theoretical value of intermittently reinforced operant behaviour derives from the fact that this type of reinforcement schedule generates stable and prolonged performance. Bijou (1961) argues persuasively that the experimental analysis of the behaviour of individual children is made feasible by this method, 'since a clear functional relationship has been shown between a stable baseline performance and the introduction of a special stimulus condition.' If this claim is borne out by research results, it will be of considerable value to clinical psychologists, who are constantly faced with the dilemma of group norms and individual patients (Meehl, 1954; Shapiro, 1961). Stable operant responding certainly lends itself to investigations designed to evaluate therapeutic (or drug) effects, or indeed any specific effect. However, there are circumstances in which an excessively stable response rate may mask drug effects; in such cases a fixed ratio schedule would be more appropriate.

Some practical recommendations which emerge from this literature (see Lovibond, 1963b) and from our own experiences with the clinical use of operant methods are as follows. Unless the purpose of the investigation is concerned with the effects of specific changes (e.g. drug effects), it is preferable to change the reward schedule from a small fixed ratio to an intermittent ratio at an early opportunity. Intermittent reinforcement schedules not only produce more stable responding but they also help to delay or avoid satiation effects. Satiation can occur fairly quickly in these operant situations, particularly when one is dealing with young children. For example, they soon tire of receiving sweets if these are given too frequently. The changes in reward schedules should be made gradually and cautiously, in order to avoid provoking emotional outbursts (see, for example, Ferster and de Meyer (1961) who describe the 'storms' which can be produced by rapid changes).

Generalization of responses

These experimental learning techniques would be of limited interest if the changes they produce failed to generalize or spread into the patient's ordinary life and behaviour. Changes produced by the reciprocal inhibition method do spread to the patient's out-of-clinic behaviour. This is well-documented, particularly in the treatment of adults (Wolpe, 1958; Eysenck, 1960a).

The clinical application of operant conditioning has not yet progressed to the point where one can reach a firm conclusion. Baer (1963), for example, was able to reduce thumb-sucking in three children during experimental sessions, but the habit promptly returned when the relevant condition were withdrawn. King et al. (1960), however, were able to record significant general improvements in a group of (adult) acute schizophrenics who were treated by operant methods. By comparison with three control groups, the operant-treated patients improved in the following areas: 'levels of verbalization, motivation to leave the ward, less resistance to therapy, more interest in occupational therapy, decreased enuresis, and transfer to better wards.' In an earlier study, King (1956) reported a 'positive relationship between rate of operant motor response in schizophrenic patients and another measure of manipulative responsiveness, i.e. energy displayed in regard to the various crafts of occupational therapy.'

A spread of experimentally-induced changes in behaviour was noted by Salzinger et al. (1962) in their study on the operant training of speech in young children. They found that 'the application of reinforcement to the response class of first person pronouns produced an increase not only in the specific class itself but also in general speech rate.' Brady and Lind (1961) obtained a dramatic change in an adult patient who had been suffering from hysterical blindness for more than two years, despite numerous earlier attempts at treatment. Their cleverly designed and simple (but highly effective) experimental procedure (see page 97 above) is a vivid example of the spread of effectiveness from the laboratory clinic to the 'outside world'.

The experimental work of Lovaas (1960, 1961a, b) promises to elucidate the relationship between the particular response which is being conditioned and the person's general behaviour. Lovaas has shown that operant conditioning of verbal behaviour can transfer to other behaviour, and hence influence eating habits (1961b), motor behaviour (1960), and aggressive behaviour (1961a). The trend of these results encourages the assumption that the effects of operant conditioning in the clinic will spread to the child's ordinary behaviour and environment.

Before leaving the topic of generalization of responses, it should be pointed out that there is also a technique which can be used in promoting the irradiation of newly-acquired responses. If the gap between the clinical and social environments is not surmounted spontaneously, the bridge of 'successive approximation' can be used. The patient can be taught intermediate responses which will enable him to cope with non-clinical situations. A theoretical account of this technique is provided in a paper by Skinner, Solomon and Lindsley (1954), and Ayllon (1960), Orlando and Bijou (1961), and Spradlin (1961) have all used it in the early stages of the conditioning process. Spradlin (1961), for example, used successive approximations in order to adapt his retarded patients to the experimental situation.

Shaping and successive approximation

The technique of shaping is best illustrated by examples from clinical experiments such as those of Spradlin (1961), Ayllon (1960, 1963), and Ferster and de Meyer (1961). In the initial stages of his study on the operant conditioning of severely retarded children, Spradlin found it necessary to train the children to use the experimental manipulanda. The first step in the shaping process was to teach the child to retrieve the rewards (candy) from the goal box. The psychologist first retrieved the candy for the child. After this demonstration, the psychologist withdrew from the situation and controlled the instruments remotely.

'Initially, the experimenter reinforced any approach to the goal box. Once the child was spending most of his time near the goal box, the experimenter withheld reinforcement until the child moved his hand towards the manipulandum. Soon the child would touch the knob. After the knob-touching response was firmly established, the experimenter withheld reinforcement until the child made a grasping motion toward the knob— this was then reinforced. Later, reinforcement was withheld until the child shook the knob of the manipulandum and still later until the child made an outward movement of the knob. Once this stage was reached, independent activation of the

Lindsley manipulandum followed readily' (Spradlin, 1961).

One of the present authors recently obtained a striking example of the effectiveness of a shaping procedure with an autistic boy, aged seven. This child was a severely disabled, non-verbal case of infantile autism who characteristically responded to environmental changes, or intrusive stimuli, with a sharp anxiety reaction. He was coaxed into the experimental room with great difficulty after several trials and frequent rewards along the way. The room contained a lever and a box consisting of ten lights, a buzzer, and a reward chute. The experimenter controlled the apparatus from a distant corner of the room. When the lights and buzzer were first sounded, the child hastily retreated to the wall opposite the manipulandum, where he stood whimpering and trembling. When he shifted his posture, a sweet was delivered through the chute and fell two feet in front of him. He quickly retrieved the sweet, returned to the wall, and then ate the sweet. The next two occasions on which he changed his posture were similarly rewarded. After that, we only rewarded postural changes which brought the boy a little closer to the manipulandum. Seven rewarded trials were needed to bring him up to the manipulandum. We then reinforced any hand movement in the direction of the lever. Within five trials he was handling the lever, and two further trials produced an appropriate lever-pulling response. The lever-pulling responses were reinforced on a 1 : 1 fixed ratio for five trials and then gradually extended to a 1 : 10 ratio. The buzzer and light stimuli were then introduced in a gradual manner, and the boy completed five minutes of regular, slow responding on the machine. The total time taken to shape the boy's behaviour in this session was twelve minutes (excluding the five minutes of operant responding proper). In subsequent training sessions he continued to respond slowly but correctly and rarely showed signs of anxiety.

The effectiveness of shaping procedures in ameliorating the condition of chronic (adult) psychotic patients is admirably demonstrated by the work of Ayllon (1960, 1963). One aspect of behaviour which he has shaped with considerable success in adult patients is feeding, and his reports suggest methods of dealing with similar difficulties as they occur in children. A striking success in the shaping of speech was reported in 1960 by Isaacs and Goldiamond (see Chapter 12).

The shaping process begins by utilizing responses which the subject is capable of making (e.g. an eye-movement in the case mentioned above). The learning is 'most easily established by starting with the reinforcement of responses that only generally resemble the one that you ultimately seek to establish, then gradually increasing the strictness of your definition of a correct response, i.e. the one that will be reinforced' (Lawson, 1960). The same procedure is used in training the organism to discriminate between stimuli. 'Ultimately only a very precise response is being reinforced, and only when it occurs in the presence of a very specific stimulus pattern' (Lawson, 1960). The shaping of increasingly accurate responses is neatly illustrated in an experiment by Sidman (1956). He trained rats to make a lever press every twenty seconds, by withholding the reward if the animals responded before the twenty-second time-period had elapsed (see Fig. 38 below).

In clinical work, it seems advisable to carry out the shaping procedures in comparatively realistic settings. Ayllon's remarkable successes in modifying the behaviour of psychotic patients were obtained within a realistic social milieu, and it is probable that Ferster and de Meyer would have had greater success in 'treating' their patients outside the experimental chamber—although they disclaimed any therapeutic intentions. Despite the loosening of experimental controls which occurs when the patient is being conditioned in a social environment, Ayllon has demonstrated very clearly that even in a psychotic ward it is possible to control and quantify the relevant variables.

Conclusions

Advances in the application of learning theory to clinical problems in adults have not been accompanied by a similar rate of development in child psychology. A probable reason for this uneven progress lies in the fact that behaviour therapy is more obviously applicable to adult disorders. Behaviour therapy has so far provided more techniques for the elimination of unadaptive behaviour than for the development of desired behaviour. The disturbances of behaviour in childhood are more often of the deficit type. Consequently, it is likely that the methods of operant conditioning will increase the applications of behaviour therapy to the clinical problems of child psychology.

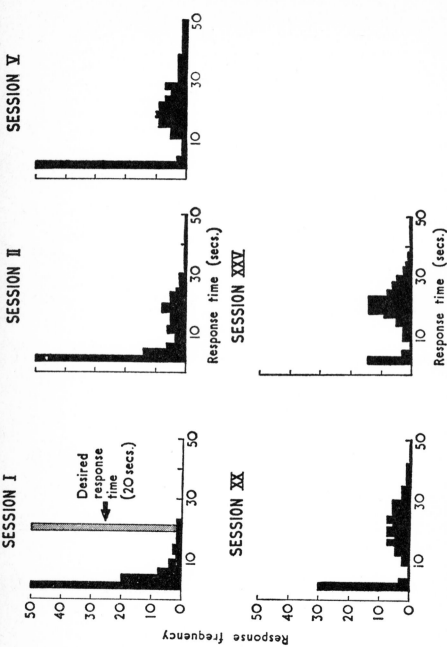

Fig. 38. In this experiment by Sidman (1956) the animal was trained to press a lever in order to obtain water. The animal was required to space his responses by 20 sec. intervals—the reward being delivered only if 20 seconds or more had elapsed since the preceding response. As the training progresses, the animal's behaviour becomes more accurate and efficient session

Operant conditioning methods can be used to generate and/or sustain stable behaviour patterns. The advantages of operant methods are that they permit, when required, (i) non-verbal operation; (ii) strict control of variables; (iii) quantification of operations; (iv) exclusion of 'clinician-variables', and (v) single-case studies. The disadvantages are both of a practical nature. Operant methods usually demand special equipment and experimental rooms, and can be time-consuming. These two factors are probably inversely related—better equipment provides for more automatic control and saves time. Information regarding equipment can be found in Spradlin (1962), Lindsley (1956), Razran (1961b), Ivanov-Smolensky (1927), Ferster and de Meyer (1961), Robinson and Robinson (1961), Simmons and Lipsitt (1961), Bijou and Baer (1960), Sidman (1962).

In regard to further research, the four selected topics discussed above (social reinforcement, intermittent reinforcement, shaping, generalization of responses) all require further investigation. What is needed above all, however, are clinical trials of operant methods. With very few exceptions, operant conditioning has not been used as a *clinical* procedure.

Both operant conditioning and the more familiar methods of behaviour therapy are likely to make a significant contribution to child psychology in the coming years.

Chapter 16

THE RESULTS OF BEHAVIOUR THERAPY

IN order to support their contention that their methods should be implemented on a widespread scale, behaviour therapists are, we feel, obliged to demonstrate at least one and preferably all of the following advantages over other methods of treatment. Does behaviour therapy produce a larger number of recoveries from neurotic illness? Does behaviour therapy produce quicker recoveries? Does behaviour therapy produce recoveries in more types of neurotic illness than other therapies? The number of people who have been treated by behaviour therapy is now in excess of one thousand. The number of cases reported in the literature is in the region of nine hundred.[1] The case history material and small-scale studies described in earlier chapters, while they are instructive and suggestive, do not and cannot permit a general appraisal of the effectiveness of behaviour therapy. This assessment must depend ultimately, on the results of properly controlled, prospective investigations of large samples of neurotic patients.

The present, interim evaluation of behaviour therapy is based on the published information available, and will no doubt be amended when the studies now in progress are completed. Of the ten large-scale reports available, seven consist of the results obtained by individual therapists in full-time practice and consequently no control groups were constructed. For the same reason, the follow-up information is, for the most

[1]This figure excludes enuretic and alcoholic patients. The results of conditioning treatment with these disorders are discussed separately in Chapters 11 and 13.

part, deficient or entirely absent. The remaining three reports provide comparisons between patients who received behaviour therapy and similar patients who were treated by other methods or not at all. The reports which included control groups are discussed separately below.

The first three series of results were all reported by Wolpe in 1952, and 1958. These results are conveniently summarized

TABLE 8

Results of reciprocal inhibition psychotherapy in 210 cases. (From Wolpe, *Psychotherapy by Reciprocal Inhibition*, Stanford University Press, 1958)

	No. of Cases	Apparently Cured	Much Improved	Slightly to Moderately Improved	Un-improved
1952 series	70	34	26	7	3
1954 series	52	20	30	1	1
Present series	88	28	50	7	3
Totals	210	82 (39.0%)	106 (50.5%)	15 (7.2%)	7 (3.3%)

in his book, *Psychotherapy By Reciprocal Inhibition* and we will deal with them as a single unit. This is possible because the type of patients and method of assessment used in all three series are the same. Wolpe reports the results obtained in the treatment of 210 neurotic patients. All of these patients had been diagnosed as suffering from some kind of neurotic disturbance and it was Wolpe's policy to accept every patient provided the diagnosis of neurosis had been confirmed. Psychotics and psychopaths were not accepted for treatment, so that the results reported are relevant to the treatment of neurotic disturbances only. Wolpe assessed the effectiveness of therapy in each case by reference to Knight's (1941) criteria. These criteria, proposed by a psychoanalyst, are as follows: symptomatic improvement, increased productiveness, improved adjustment and pleasure in sex, improved interpersonal relationships, and ability to deal with reasonable reality stresses. In addition, each patient was asked to fill out the Willoughby Neurotic Tendency Scale before and after treatment. This scale is a measure of general neuroticism, and the hypothesis was that these neurotic scores would decline with success of the treatment. Each patient was assessed in terms of

Knight's criteria and then classified according to the system proposed by Knight. The five descriptive categories are: (1) apparently cured; (2) much improved; (3) moderately improved;
(4) slightly improved, and (5) unimproved. The total number of
patients treated in all three series was 210 (see Table 8). Of these
210, approximately 90 per cent were apparently cured or much
improved after treatment. This figure is, of course, in excess of

TABLE 9

The duration of reciprocal inhibition therapy. (From J. Wolpe,
Psychotherapy by Reciprocal Inhibition, Stanford University Press, 1958.)

	Mean Therapeutic Time Span (Months)	Mean No. of Interviews	Median No. of Interviews
Apparently cured and much improved groups	10.8	43.6	22.0
Slightly to moderately improved and unimproved groups	10.2	51.0	40.5
Whole series	10.7	45.6	23.0

the figures reported by other types of therapy, and also in excess
of the hypothesized remission rate of 65-70 per cent. The median
number of interviews required to achieve improvements was 22
(mean= 43); the median number of interviews taken up by the
patients who improved only slightly or who failed to improve at
all was 40 interviews. The median number of interviews for the
whole series was 23 (see Table 9).

The Willoughby Neurotic Scores are of considerable interest
and show a significant decline with successful treatment. In
the apparently cured group, the mean neuroticism score
dropped from 45·2 to 12·2, and in the case of the much improved patients, the mean Willoughby score of 34·8 dropped
to 25·6 after successful treatment. Unfortunately, the demands
of private practice prevented Wolpe from carrying out
systematic follow-up investigations of all of these patients. He
was, however, able to trace forty-five apparently cured or much
improved patients, from two to seven years after the completion of treatment. Of these forty-five, only one had relapsed
to any significant extent after one year. It was impossible, in
this case, to obtain sufficient information to analyse the
possible causes of this relapse. A second inadequacy of Wolpe's

results is to be found in the absence of a control group. He attempted to make good this deficit by comparing his results with results obtained and reported from two psychoanalytic institutes. While this comparison indicates a clear superiority of the methods of behaviour therapy, a final decision will have to await a large-scale controlled study. It is worth mentioning, however, that the percentage improvement obtained at these other institutes varied between 38 per cent to 60 per cent apparently cured or much improved.

These series reported by Wolpe were the first systematic and protracted attempts to apply the principles of learning theory to the treatment of neurotic disturbances. As a pioneering work, they cannot be expected to provide a full answer to the problems of psychotherapy. Nevertheless, it would be unwise and ungenerous not to acknowledge the tremendous importance of this work. In addition to demonstrating the possibility of providing a new type of therapy based on sound psychological principles, Wolpe also succeeded in developing some very successful therapeutic techniques. He was able, in these studies, to prepare the ground for later work.

In 1963, Lazarus reported on the treatment of 408 patients. These neurotic patients were treated along the lines proposed by Wolpe, and were assessed in a manner like that used by Wolpe in his original series. Lazarus was able to obtain significant improvements in 321 patients: that is, 78 per cent. He then went on to do a detailed analysis of the results obtained with 126 patients who were suffering from what he describes as severe neuroses. Lazarus's purpose in carrying out this sub-analysis of his information was to enable him to evaluate the effectiveness of behaviour therapy in treating people who were suffering from 'widespread, diffuse and pervasive neurotic disorders.' He felt obliged to carry out this analysis because of the commonly-held belief that behaviour therapy is able to cope only with those neurotic conditions which are relatively simple and monosymptomatic. The overall results obtained in the treatment of these 126 severe cases was 62 per cent apparently cured or much improved. This figure, it will be noticed, is lower than that obtained by Wolpe in his total series, and also lower than that reported by Lazarus for the whole series of 408 patients. The suggestion arising from this analysis is that while behaviour therapy is probably effective in treating complex neurotic disorders, it may well turn out that it is *more* effective in treating simple monosymptomatic disorders. One point worthy of notice is that the average number of sessions required by Lazarus for treating his patients is probably significantly lower than that required by Wolpe; in the case of those patients who were completely or markedly improved, the average number of sessions required was only fifteen. The two differences which emerge most clearly are that Wolpe took a longer time to treat his patients and also obtained a higher recovery rate. It seems possible that Wolpe's higher recovery rate may be accounted for by the fact that he was more persistent and more painstaking in his treatment of severe cases. Wolpe reports having taken many more sessions for the treatment of difficult cases than he did in the treatment of relatively un-complicated cases. On the other hand. Lazarus reports no difference in the number of sessions required to treat severe and uncomplicated types of patients.

Lazarus obtained follow-up information on each of the 126 severely neurotic patients. Each patient was interviewed and in addition, at least one other relevant person was also seen at follow-up. The mean duration of follow-up was 2·15 years. Only one of the patients who had recovered or was markedly improved had relapsed in the interim. Special attention was paid to the possibility of symptom substitution in these patients, but Lazarus was able to uncover only the most tenuous sugges-tions that symptom substitution had occurred at all. This study confirms that a large number of patients suffering from severe and complex neuroses can benefit from behaviour therapy.

In another series reported by Lazarus, twenty-one children suffering from phobic conditions were all successfully treated. Unfortunately, no follow-up data were provided, so that it is difficult to assess the long-term value of these improve-ments.

In 1962, Hussain reported successful outcomes in 95 of the 105 neurotic patients he treated. Although Hussain describes his method as consisting of reciprocal inhibition and re-condition-ing, there is reason to doubt whether some of the methods actually employed can fairly be described by these terms. In particular, he appears to have used the hypnotic sessions more as a means of providing direct hypnotic suggestion, rather than as a vehicle for inducing relaxation and desensitization. Hussain does not give complete details about the composition of his group of patients, but he does point out that none of these patients had been specially selected and that the only patients who had been excluded from treatment were those who had been diagnosed as psychotic. The majority of his patients appear to have been suffering from anxiety states, although fifteen patients had hysterical disorders. The time taken to complete the treatment varied from between four to sixteen weeks. The extent of improvements were assessed in terms of Knight's criteria and, in some cases, the patient's relatives were also interviewed, to help in determining the degree of change. Hussain states that the follow-ups were carried out over periods ranging from six months to two years. He reported only one relapse in the improved group, and could find no evidence whatever of symptom substitution. Hussain does not provide sufficient information either about the patients treated or about the methods which he employed in therapy. The follow-up information is scanty and anecdotal in nature, and no control subjects were provided.

Burnett and Ryan (1963) treated 100 patients with a modified form of behaviour therapy. They describe their treatment in this way. 'Our treatment procedure in summary, is as follows: (a) education regarding the effects of emotion on the body (group psychotherapy); (b) illustration of simple conditioning, generalization, and desensitization (group psychotherapy); (c) motivation towards relaxation when in fear-provoking situations.' Of this original group, only twenty-five could be located for systematic follow-up study. Follow-ups, which lasted for one year, consisted of regular interviews with the patient and, on occasion, with relations. Improvements in the patients' condition were assessed after the manner of Wolpe, by using Knight's five criteria. Burnett and Ryan's results with these twenty-five patients are as follows. Fifteen patients were either cured or much improved. Eight patients were moderately improved, and two showed only slight improvement. Combining the apparently cured and the much improved patients, we have a recovery rate of 60 per cent. Apart from the absence of control data, there is another serious deficiency in Burnett and Ryan's study (although it should be pointed out that they are themselves aware of the deficiencies of the study). The 100 patients who received this modified form of behaviour therapy were themselves selected from a total patient intake of 550. The basis on which the selection was made is not given. This sample bias, coupled with the fact that only one in four of the treated group were ascertained at follow-up and indeed included in the analysis, makes it difficult to draw conclusions from their findings. Burnett and Ryan's study does, however, have two interesting features; the first is that they were dealing with a rurally isolated and educationally below average population. It was these demographic and educational factors which actually provoked them into attempting behaviour therapy methods at their clinic. They felt that the more conventional types of psychotherapy demanded a high degree of verbal intelligence which was frequently absent in their patients, and they were very much concerned with the possibility of finding an alternative type of treatment which does not make such intellectual demands on the neurotic patient. The second is that much of the treatment was carried out in groups. It is a pity, therefore, that the study is inadequate, as it might have provided some useful information about the possibilities of group behaviour therapy.[1] Burnett and Ryan's own assessment of behaviour therapy is as follows. 'We feel that the results have been consistently good on the type of patient attending this clinic and we postulate that his type of technique can be successfully used to treat a fairly large number of rural, unsophisticated patients who have limited formal education.'

The evidence afforded by these studies is suggestive but not conclusive. A definitive conclusion must await carefully controlled studies in which careful selection procedures, methods of assessment, follow-up studies, and control subjects are used. However, reports like Wolpe's contribute to the development of a scientifically-based psychotherapy in two ways. Firstly, they lead to the refinement of the techniques which may be used in treating neurotic patients; and secondly, they enable one to construct hypotheses on which to base further investigations. Two hypotheses which arise out of this information may be stated as follow. (1) Neurotic patients treated by means of psychotherapeutic procedures based on learning theory improve significantly more quickly than do patients treated by

[1]Some exploratory work on the use of group behaviour therapy with agoraphobics is at present being carried out at Bexley Hospital, Kent.

other types of therapy, or not treated by psychotherapy at all. (2) Behaviour therapy is able to achieve a higher recovery rate that other types of therapy, or no therapy at all.

Studies employing control groups

To date, three studies have been carried out into the effectiveness of behaviour therapy employing control groups. These studies were carried out by Lazovik and Lang (1960, 1963), by Lazarus (1963), and by Cooper (1963). Cooper's study, unfortunately, is of a retrospective nature and, as such, brings with it numerous serious problems. Cooper carried out a follow-up study of thirty patients who had received behaviour therapy at the Maudsley Hospital between 1954 and 1960. He attempted to construct a retrospective control group by matching them with another thirty patients who had been treated at approximately the same time. Cooper was able to extract only sixteen matched controls from the hospital records. The progress of these sixteen individually matched pairs of patients (ten phobias, four obsessionals, one stammerer, and one case of writer's cramp) was then estimated by two independent assessors. Retrospective assessments were made of their progress at the end of treatment, one month and one year after treatment. Cooper stated that, 'The only striking finding is at the end of treatment in the ten phobic patients, nine of whom showed improvement in the symptom treated, compared to only five of the control cases. A month and a year later, however, this difference had disappeared; so, if behaviour therapy is a worthwhile addition to other therapy in this type of patient, as seems likely, its effect is transient.' Cooper also points out that none of the patients had developed substitute symptoms.

The value of Cooper's study is undermined by several factors. Firstly, the selection of patients could not be properly randomized for control purposes as the matching was carried out retrospectively, and, as Cooper himself points out, 'In some of these cases, behaviour therapy suffered the fate of all new forms of treatment and was tried as a last resort, and some cases were taken on experimentally as much as therapeutically. This was particularly so in the obsessional patients. . . . '

Secondly, some of the treatment was carried out by students

or by psychologists who had had no previous experience of behaviour therapy. (Many of the control patients were treated by trainee psychiatrists.) Thirdly, Cooper provides few details about the nature of the behaviour therapy which was employed. His statement that the phobic patients were treated by Wolpe's methods of reciprocal inhibition and desensitization is misleading. In fact, less than 20 per cent of the patients (in the matched group of behaviour therapy cases) were treated by the method whichWolpe used in practically all of his phobic cases, namely, desensitization based on relaxation. Consequently, Cooper's comparison of these results with those reported by Wolpe also tends to be misleading. Cooper failed to indicate in a clear manner that he was in fact comparing different types of behaviour therapy. He was also comparing different types of patients—many of the Maudsley group were people who required in-patient, hospital care. The great majority of Wolpe's patients were treated on an out-patient basis. A fourth drawback to Cooper's study lies in the fact that the independent assessors worked solely from the case notes, and did not interview any of the patients in the treatment or the control groups. Cooper himself interviewed fourteen of the thirty behaviour therapy patients and none of the controls.

For these four reasons, Cooper's conclusions cannot be accepted at face value. They do, however, underline the need for well-designed controlled trials, in which particular care should be taken to ensure that adequate follow-up facilities are arranged.

Cooper's study was concerned primarily with phobic patients (the four obsessional patients were chiefly treated on an exploratory basis). The two other controlled studies both deal with the same type of disturbance. Lang and Lazovik (1963) investigated the treatment of snake phobias, and Lazarus (1961) examined phobias and cases of impotence.

Lang and Lazovik's experiment is a development of an earlier, pilot study on the same topic (Lazovik and Lang, 1960). The methods used in their experiment were carefully and elaborately prepared, and their experimental design and execution are of a high quality. The stringent controls which they employed enhance the significance of their findings and because of their importance, we will describe their experiment in some detail.

The aims of the experiment are described by the authors as follows. '(1) To evaluate the changes in snake phobic behaviour that occur over time, particularly the effects of repeated exposure to the phobic object. (2) Compare these changes with those that follow systematic desensitization therapy. (3) Determine the changes in behaviour that are a direct function of the desensitization process.' They chose to study snake phobias because of their common occurrence and also because of the assumed symbolic sexual significance attached to this disorder. Twenty-four subjects participated in the research. They were all college student volunteers and were selected by a combination of interview, questionnaire, and direct exposure to a non-poisonous snake. Only those subjects who rated their fear as intense, and whose behaviour in the presence of the snake confirmed this subjective report, were used in the experiment. The subjects were divided into two matched groups, an experimental group consisting of thirteen subjects and a control group comprising eleven subjects. The experimental treatment consisted of two essential parts, training and desensitization proper. The training procedure consisted of five sessions of forty-five minutes' duration, during which an anxiety hierarchy consisting of twenty situations involving snakes was constructed. The subjects were then trained in deep relaxation and taught how to visualize the feared scenes vividly while under hypnosis.

Following this training period, the experimental subjects were given eleven sessions of systematic desensitization during which the subject was hypnotized and instructed to relax deeply. The anxiety items from the hierarchy were then presented, starting with the least frightening scenes, and working up the scale to the most frightening scenes. As the experimental design demanded that each treated subject received only eleven treatment sessions, some of the subjects were not desensitized to all of the items in the hierarchy. In order to assess the effectiveness of reality training, half of the experimental subjects were exposed to the snake before treatment on a number of occasions. The control subjects did not participate in desensitization, but they were evaluated at the same time as their opposite numbers in the experimental series, and their behaviour in the presence of the snake was ascertained at the beginning and end of the experiment. All of the available subjects were seen and evaluated six months after the completion of therapy.

The authors summarize their results in the following way. 'The results of this present experiment demonstrate that the experimental analogue of desensitization therapy effectively reduces phobic behaviour. Both subjective rating of fear and overt avoidance behaviour were modified, and these gains were maintained or increased at the six months' follow-up. The results of objective measures were in turn supported by exten-

TABLE 10

Results of an experiment on desensitization. (From Lang and Lazovik, *Journal of Abnormal and Social Psychology*, 1963.)

Mean Snake Avoidance Scale Score at Test 2 and 3, Mean Change Scores, and the Mann-Whitney Test of Significance

	Test 2	Test 3	Change Scores	U
Experimental Groups	5·35	4·42	0·34	34·5*
Control Groups	6·51	7·73	0·19	

*P·05

sive interview material. Close questioning could not persuade any of the experimental subjects that they desire to please the therapist had been a significant factor in their change. Furthermore, in none of these interviews was there any evidence that other symptoms appeared to replace the phobic behaviour. The fact that no significant change was associated with the pre-therapy training argues that hypnosis and general muscle relaxation were not in themselves vehicles of change. Similarly, the basic suggestibility of the subject must be excluded . . . Clearly the responsibility for the reduction in the phobic behaviour must be assigned to the desensitization process itself.' (See Table 10.)

Lang and Lazovik also found a very close connection between the degree of improvement and the amount of progress made in the desensitization of hierarchy items within the eleven sessions provided by the experiment.

The differences between those experimental subjects who completed more than fifteen of the twenty hierarchy items and those who completed less than fifteen of the anxiety items are shown in Tables 11 and 12.

The authors also make three general points on the basis of their results. Firstly, as has been argued on previous occasions (see Wolpe, 1958; Rachman, 1958), it is not necessary 'to explore with a subject the factors contributing to the learning of a phobia or its unconscious meaning in order to eliminate the fear behaviour.' Secondly, they were not able to find any evidence to support the presumed claim that symptom substitution will arise if the symptoms are treated directly. Thirdly, they point out that in reducing phobic behaviour, it is not necessary

TABLE II

Results of an experiment on desensitization. (From Lang and Lazovik, *Journal of Abnormal and Social Psychology*, 1963.)

Avoidance Test Behaviour Change from Test 2 to Test 3 for Therapy Ss who Completed More than 15 Hierarchy Items, for Those who Completed Less than 15, and Mann-Whitney Tests of Significance.

Number of Hierarchy Items Successfully Completed	Snake Avoidance Scale			
	Test 2	Test 3	Change Score	U
More than 15 (N = 7)	6·71	3·93	0·49	
				5·0**
Less than 15 (N = 6)	4·17	5·00	−0·07	
	Fear Thermometer			
	Test 2	Test 3	Difference	U
More than 15 (N = 7)	7·57	4·00	3·57	
				8·0*
Less than 15 (N = 6)	7·67	6·50	1·17	

Note—All scores are mean values.

*$p < 0.08$
**$p < 0.03$

to alter the basic attitudes, values, or personality of the subject.

The third control experiment was carried out by Lazarus in 1961 and affords some convincing evidence in support of the effectiveness of systematic desensitization. This study was unusual in that the treatment was carried out in groups rather than in individual treatment sessions. This variation introduces a new factor into the examination of the effectiveness of desensitization. The group desensitization technique had never been used before, so that Lazarus's studies, to quite a large extent, were exploratory rather than confirmatory. The results are nevertheless favourable to the systematic desensitization technique.

Altogether, Lazarus treated seventeen control subjects and eighteen experimental subjects. The samples consisted of four types of patients. These were eleven acrophobics, fifteen claustrophobics, five cases of impotence. The experimental subjects were treated in four separate groups, varying in size from two to five subjects and the control subjects were treated in groups of no less than three subjects. The experimental

TABLE 12

Results of an experiment on desensitization. (From Lang and Lazovik, *Journal of Abnormal and Social Psychology*, 1963.)

Changes in the Fear Survey Schedule (FSS) following Desensitization Therapy for Ss who completed more than 15 Hierarchy Items, for those who completed less than 15, and Mann-Whitney Tests of Significance

Number of Hierarchy Items Successfully Completed	Fear Survey Schedule			
	Pre-therapy	Post-therapy	Difference	U
More than 15 (N = 7)	2·34	1·85	0·49	
				4·5*
Less than 15 (N = 6)	3·21	3·20	0·01	
	FSS–S's Rating of Snake Fear			
	Pre-therapy	Post-therapy	Difference	U
More than 15 (N = 7)	6·71	4·14	2·57	
				3·0**
Less than 15 (N = 6)	6·67	6·67	0·00	

Note.—All scores are mean ranks or mean rank differences.
*p <0·02
**p <0·01

subjects were trained in relaxation and were given desensitization training and, eventually, desensitization treatment. The first control group was given group interpretative therapy and the second control group (consisting of eight patients) received interpretative therapy and relaxation. Although the patients treated by Lazarus were not drawn from a psychiatric population, they were nevertheless severely limited in their social relationships and general psychological adjustment because of their complaints. Before commencing treatment, each control and experimental subject was interviewed and given psychometric tests and was also observed in a real-life, fear situation. The assessment of treatment was carried out by interview methods and also by a further exploration into the relevant feared situation. The results obtained with these patients is illustrated in Table 13 below. It will be seen that a high degree of success was obtained with the group desensitization method, whereas those patients who received interpretative treatment did not show any recoveries. Of the eight patients

TABLE 13

The number of patients assigned to each condition, and outcome of therapy in an experiment on systematic desensitization. (From A. Lazarus, Journal of Abnormal and Social Psychology, 1961.)

Patients	Treated by Desensitization	Recovered	Treated by Interpretation	Recovered	Interpretation and Relaxation	Recovered
Acrophobics	5	4	3	0	3	1
Claustrophobics	7	4	3	0	3	1
Impotence	2	2	3	0	–	–
Mixed	4	3	–	–	–	–
	18	13	9	0	8	2

treated by group interpretative therapy and relaxation, only two recovered. Follow-up studies were carried out on all the patients who had shown any sign of recovery. The follow-ups were carried out by means of a questionnaire, and any patient who revealed even a slight phobic recurrence was considered to have relapsed. Although Lazarus paid attention to the question of possible symptom substitution, no evidence of this phonomenon was encountered. Lazarus summarized his results in this way:

'Group desensitization was applied to eighteen patients of whom thirteen initially recovered and three subsequently relapsed. Group interpretation was applied to nine patients. There were no recoveries in this group. Group interpretation plus relaxation was applied to eight patients of whom two recovered and one subsequently relapsed. The fifteen patients who had not benefited from the interpretative procedures were then treated by group desensitization. There were ten recoveries of whom two subsequently relapsed.'

Of the eighteen subjects who were treated by direct group desensitization, thirteen recovered in a mean of 20·4 sessions. The fifteen patients who were not symptom-free after undergoing interpretative group therapy and who were subsequently treated by desensitization showed a 66 per cent recovery rate after a mean of only 10·1 sessions. Lazarus suggests that the fact that these patients recovered in a shorter time than the original experimental subjects indicates that they may have received some form of non-specific benefit from either the relaxation training, or from the relaxation training in association with the interpretative group therapy.

The control studies, which have been described above, are almost totally concerned with phobic conditions and the evidence which they provide is very striking. They indicate, beyond question, that behaviour therapy (in these instances, desensitization based on relaxation) is highly effective in eliminating phobic disorders and, furthermore, the great majority of these therapeutic improvements are lasting. These experimental demonstrations are particularly valuable because of the commonly-held view that phobic conditions are notoriously resistant to treatment. Lazarus in fact mentions no less than four well-known textbooks which echo this view.

Another suggestive piece of evidence comes from Lazarus's (1964) account of the treatment of three pairs of identical twins. In each case the treated twin recovered after behaviour therapy while his co-twin remained ill. In two of the three pairs, the untreated co-twin subsequently sought treatment after observing the improvement obtained by his twin. Following behaviour therapy the previously 'untreated' patients also recovered. The third co-twin remained untreated and apparently continued to display neurotic behaviour. Despite the small number of patients described in this report, it nevertheless provides strong supporting evidence for the claim that behaviour therapy effects improvements in neurotic illnesses—because an ideal control group was fortuitously provided.

The effective act

What is the effective act which produces improvements in the patient's condition? It has been argued that behaviour therapists tend to ignore the importance of the patient-therapist relationship in producing therapeutic changes (Cooper, 1963; Meyer and Gelder, 1963; Murray, 1962). If one adopts an extreme position on this point (and none of the people quoted above has done so) and claims that the patient-therapist relationship is the primary cause of the therapeutic improvements, then it is difficult to explain why behaviour therapy apparently produces better results than other types of therapy. Fortunately, we are in a position to estimate the contribution made to the progress of the therapy by this relationship.

The first point which needs to be stressed is that the contribution made by the relationship varies with the type of disorder under treatment. In certain disorders such as enuresis, the relationship is of virtually no significance in determining the course of the treatment. In other types of disorder, which are complex and longstanding, the relationship is of some significance (see, for example, the agoraphobic patients described by Meyer and Gelder, 1963). Costello (1963) has, however, drawn attention to an important difference between conventional types of psychotherapy and behaviour therapy. Many psychotherapists actively encourage the patient to form a close, and even dependent emotional relationship with the therapist. In behaviour therapy, *this type of emotional bond* is discouraged, as it may interfere with the relearning process. Naturally, the behaviour therapist requires the co-operation of his patients and must avoid giving them cause for distrust or distress.[1] It is also recognized that the therapist is a potential source of social reinforcement (see Ferster's (1958) excellent discussion). He can also facilitate the reduction of anxiety in a formal manner (by relaxation, etc.), or in an informal manner by verbal conditioning and reassurance. In the treatment of children, he can reduce anxiety by directly comforting the patient (e.g. Bentler, 1963). In certain instances, the relationship is of little significance in determining the course of the treatment (e.g. conditioning treatment of enuresis) while in other cases if has been found to play an important role (e.g. Meyer and Gelder, 1963). It is preferable and indeed necessary, to analyse the effects of the

---

[1] It is, of course, inevitable that therapists will differ in quality in the same way that there are good surgeons and bad surgeons. The minimal requirements for a behaviour therapy practitioner are that he should have a sound knowledge of learning theory, training and practice with the techniques and no serious psychological disorder.

THE RESULTS OF BEHAVIOUR THERAPY

relationship in learning theory terms rather than in a psycho-analytic or psychodynamic manner. Explanations which rely on the concepts of psychosexuality and/or unconscious motives and ideas cannot accommodate some of the available evidence. In particular, the results obtained in the treatment of enuresis defy explanation in dynamic terms. Similarly, it is impossible to speak of transference and counter-transference effects in attempting to account for the successful reduction of neurotic disturbances in animals by means of direct comforting and soothing (see the work of Anderson and Parmenter (1941) Massermann (1943), Haslerud et al. (1954) for examples).

The chief therapeutic contribution is made by the *deliberate and systematic* inhibition or extinction of the neurotic habit patterns —by deliberately facilitating the learning process. This conclusion is supported by the control studies conducted by Lazarus and by Lang and Lazovik, and also by some direct observations of the changes which occur during the treatment process (Wolpe, 1962b, 1963a; Clark, 1963b). Lang and Lazovik, for example, were able to exclude the possibility that any, or all, of the following factors played any role in the improvement of ten of their phobic subjects—sheer muscle relaxation, suggestibility, rapport, or hypnosis. Lazarus's control group actually received 'depth therapy'. It was found that the treated group (i.e. behaviour therapy) improved to a significantly greater extent than the patients who received 'depth therapy'.

Clark (1963b) successfully treated a patient who suffered from a monosymptomatic phobia of birds and feathers. During the treatment he recorded her GSR changes and observed a progressive increase in basal skin resistance (i.e. decreased GSRs) which corresponded closely with her progress up the desensitization hierarchy. Along similar lines, Wolpe (1962b) described in great detail the close correspondence between (a) the steps completed in desensitization of the anxiety hierarchy, and (b) the changes in the behaviour of a patient who was suffering from travel anxiety. The argument that re-learning is the effective act is further supported by the fact that this patient's behavioural improvement continued to mirror her progress in the desensitization sessions, even when the therapist was changed.

In another paper, Wolpe (1963a) presented further convincing evidence in support of the argument that behaviour therapy is a learning process which can be manipulated and measured in the same manner as other, more familiar, learning processes. He quantified the relationships between the amount of training (learning trials) and the development of the learned reaction, and was able to demonstrate some interesting differences between 'proximation' phobias and other phobias. He found that 'in claustrophobias and phobias in which the anxiety arises

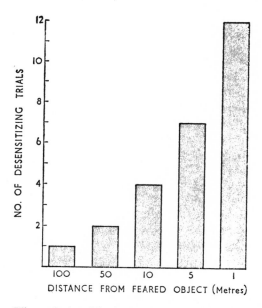

FIG. 39. The relationship between the number of treatment sessions and speed of recovery in a theoretical case of an animal phobia.

with increasing proximity to a feared object' only a small number of practice trials (desensitization presentations of the scene) were required to eliminate the anxiety experienced at a far distance from the feared object, e.g. 200 yards from a hospital. As the feared object is approached, however, an increasing number of practice trials are required (a positively accelerating curve). We may illustrate this finding by the following diagram (Fig. 39) which depicts a theoretical case of an animal phobia.

In the case of agoraphobias and phobias which increase in intensity with the number of objects involved, the initial items are difficult to overcome (i.e. require many practice trials). This learning curve 'corresponds to a negatively accelerating function', illustrated in Figure 40 by a theoretical case of a housebound, agoraphobic patient.

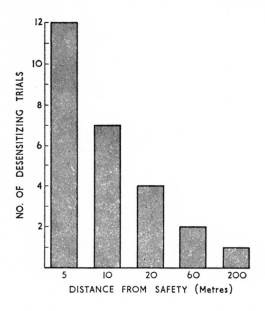

FIG. 40. The relationship between number of treatment sessions and speed of recovery in a theoretical case of agoraphobia.

Three of Wolpe's figures, which were derived from actual case material, are reproduced below (see Figs. 41, 42, 43). They illustrate the different types of learning curves obtained in treating proximation phobias (Fig. 41), claustrophobias (Fig. 42), and agoraphobias (Fig. 43). Apart from their relevance to the present discussion concerning the effective act in behaviour therapy, these findings show how therapeutic actions and reactions can be measured. Furthermore, they indicate how the lawful progression of the therapeutic learning process can be brought under examination.

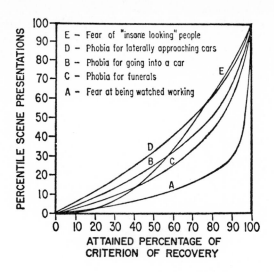

Fig. 41. Response to treatment in proximation phobias. (From Wolpe, *American Journal of Psychiatry*, 1963a.)

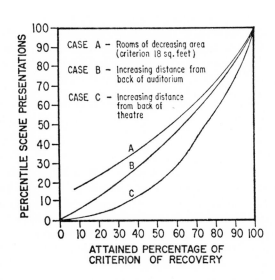

Fig. 42. Response to treatment in claustrophobia. (Wolpe, 1963a.)

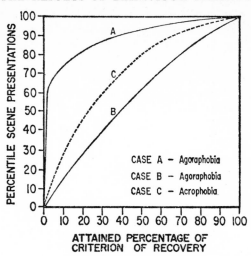

F IG. 43. Response to treatment in agoraphobia and acro-
phobia. (Wolpe, 1963a.)

The range of applicability of behaviour therapy

In considering the range of application of behaviour therapy,
we will concentrate on two aspects of this question; namely,
the influence of (a) personality factors, and (b) severity of
illness on therapeutic outcome. Therapeutic successes have
been obtained in a wide range of neurotic conditions. Rachman
(1963c) summarized the position early in 1963 and concluded
as follows.

'Behaviour therapy had been successfully used in the treatment of a wide range of neurotic conditions including: *phobias*
(e.g. Wolpe, 1958; Lazarus, 1963; Meyer, 1957; Eysenck,
1960b), *hysteria* (e.g. Brady and Lind, 1961; Sylvester and
Liversedge, 1960; Wolpe, 1958), *enuresis* (e.g. Jones, 1960;
Mowrer, 1938; Lovibond, 1963), *sexual disorders* (e.g. Blakemore *et al.*, 1963; Rachman, 1961b), *tics* (e.g. Yates, 1958;
Walton, 1961; Barrett, 1962), *obsessional neuroses* (e.g. Wolpe,
1958; Lazarus, 1963; Hussain, 1962), *tension states* (e.g. Wolpe,
1958; Eysenck, 1960), *children's disorders* (e.g. Rachman, 1962).
Recently, some relative improvements have been obtained
even in psychotic illnesses (e.g. Cowden and Ford, 1962; King
et al., 1960; Ayllon, 1963).'

Wolpe's combined series of 210 cases fall into six diagnostic categories (see Table 14). It will be seen that nearly two-thirds of his patients were suffering from anxiety states and only a small fraction of the total number conform to Eysenck's description of the neurotic extravert (hysterics). Commenting on the composition of Wolpe's sample, Eysenck (1957) posed the problem of the influence of personality on thera-

TABLE 14

The diagnostic classification of Wolpe's 210 cases. (From Wolpe, *Psychotherapy by Reciprocal Inhibition*, Stanford University Press, 1958)

	1952 Series	1954 Series	Present Series	Totals
Anxiety state	39	33	63	135
Hysteria	6	3	4	13
Reactive depression	7	3	5	15
Obsessions and compulsions	5	6	8	19
Neurasthenia	3	0	0	3
Mixed and unclassified	10	7	8	25
	70	52	88	210

peutic outcome. In view of the poor conditionability of extraverts, he predicted that these types of patients might raise serious difficulties in treatment. Wolpe did not distinguish between introvert and extravert personality types, and did not analyse the percentage of recoveries in each diagnositic category. He did show, however, that behaviour therapy can be applied to many types of neurotic disorder, including cases of a complicated nature. The recovery rate obtained with complex cases did not differ from that obtained with the more straightforward type of cases. On the other hand, Lazarus reported greater overall success with these less severely ill patients. As we have already mentioned, Wolpe's success rate exceeds that obtained by Lazarus, but Wolpe used a considerably larger number of treatment sessions. It is possible that Wolpe's superior results were gained by his greater persistence. Both these workers agree, however, that there are numbers of neurotic patients who pose considerable and intricate therapeutic problems. The treatment of stammerers, for example, has resulted in several failures in behaviour therapy. The possible reasons for the particular difficulty encountered in treating this condition are mentioned in Chapter 13 above, and may be said to stem from our ignorance of the aetiology of stammering. It seems likely that special behavioural techniques will have to be developed in order to overcome this disturbance, and fortunately there are some indications of progress already available (Cherry and Sayers, 1959; Meyer and Mair, 1963).

TABLE 15

Therapeutic results obtained with severe, mixed neurotic disorders. (Adapted from A. Lazarus, *Behaviour Research and Therapy*, 1963)

Symptoms	No. of Patients	Per cent improved
General anxiety	61	57
Pervasive anxiety	26	43
Obsess. compulsive	22	55
Sexual disorders	10	70
Interpersonal problems	47	81
Phobias	47	59
Depression	50	60
Panic	11	45
Hysteria	27	71
Passivity	16	63
Psychosomatic	13	69
Stuttering	5	20

Lazarus has provided a breakdown of his successes and failures with 126 severe cases in terms of their diagnoses (see Table 15). It is evident that the three types of disturbance which yielded the least satisfactory results were: pervasive anxiety states, panic states, and stammering. While Wolpe (1963b) has drawn attention to some of the complexities which are encountered in treating cases suffering from pervasive anxiety, he does not indicate that their improvement rate was significantly inferior. A possible reason for Lazarus's comparative lack of success with this type of patient may be traced to the fact that he does not include carbon dioxide therapy in his list of techniques, whereas Wolpe recommends the use of this procedure precisely in those patients who experience pervasive anxiety. Whether this observation has any substance or not will, of course, depend on further information. The inferior results obtained with panic states cannot be accounted for at this stage.

In regard to personality variables, Lazarus found that 75 per cent of his patients were dysthymics. Contrary to expectation, the group of patients who failed to improve had lower extraversion scores than the improved group. (E = 16·9 in the failure group, E = 22·2 in the success group). This apparent contradiction of the postulated relationship between extraversion and recovery rate needs to be interpreted with reserve because of two complicating factors. Firstly, the failure group differed from the success group in respect of *neuroticism* as well as extraversion. They were significantly more neurotic (N = 39·8) than the success group (N = 28·7). Secondly, neither the success group nor the failure group can properly be described as comprising neurotic extraverts (hysterics). The majority of the patients were in fact dysthymics. While there is some sound evidence to support the postulate of differential recovery rates in extraverts and introverts, especially in the conduct disorders and enuresis (see Chapter 13 above), the high recovery rate of 71 per cent obtained by Lazarus in his group of 27 hysterics cannot be ignored.

In regard to the intensity of the neurotic illness, Lazarus found that this variable was related to outcome in some types of illness (hysteria, obsessions, inter-personal problems, psychosomatic disorders) but not in others (anxiety states, phobias, depression, passivity). The finding that there is no direct relationship between the intensity of a phobic illness and the success of therapy receives support from Lang and Lazovik's control study.

Hussain (1962) treated a wide range of neurotic patients and reported a 95 per cent recovery rate. Although his patients included anxiety cases, phobics, obsessionals, hysterics, psychosomatic disorders, the majority of patients were again of the dysthymic type. He does not provide separate recovery figures for the different types of disorders. At this juncture, it is worth remarking that the accumulation of large-scale studies in which dysthymics feature so largely brings in its wake another matter of general interest and concern. Are there more introverted neurotics in the general population than there are extraverted neurotics, or is there some sort of selection bias operating? This skewed distribution in the composition of neurotic groups can best be explained as a manifestation of 'natural selection'. Neurotic extraverts will tend to develop anti-social conduct disorders rather than anxiety conditions—for the reasons discussed earlier (Chapter 2). Prison populations also show a skewed distribution—with *extraverts* in the clear majority. (Eysenck, 1964*b*).

The evidence shows that behaviour therapy can be successfully used in a wide range of neurotic conditions. It can also be successfully used in severe cases, but may require a longer period of treatment. The disorders which undoubtedly respond well and reasonably quickly are phobias, certain types of sexual disorders, hysterias, anxiety states, and tension states. The obsessional disorders and conditions in which pervasive anxiety is present, while they do respond to treatment, often present problems during the process of therapy. Stuttering and conduct disorders have not responded well to the techniques in use at present.

Conclusions

Considering its short history, we feel that behaviour therapy has accomplished a great deal. It has opened the gate for what may yet prove to be a most significant advance in the treatment of neurotic illness. Behaviour therapy starts off with several important advantages. It has developed out of established psychological theories and has a large body of experimental evidence on which to proceed. The therapeutic process and its outcome are both open to quantification. It permits precision and a systematic planning of the treatment required in individual cases.

Since the publication of Wolpe's first reports, eleven years ago, more than a thousand patients have received behaviour therapy. A rough estimate, based on published, large-scale reports, suggests that something in the region of 80 per cent of the patients treated were apparently cured or markedly improved. These reports also indicate that the length and amount of treatment required to effect these recoveries is significantly smaller than that required by prevailing types of psychotherapy, particularly psychoanalysis. Behaviour therapists have reported successful results in a wide range of neurotic conditions and, in the studies described above, no patients suffering from neurotic complaints were refused treatment. This in itself is an advance on the current tendency of many psychotherapists to demand that the patient fit the treatment instead of tailoring the therapy to meet the needs of the patient.

Many new methods of treatment have already been developed and more can be confidently expected—the very extensive literature on the psychology of the learning process can provide a valuable source for these new ideas. What is now required is a thorough investigation of this new form of therapy which promises to benefit more patients, more quickly. New departures such as behaviour therapy always produce a plethora of problems, and it can be stated with certainty that at present we have more problems than we have answers. Some of the topics which seem to require prompt attention are these. What is the influence of personality factors on the aetiology and treatment of neurotic disorders? How can drugs be used to facilitate behaviour therapy? How can we ensure that the therapeutic improvements are of a stable nature? What is the nature of pervasive anxiety and how is it best treated? Other conditions which require a great deal of investigation include conduct disorders, stuttering, obsessional-compulsive disorders, and psychosomatic disorders. And, of course, many controlled studies of behaviour therapy will be needed.

It will be extremely interesting to re-consider the contribution of behaviour therapy in five or ten years' time.

Chapter 17

RECOVERY AND RELAPSES

The effects of psychotherapy

In a recent article, Rosenthal (1962) recalled the observation of a group of psychologists that psychotherapy is 'an unidentified technique applied to unspecified problems with unpredictable outcomes. For this technique we recommend rigorous training.'

There is no satisfactory evidence that psychotherapy benefits people suffering from neurotic conditions. Examinations of the effects of psychotherapy on adults (Eysenck, 1952b; 1960a) have shown that there is no reason to suppose that this technique is capable of producing relief from neurotic illnesses. Eysenck's conclusions were based on the published reports of the effects of psychotherapy and the gross number of patients covered in the survey was 7,293. The evidence 'fails to prove that psychotherapy, Freudian or otherwise, facilitates the recovery of neurotic patients. They show that roughly two-thirds of a group of neurotic patients will recover or improve to a marked extent within about two years of the onset of their illness, whether they are treated by psychotherapy or not. This figure appears to be remarkably stable from one investigation to another, regardless of type of patient treated, standard of recovery employed or method of therapy used,' (Eysenck, 1960a). These conclusions were, at first, vehemently rejected by many psychotherapists and analysts. Recently, however, there have been indications that the validity of this argument is gaining widespread acceptance, even among psychoanalysts. Among those who appear to have accepted these conclusions are Dr. Weinstock (Chairman of the Fact-Gathering Committee of the American Psychoanalytic Association), Dr. Glover (doyen of British psychoanalysts), Professor Mowrer (a past President of the American Psychological Association and a former adherent of analysis), and Dr. Malan, Senior H.M.O. at the psychoanalytic Tavistock Clinic.

Weinstock has stated that 'no claims regarding the therapeutic usefulness of analytic treatment are made by the American Psychoanalytic Association. We are not responsible for claims made by individuals whose enthusiasm may outrun knowledge.' Dr. Glover (1955), in his book, *The Technique of Psychoanalysis*, wrote: 'We have next to no information about the conduct of private analytic practice . . . such figures as are published regarding clinic practice would, in the majority of cases, be rejected as valueless by any reputable statistician, uncorrected as they are for methods of diagnosis and selection, for length of treatment, for method of treatment, for after-history, and for spontaneous cure. Indeed, apart from an occasional reference to a case that may have remained well for some years, we have no after-histories worth talking about . . . we cannot attach *any* scientific significance to general impressions or assumptions regarding *any* form of psychotherapy,' (pp. 376-377). Malan (1963) writes: ' . . . it nevertheless remains true that there is not the slightest indication from the published figures that psychotherapy has any value at all. If psychotherapy really is of value—and as a psychotherapist I find difficulty in believing that it is not—then how can this paradox be resolved?' (p. 164). Professor Mowrer (1959) concludes: 'From testimony now available from both the friends and foes of analysis, it is clear that, at best, analysis casts a spell but does not cure (p. 121) . . . there is not a shred of evidence that psychoanalysed individuals permanently benefit from the experience, and there are equally clear indications that psychoanalysis, as a common philosophy of life, is not only non-therapeutic but actively pernicious' (p. 161).

An examination of the evidence concerning the effects of psychotherapy on children was carried out by Levitt in 1957. He reached the same conclusions as Eysenck—there is no proof that psychotherapy with children is effective. Of the 8,000 child patients included in this survey, two-thirds were improved when treatment ended (see Table 16). This statistic is no greater than that obtained from children who had received no psychotherapy; if anything, the treated group showed fewer improvements.

Levitt (1963) has now brought his examination of the evidence up-to-date, and the reports on the effectiveness of psychotherapy which have appeared in the past six years bring no comfort. He concluded that there still 'does not seem to be a sound basis for the contention that psychotherapy facilitates

TABLE 16

A summary of results of psychotherapy with children at close of treatment.
(From E. Levitt, *Journal of Consulting Psychology*, 1957.)

N	Much Improved	Partially Improved		Unimproved		Per cent Improved
57	16	18	12	8	3	80·7
100	13	18	42	26	1	73·0
70	12	29	19	10		85·7
250	54	82	46	68		72·8
196	76	52		68		65·3
50	15	18		17		66·0
126	25	54		47		62·7
290	75	154		61		79·0
814	207	398		209		74·3
72	26	31		15		79·2
196	93	61		42		78·6
27	5	11		11		59·3
31	13	8		10		67·7
23	2	9		12		47·8
75	35	22		18		76·0
80	31	21		28		65·0
522	225			297		43·1
420	251			169		59·8
3,399	1,174	1,105		1,120		67·0
100·00	34·54	32·51		32·95		

recovery from emotional illness in children.' Once again, the overall recovery rate shows that two out of three children are improved when treatment ends (see Table 17). Psychotherapy does not produce more recoveries than might be expected to occur without treatment.

It will be seen that in this second assessment Levitt attempted to analyse the results in diagnostic groups. He reached the tentative conclusion that 'the improvement rate with therapy is lowest for cases of delinquency and anti-social acting-out, and highest for identifiable behavioural symptoms like enuresis and school phobia.' This suggestion is interesting in the light of the prediction that 'extinctions occurring naturally during the life history of the individual should produce spontaneous remissions in patients suffering from dysthymic conditions' (Eysenck, 1963e). A re-examination of survey material also tends to support this prediction. O'Neal and Robins (1958)

TABLE 17

A summary of evaluation data from twenty-four studies of child therapy.
(From E. Levitt, *Behaviour Research and Therapy*, 1963.)

Type of Disorders	Number of Studies	Much improved		Partly Improved		Unimproved		Total	Overall % Improved
		N	%	N	%	N	%	N	
Neurosis	3	34	15	107	46	89	39	230	61
Acting-out	5	108	31	84	24	157	45	349	55
Special symptoms	5	114	54	49	23	50	23	213	77
Psychosis	5	62	25	102	40	88	35	252	65
Mixed	6	138	20	337	48	222	32	697	68
Totals	24	456	26·2	679	39·0	606	34·8	1741	65·2

carried out a long-term (thirty year) follow-up of 150 patients who had attended a child clinic but who had not received treatment. These former patients did not display more neurotic disturbances in adulthood than the control subjects. They did, however, show more sociopathic disorders than the controls, and it was precisely those patients who had been referred for extraverted disorders during childhood who had failed to adjust satisfactorily as adults. Morris, Escoll and Wexler (1955) followed up sixty-six children who had originally been referred because of their aggressive behaviour disorders (truancy, lying, stealing, cruelty, tantrums, destructiveness, defiance, restlessness). At the age of eighteen, only 21 per cent (fourteen) of the children had made a satisfactory adjustment; 59 per cent (thirty-nine) had failed to adjust and of these thirty-nine, twelve had committed at least one crime; 20 per cent (thirteen) had developed psychotic disorders. A group of introverted children who had received no treatment showed a very different outcome. Fifty-four adults 'who were sufficiently shy and withdrawn as children, sixteen to twenty-seven years previously, to be brought to a child guidance clinic' were followed up by Morris, Soroker and Burruss (1954). They found that two-thirds were satisfactorily adjusted and the other third were 'marginally adjusted.' Only two of the fifty-four were considered to be psychologically disturbed, and one of these was actually in a mental hospital. The association between improvements and the passage of time is illustrated by Cummings' (1946) study of emotional disturbances in school-children. The improvement index (without treatment) increased from 29 per cent after six months to 65 per cent after eighteen months in a group of 142 children.

In view of Eysenck's and Levitt's findings, we must argue that until substantial evidence is produced, the use of psychotherapy will continue to be viewed with serious misgivings. Clearly, *behaviour therapy* will have to do better than this. In view of the failure of psychotherapists to produce justifiable grounds for the continued use of a dubious technique, the proper exploration of behaviour therapy is overdue. The clinical investigation of behaviour therapy also seems to be recommended for more positive reasons. It has been developed from a broad background of information about the nature of learning processes in both normal and disordered organisms. Secondly, its applications have already achieved an encouraging degree of success, notably in the treatment of adult neurotics (Wolpe, 1958; Eysenck, 1960b). It has now to be demonstrated unequivocally that behaviour therapy produces more and/or quicker improvements than might be expected to occur spontaneously.

Behaviour therapy, spontaneous remissions and relapses

It has been argued elsewhere (Eysenck, 1963c) that a satisfactory theory of neurotic behaviour must account for the main phenomena in this field. As we pointed out in Chapter 1, the fact that approximately two out of three people with neurotic illnesses can be expected to recover without receiving any formal treatment cannot be ignored by any serious theory.

Levitt (1957) calculated that the overall improvement rate for 160 cases who defected from a children's clinic before receiving treatment was 72·5 per cent. This spontaneous remission rate was adduced from two reports in which disturbed children who had received no treatment were re-assessed one year later in one study, and eight to thirteen years later in the other study. In evaluating the significance of these findings, it is necessary to emphasize that Levitt (1963) was unable to find any evidence which might indicate that the defector cases were less disturbed than children who had received psychotherapy. In the first study, Levitt showed that the 'defector cases and those who have had some treatment *do not differ on sixty-one factors*, including two clinical estimates of severity of symptoms and eight other factors relating to symptoms' (our italics). In Levitt's second study, the treated and defector children were compared on a five-point severity scale by experienced workers; the mean severity rating for the treated group was 2·98 and that of the defector group 3·02. Although Ross and Lacey (1961), and Lake and Levinger (1960) have found some differences between treated and defector groups, Levitt's (1963) criticisms of these studies appear to be well taken. Either way, Levitt's findings can scarcely be ignored. Additional information about spontaneous improvements is provided by MacFarlane *et al.* (1954). In their survey of the behaviour disorders of *normal* children they found that the frequency of most disorders declines with increasing age. Some of their findings are reproduced here (see Figs. 44 *a-f*). Further data on the spontaneous remission of children's fears is provided by Holmes (see Table 6, page 203).

One of the highest spontaneous remission rates ever recorded was that obtained by Clein (1959), in a study carried out at the Maudsley Hospital. Thirty-eight non-attenders were traced, three to five years after applying for treatment. None of these children had received psychological treatment in the interim, but 86·9 per cent of them were found to be improved or much improved at follow-up. It should be pointed out, however, that the composition of this group of non-attenders was slightly atypical.

Spontaneous remission, although one of the best documented facts in the whole field of neurotic disorders, has received very scant attention from theoreticians; that is possibly due to the

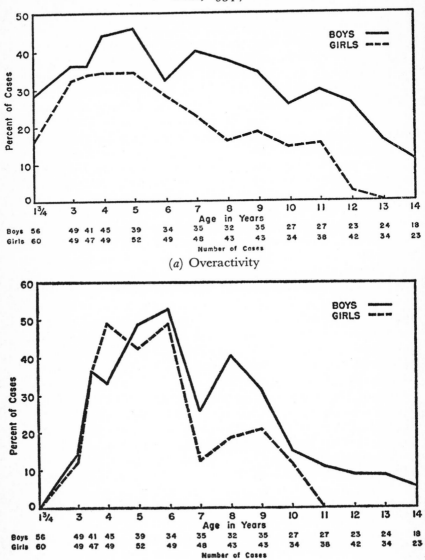

FIGS. 44 (*a-f*). Behaviour disorders in normal children. (Adapted from MacFarlane *et al.*, *A Developmental Study of the Behaviour Problems of Normal Children*. University of California Press, 1954.)

(*a*) Overactivity

(*b*) Lying

274

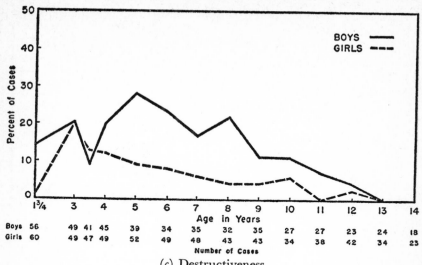

(*c*) Destructiveness

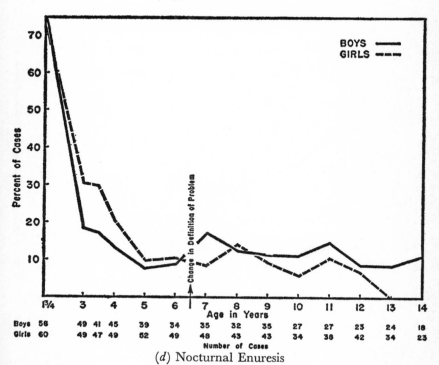

(*d*) Nocturnal Enuresis

275

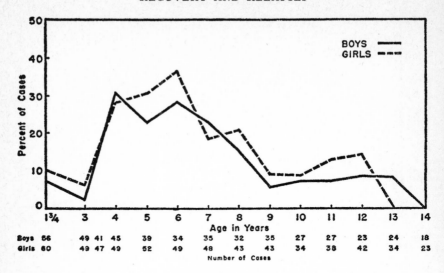

(*e*) Insufficient Appetite

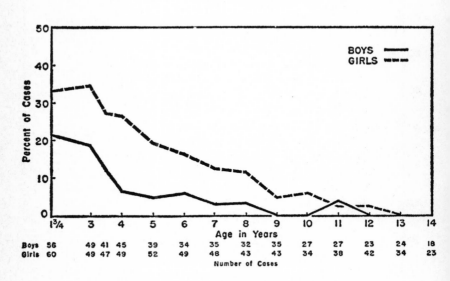

(*f*) Thumbsucking

fact that, according to psychoanalytic theory, the phenomenon itself simply should not happen. If neurotic disorders are always due to oedipal and other early conflicts in the child's history, which are repressed and require to be 'uncovered' before the nefarious symptom-producing results can be undone, then clearly spontaneous remission cannot take place, or if it does, cannot be lasting. Indeed, the demonstration that spontaneous remission occurs in the great majority of cases, even of severe illness, and does not normally result in relapse, is a very powerful argument against the psychoanalytic interpretation.

The improvement of neurotic patients without treatment appears to be function of time. As pointed out in an earlier chapter, Eysenck (1960a) has suggested that the following formula is descriptive of the situation:

$$X = 100(1\text{-}10^{-0.00435N})$$

where X stands for the amount of improvement achieved in per cent and N for the number of weeks elapsed. While the exact values in this formula should not be taken too seriously, its general form is of course that of the typical learning curve with which psychologists are familiar.

It may be worthwhile to take a closer look at the phenomenon of spontaneous recovery from a theoretical point of view, in order to determine possible causative factors; it is clearly impermissible to implicate 'time' as such, because it can only be *events* happening in time which can exert a causal influence, and our formula does not tell us very much about the possible nature of these events.

How does behaviour therapy deal with spontaneous remission? In order to answer this question, we must first summarize the main tenets of the general theory. For convenience, we may number the points in order.

(1) Neurotic behaviour consists of maladaptive conditioned responses of the autonomic system and of skeletal responses made to reduce the conditioned (sympathetic) reactions.

(2) While the term 'symptom' may be retained to describe neurotic behaviour, there is no implication that such behaviour is 'symptomatic' of anything.

277

(3)   It follows that there is no underlying complex or other 'dynamic' cause which is responsible for the maladaptive behaviour; all we have to deal with in neurosis is conditioned maladaptive behaviour.

(4)   Treatment consists of the *deconditioning*, by reciprocal inhibition, extinction, conditioned inhibition, or in some other way, of the maladaptive behaviour, and the *conditioning*, along orthodox lines, of adaptive behaviour.

(5)   The treatment is a-historical and does not involve any 'uncovering' of past events.

(6)   Conditioning and deconditioning will usually proceed through behavioural channels, but there is no reason why verbal methods should not also be used; there is good evidence that words are conditioned stimuli which have an ascertainable position on the stimulus and response generalization gradients of the patients (Eysenck, 1960*b*).

Our theory of spontaneous remission is a direct development of our theory of neurosis as a form of maladaptive autonomic conditioning. More specifically, spontaneous remission may be seen to be a simple example of the well-known mechanism of *extinction* which occurs in laboratory experiments on conditioning whenever the conditioned stimulus is applied without reinforcement, i.e. without the application of the unconditioned stimulus.[1]

Consider now a typical case history involving the establishment and cure of a cat phobia (Freeman and Kendrick, 1960). A traumatic event, involving the patient's favourite cat, produces a conditioned fear of cats; this develops to such an extent that she is effectively home-bound for many years, refusing to go out for fear of encountering cats. Treatment is by means of graduated presentations of cats (firstly symbolically, i.e. by words and pictures, then bodily, but at a distance, etc.) under conditions of relaxation and parasympathetic stimulation (desensitization, reciprocal inhibition). After a few weeks, treatment is completely successful, and a permanent cure achieved (no relapse for several years). In this case history there is no spontaneous remission, and we may enquire (a) why such a

---

[1]The present theory received strong support from a recent experiment by Willmuth and Peters (1964).

remission might have occurred, and (b) why in fact it did not do so.

First, we have a traumatic event which, by means of classical conditioning, produces a conditioned fear reaction to a previously neutral set of objects, i.e. cats. It is easy to see how this conditioned fear arose, but it is not so easy to see just why it should have persisted so long. Solomon and Wynne (1954), on the basis of their work with dogs, have offered the principle of 'partial irreversibility' in avoidance conditioning, but it should be noted that the aversive stimuli in their case were probably stronger than in the case of the patient, and also that they report no single-trial learning, as seems to have occurred in this patient. On general learning-theory principles, one would have expected the gradual *extinction* of the conditioned fear response in the course of time. Each time the patient saw a cat (the CS), without a recurrence of the traumatic events which precipitated her original fear (the UCS), this unreinforced presentation of the CS should lead to an increment of inhibition potential leading to extinction. Similarly, each time she discussed her troubles with a sympathetic listener, this should have had an effect similar to that of 'reciprocal inhibition', also leading to extinction of the fear response. In other words, behaviour theory seems to have no difficulty in explaining the extinction of neurotic symptoms by 'spontaneous remission'; this extinction is the natural result of the inevitable recurrence of the CS in the absence of reinforcement. We may thus re-interpret our formula for the time-course of spontaneous remission by saying, not that it resembles the typical learning curve, but rather that it resembles (and indeed is nothing but) the typical extinction curve. Our hypothesis, then, is that *all neurotic symptoms are subject to extinction*, and that this process of extinction is reflected in observable behaviour in the form of 'spontaneous remission'. The theory would appear to fit the facts reasonably well, but it would also appear to assert too much; not all cases of neurosis do in fact remit, and a theory predicting universal remission is clearly in need of an extension.

Such an extension is indeed implied in the first of our numbered postulates of behaviour therapy, given above, in which attention was drawn to the importance of 'skeletal responses made to reduce the conditioned (sympathetic) reaction.' What is asserted here is that in many cases of neurosis the original

stage of classical conditioning is followed by a stage of instrumental conditioning, and that it is this secondary development
which makes impossible the process of extinction by removing
the conditions of its occurrence, i.e. the presentation of the CS
under conditions of non-reinforcement. Consider the events in
the laboratory during the extinction of a conditioned response.
The dog, lashed to his stand, is presented with the CS a number
of times; his conditioned responses get weaker and weaker, until
finally they cease altogether. This paradigm differs profoundly
from that of our patient encountering a cat in the street after
her conditioned fear has been established. The patient is not
lashed to a stand, and thus forced to witness the conjunction:
CS—non-reinforcement; she is free to turn her back and run
away. This course of conduct produces an entirely different
paradigm, one favourable to the growth of an instrumental
response of running away from cats. Simplifying the situation
grossly, we may say that what happens is something like this.
The patient approaches the cat and experiences a conditioned
sympathetic response (fear) which is profoundly disturbing and
(negatively) reinforcing. She turns and runs, thus excluding the
cat from her field of vision, and also increasing the distance
between herself and the feared object. This behaviour reduces
the sympathetic arousal, and is thus reinforced by the resulting
lessening of fear. The next time the patient encounters a cat,
the newly-acquired habit of running away will again, and more
easily, be brought into play, until finally an instrumental
conditioned response of running away is developed to such
an extent that it permanently excludes the possibility of encountering the CS at all. In this way, the secondary process of
instrumental conditioning 'preserves' the primary conditioned
response; putting the whole matter into psychiatric terminology
instrumental conditioning makes impossible the 'reality testing'
of the classically conditioned response.

There is no doubt, of course, that in most cases the situation
is much more complex than this. The original conditioning is
not always, and perhaps not even usually, a traumatic, single
trial event; repeated sub-traumatic trials may produce an even
stronger conditioned fear response than a single traumatic
event. Little is known about the precise dynamics of this
process in individual cases, largely because psychiatric attention has not usually been directed at these events from the

point of view of learning theory. Again, few neuroses are monosymptomatic, and there may be a very complex inter-weaving of several different habit-family hierarches (Hull, 1943; Wolpe, 1958), each subject to extinction at different rates, and by exposure to different events (CSs). Lastly, experience indicates, and theory suggests, that extinction of conditioned fear responses in one habit-family hierarchy facilitates (through a process of generalization) extinction in others, whether this extinction is occurring during 'spontaneous remission' or during behaviour therapy. To mention these complications, to which many others could have been added, is simply to remind the reader that while in principle the explanation of spon-taneous remission here given is perhaps correct, nevertheless much experimental and observational work remains to be done before the details of the process can be said to be at all well understood.

We may use this theory of spontaneous remission in trying to deal with the problem often raised by psychotherapists, namely that of relapse. On the hypothesis that neurotic symptoms are merely the outcrop of repressed complexes, it would seem to be argued that no treatment of the symptoms alone could possibly have any long-term beneficial effects, as either a recrudescence of the old symptoms or the growth of new symptoms would be predicted to follow. This is a case where there appears to be complete agreement between all psycho-analysts on a specific behaviourally testable outcome, and the disconfirmation of this prediction (Eysenck, 1963c) is, therefore, of considerable theoretical, as well as practical, importance. The position seems to be that in the great majority of cases there is no relapse; it is also true, however, that under certain circumstances the neurotic who apparently has been cured does later on develop similar or different symptoms again. How can this fact be explained?

There are several points to be borne in mind here. The first and most obvious perhaps is that behaviour therapy is some-times carried out by individuals not properly trained in the procedures, and without a proper background in modern learning theory; they may fail to carry the process through to its proper conclusion, they may break off treatment too early, or they may make other mistakes which may lead to undesirable consequences. Eysenck (1963c) has drawn attention to the more obvious faults committed by some writers in the literature, and it must be clear that where treatment is carried out under conditions which violate the laws of learning theory, the results cannot be held to be damaging to the claims of behaviour therapy.

The second point to be considered is this. Let us assume that there is a one in ten chance of any particular individual undergoing a severe neurotic attack. If this occurs on a purely random basis, then one person in a hundred will contract two serious neurotic illnesses in the course of his life, one in a thousand will contract three, and so on. These calculations are, of course, not to be taken too seriously, as predisposition is known to weight the balance against any kind of random distribution; nevertheless, the point remains that a person may contract the same illness twice during the course of his life without this being in any case a relapse. A rugby player may break his nose in 1959 and, after it has been completely healed, may break it again in 1962; this is not to be regarded as a relapse. Similarly, a child prone to neurotic disorders may reproduce symptoms as a result of a certain conditioning process involving his parents, say, and he may, after cure, produce another set of symptoms on another occasion as a result of a new conditioning process involving, say, his girl friend. This does not necessarily constitute a relapse. It is clearly necessary to define, with considerable care and accuracy, precisely what is meant by a 'relapse', and how it is to be distinguished from a new and entirely separate breakdown.

However, there is a third consideration which suggests that certain types of neurotic disorder should hardly ever result in relapse after treatment while others are very much more likely to do so (Eysenck, 1963c). In Chapter 1 we made a distinction between two types of neurotic disorder. When the symptom is of a dysthymic character (anxieties, phobias, depression, obsessive-compulsive reactions, etc.) it is assumed that the disorder consists of conditioned *sympathetic* reactions, and the treatment consists of reconditioning the stimulus (or stimuli) to produce *parasympathetic* reactions which, being antagonistic to the sympathetic ones, will weaken and finally extinguish them. These disorders were described as 'disorders of the first kind'.

When the symptom is of a socially disapproved type in which

the conditioned stimulus evokes parasympathetic responses (alcoholism, fetishism, homosexuality), or where there is an entire absence of an appropriate conditioned response (enuresis, psychopathic behaviour), treatment (aversion therapy) consists of the pairing of the stimulus in question with strong aversive stimuli producing sympathetic reactions. These disorders are called 'disorders of the second kind'. (In putting the distinction between these two types of treatment in this very abbreviated form, we have used the terms 'sympathetic' and 'parasympathetic' in a rather inexact shorthand notation to refer to hedonically positive and negative experiences, respectively; the reader familiar with the complexities of autonomic reactions will no doubt be able to translate these blanket statements into more precise language appropriate to each individual case. We have retained this use of the terms here because it aids in the general description given, and indicates the physiological basis assumed to exist for the hedonic reactions.)

Let us now consider the role which extinction should play in these two types of disorder. It is our belief that in tracing the fate of those conditioned responses we call neurotic symptoms, too little attention has been paid to the facts of extinction, and the conditions giving rise to them. It is suggested that extinction affects, in a profoundly different manner, neurotic disorders of the first and second kind, respectively, and that the problem of relapse cannot be discussed in any satisfactory manner without paying attention to these differences.

Consider neurotic disorders of the first kind, i.e. the dysthymic disorders. Here it is hypothesized that the original cause of the symptom is a conjunction of a single traumatic event (or several repeated sub-traumatic experiences) with the presence of a previously neutral stimulus. Through the process of classical conditioning, the previously neutral stimulus (CS) now acquires the properties properly belonging to the traumatic event (UCS) itself, and produces the autonomic disturbances originally produced by the UCS.

Extinction, as explained above, should lead to spontaneous remission in cases of this type, and it is clear that in the case of neurosis of the first kind, extinction works in favour of the therapist and may even, unaided, lead to improvement and cure. Where the random events of life, acting in this fashion, do not produce a cure, the therapist can aid the process along the lines laid down by Wolpe (1958) and others and described in this text. Relapses should not occur in the ordinary way unless a new, repeated traumatic event occurs to produce a new symptom and a new neurotic disorder, This, of course, could not be considered a relapse, just as we would not consider it a relapse if a patient with a broken scapula should, years after recovery, suffer a Pott's fracture. Cure from one set of symptoms does not confer immunity on the patient.

Now consider the situation in relation to disorders of the second kind. Here the situation is clearly exactly the opposite to that which we have encountered so far. The patient is suffering from a maladaptive habit which is either itself an unconditioned response, as in the case of enuresis, or where the conditioned stimulus has become associated with consequences which are immediately pleasurable to the patient, although they may be socially undesirable and highly unpleasant in their long-term consequences for the individual himself (fetishism, alcoholism, and the like). Some types of disorder, such as homosexuality, may pertain to either one or the other of these two categories. In any case, what is true in all these types of disorder is that a strong bond has been created between a previously neutral stimulus and a strongly positive reinforcement. Ordinary events of life occurring randomly are not likely to lead to extinction, as they are not likely to associate the conditioned stimulus with lack of reinforcement.

The formal or informal punishment which is often provoked by socially unacceptable behaviour (as we have already seen in Chapter 1) seldom succeeds in extinguishing the undesirable act. If the behaviour pattern is immediately followed by reward and only much later by punishment, it can be expected to persist.

It is with respect to this temporal sequence that aversion therapy differs from punishment in the ordinary sense of the term. Punishment is a relatively arbitrary and long delayed consequence of action which, according to Mowrer's principle (see page 9) should have very little, if any, influence upon the habit in question. Aversion therapy attempts to apply the aversive stimulus *immediately* after the conditioned stimulus, and in such a way that it eliminates, or at least precedes, the positive reinforcement resulting from the act. This is often difficult to do, as clearly split-second timing is of the utmost importance ;

as has been pointed out before, many people who attempt aversion therapy do so without a full appreciation of the complexities of conditioning, and failure easily results from the haphazard manipulation of time relationships.

Consider now a case where aversion therapy has been successful and where the conditioned stimulus has been successfully linked with the aversive stimulus; we will call this link 'aversive conditioning'. Now clearly aversive conditioning, like all other types of conditioning, is subject to extinction, and we must consider how extinction can arise, and how it would influence the future course of the symptom. The first point to be borne in mind is that aversive conditioning tends to stop when conditioning has only just been achieved, i.e. without any considerable degree of over-learning. As an example, take the treatment of enuresis by means of the bell and blanket method. According to the theoretical analysis of Lovibond (1961), urinating in bed is the conditioned stimulus which becomes linked with the aversive stimulus, the bell, which in turn produces the immediate reflex cessation of urination. Now it is clear that conditioning can only proceed while the patient still produces the conditioned stimulus, i.e. while conditioning is still far from complete. The moment the patient ceases to urinate in bed, further conditioning becomes impossible. With modifications, the same argument would hold for other types of aversion therapy. Where the conditioned stimulus can be voluntarily applied, as in the case of consumption of alcoholic beverages, consideration of time, expense, and the great discomfort produced usually limits the number of conditioning trials to a relatively small proportion of what may be required to produce any considerable degree of over-learning.

After successful aversion therapy, the patient emerges with a central nervous system into which has been built a certain amount of 'aversive conditioning' which is subject to what has been called oscillation by Spearman (1927) and Hull (1943). Oscillation is a feature of all biological systems, and produces random variations in the strength of inhibitory and excitatory potential; these oscillations may be quite considerable in relation to the total amount of potential under consideration.

Consider now an individual who has submitted to a course of aversive conditioning, and whose degree of conditioning is just at the point where the original behaviour does not occur in relation to the stimuli which used to set it off before the course of aversive conditioning. Owing to the process of oscillation, the effectiveness of aversive conditioning will be much weaker on certain occasions than on others, and if by accident the original stimuli are present at a time when the excitatory potential of the aversive conditioning is low, the individual will be liable to give way to temptation. If he does, then the extinction process phase of the aversive conditioning will have begun, because the conditioned stimulus has been presented without the (negative) reinforcement. It would follow that on subsequent occasions the excitatory potential would already be weaker to begin with, even without the action of oscillation, so that further extinction trials are even more likely to occur. We thus find that in neurotic disorders of the second kind, the random events of everyday life, far from leading to spontaneous remission, will rather lead to relapse, other things being equal. Thus our prediction, on theoretical grounds, would be that relapse should be rare or even non-existent in disorders of the first kind, but relatively frequent with disorders of the second kind. There are no empirical studies the results of which could be used to support this deduction in any conclusive manner, but it is noteworthy that those who have denied the importance of relapse, like Wolpe (1958), have concentrated largely on disorders of the first kind. Writers dealing with disorders of the second kind, like Gwynne Jones (1960), Freund (1960), and others, have drawn attention to the frequency of relapse in patients of this type. It would seem, therefore, that the distinction made is a potentially fruitful one, although the differences in relapse rates may be attributable, in part at least, to other causes as well. Thus, the symptoms of disorders of the first kind are usually such as to motivate the patient very strongly to undergo a process of therapy in order to get relief from these symptoms. The symptoms of disorders of the second kind, however, are much less painful to bear, as far as the individual is concerned; indeed, they may appear quite pleasant and agreeable to him. It is society, through one of its various agencies, which provides the motivation for therapy, and this imposed drive is likely to be much weaker. This is important, because it is well-known that the strength of conditioned responses is very much determined by the strength of the drive under which the individual is working. Here we may have, therefore, an additional principle accounting for the high relapse rate predicted for disorders of the second type.

There are, of course, several ways in which we can overcome the difficulty presented by disorders of the second type. Eysenck (1963c) has suggested over-learning, partial reinforcement, and repeated 'booster' doses of reconditioning as weakening the forces of extinction, and there is evidence to show that either alone or in combination they may be sufficient to counteract the difficulties of conditioning treatment in cases of this kind.

On the basis of observations made on therapeutic changes in children with behaviour disorders, it seems possible that another learning process may also be involved in spontaneous remissions. This process, known as latent learning, may be responsible for spontaneous remissions in disorders which arise from the patient's failure to learn an adequate way of responding. These disorders are typified by enuresis, aphemia, dyslexia, encopresis, and so forth, and most commonly occur during childhood. They differ from the common neuroses in adults (e.g. phobias, obsessions) in an important respect. Phobias and obsessions, for example, are persistent, unadaptive, and *surplus* response-patterns. Enuresis, dyslexia, and encopresis, on the other hand, are persistent, unadaptive failures to respond adequately.

Latent learning was first studied by Blodgett in 1929. It attracted the attention of numerous investigators because of its importance in the controversy between the learning theories propounded by Hull and by Tolman. The essence of latent learning is as follows. If, after a period of practice during which no improvement in performance occurs, an appropriate reward is introduced, sudden and large increments appear. The phenomenon is best described by reference to experimental findings such as those presented in Figure 45.

Since Blodgett's early demonstration of latent learning, the accumulation of experimental findings has given rise to five varieties of latent learning (Thistlethwaite, 1951; Hilgard, 1958). The best substantiated and most germane varieties are: (i) unrewarded trials with the later introduction of appropriate rewards; (ii) free exploration followed by appropriate rewards; (iii) detection of rewards learned under satiation and re-located when the rewards become relevant. The occurrence of latent learning in children has been described by Stevenson (1954), who showed that latent learning ability shows a striking increase during the pre-school years.

The laboratory evidence suggests a possible explanation for those sudden, striking improvements in performance which are often observed by clinicians. If the following three features are encountered when sudden improvements occur, we may, with

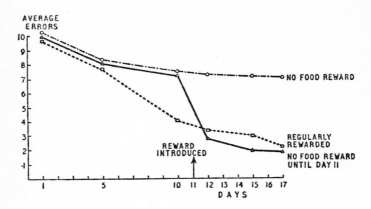

FIG. 45. Latent learning. Three groups of rats were run in a maze. Prior to receiving food rewards on the 11th day, the experimental group of rats had learned very little. The introduction of an appropriate reward on Day 11 produced a sudden, marked improvement of performance. The implication of this result is that some latent learning occurred during the first ten days but only became apparent in the rats' performances when activated by the food reward. (Adapted from Tolman and Honzik, University of California Publications in Psychology, 1930.)

reasonable certainty, conclude that latent learning has taken place.

   (a)   The patient has been exposed to the learning situation for a prolonged period—has had ample opportunity to learn the correct response.

   (b)   A new incentive has been introduced.

   (c)   The improved performance is of a rapid and/or sudden nature.

We may illustrate this process with a case of dyslexia (Rachman, 1962). Despite his four years of ordinary school attendance and nine months of special coaching, M.R., a nine-year-old boy, had learned to read only a few simple words (condition (a) above is satisfied). He was then given a period of remedial training, using an operant conditioning technique. Each correct word-recognition response was rewarded with a small piece of

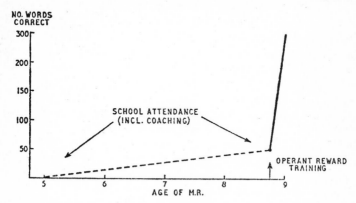

FIG. 46. Latent learning in a case of dyslexia. M.R. attended school from the age of five years. When remedial training was started at the age of 8 years 9 months he knew very few words. The dotted line is an estimate of his reading progress over the years. When he was changed to a rewarded operant training method he acquired 257 new words in five weeks.

candy (condition (b) is satisfied). In less than nine hours of practice, spread over five weeks, he learned 257 new words (condition (c) above is satisfied). M.R's extremely rapid acquisition of new words (despite the comparative absence of improvement in the preceding four years) was, in large measure, a reflection of the latent learning which had taken place prior to the start of the remedial training (see Fig. 46).

These sudden and striking improvements are very commonly seen in cases of enuresis. The case of D.H., a seven-year-old enuretic, is fairly typical. This boy had never been dry, despite the application of parental pressures which ranged from stern rebukes to affectionate encouragement. A bell-and-pad conditioning technique was then tried, and D.H. became dry overnight. He has remained completely dry for the past four years. This example of an 'incidental' cure of enuresis can be matched by any clinician, and no doubt explains why there are so many different types of folk and other remedies for this complaint. Kanner (1960) comments on this state of affairs and lists some suggested remedies; they include twenty-five mechanical and surgical procedures, twenty-three types of drugs, three types of diet, and endless psychological methods.

Sudden improvements are not restricted to cases of enuresis however. If many of these improvements are the result of latent learning, we would then expect such rapid changes to occur in other disturbances which are reflections of inadequate learning. Apart from the case of dyslexia described above, other instances can be quoted. An encopretic child was recently put on an operant training procedure. While three other children required periods of training ranging from four weeks to four months before improving, the fourth child achieved almost total control in two days. Certain defects of speech comprise another group of disorders which can be expected to be subject to latent learning and which should yield examples of sudden improvements. When confronted by a patient who has been cured by the application of leeches or a flash of lightning, one's customary reaction is to shrug and smile. If the operation of latent learning described here has any validity, we may in future be able to omit the shrug.

In conclusion, it is proposed that latent learning be added to the two processes (inhibition and extinction) which are presumed to effect spontaneous remissions. Latent learning may be presumed to be operating when clinical improvements are of a sudden and/or rapid nature and occur after the introduction of a new incentive. The presumption is strengthened if the patient has previously been exposed to the situation for a reasonable length of time and if the evidence indicates that the improvement is unlikely to have resulted from the effects of new practice. Remissions arising from the action of latent learning can be expected to occur most commonly in 'deficit' disorders, where the complaint involves a failure to learn adequate responses (e.g. dyslexia, enuresis). It is probable that latent learning remissions can be cultivated by the introduction of new, powerful incentives when the disorder is of the deficit type and the patient has already experienced prolonged exposure to the learning situation.

BIBLIOGRAPHY AND
AUTHOR INDEX

*Numbers in italic type at the end of each entry refer
to the page on which the reference is quoted.*

Al-Issa, I. (1961) An experimental investigation of the effects of attitudinal factors in eyeblink conditioning. London: Unpublished Ph.D. Thesis, Univ. of London Library. *37*

Al-Issa, I. (1964) The effect of attitudinal factors on the relationship between conditioning and personality. *Br. J. clin. Soc. Psychol.*, **3**, 113–119. *37*

Allport, G. (1951) *Personality.* London: Constable. *82*

Anderson, O. D. and Parmenter, R. (1941) A long-term study of the experimental neurosis in the sheep and dog. *Psychosom. Med. Monogr.*, **2**, Nos. 3 and 4. *123, 258*

Ardis, J. A. and Fraser, B. (1957) Personality and perception: the constancy effect and introversion. *Brit. J. Psychol.*, **48**, 48–54. *42*

Ayllon, T. (1960) Some behavioral problems associated with eating in chronic schizophrenic patients. Paper read at A.P.A. meeting, Chicago. *185, 232, 237, 238*

Ayllon, T. (1963) Intensive treatment of psychotic behaviour by stimulus satiation and food reinforcement. *Behav. Res. Ther.*, **1**, 47–58. *174, 186, 187, 188, 189, 237, 238, 262*

Ayllon, T. and Haughton, E. (1962) Control of the behavior of schizophrenic patients by food. *J. exp. Anal. Behav.*, **5**, 343–352. *185*

Ayllon, T. and Michael, J. (1959) The psychiatric nurse as a behavioral engineer. *J. exp. Anal. Behav.*, **2**, 323–334. *186, 232*

Azrin, N. (1961) Effects of punishment intensity during variable-interval reinforcement. *J. exp. Anal. Behav.*, **3**, 123–142. *168*

Azrin, A. H. and Lindsley, O. R. (1956) The reinforcement of cooperation between children. *J. abn. soc. Psychol.*, **52**, 100–102. *223*

Bachrach, A. L. (Ed.) (1962) *Experimental Foundations of Clinical Psychology.* New York: Basic Books. *82, 241*

Baer, D. M. (1960) Escape and avoidance response of pre-school children to two schedules of reinforcement withdrawal. *J. exp. Anal. Behav.*, **3**, 155–159. *224*

Baer, D. M. (1961a) Effect of withdrawal of positive reinforcement on an extinguishing response in young children. *Child Develpm.*, **32**, 67–74. *233*

Baer, D. M. (1961b) Modes of presenting social reinforcers. Paper read at A.P.A. meeting, New York. *233*

Baer, D. M. (1963) Laboratory control of thumbsucking in three young children by withdrawal and re-presentation of positive reinforcement. *J. exp. Anal. Behav.* (to appear). *193, 224, 236*

Baer, D. M., Harris, F. R. and Wolf, M. M. (1964) Control of nursery school children's behaviour by programming social reinforcement from their teachers. (To be published). *226, 233*

Bakan, P. (1957) Extraversion-introversion and improvement in an auditory vigilance task. *Med. Res. Council* A.P.U. 311/57. *43*

Baller, W. and Shalcock, H. (1956) Conditioned response treatment of enuresis. *Except. Child.*, **22**, 233–247. *196, 198*

Bandura, A. (1961) Psychotherapy as a learning process. *Psychol. Bull.*, **58**, 144–159. *119, 233*

Bandura, A. (1962) Social learning through imitation. In: Jones, M. R. (Ed.) *Nebraska Symposium on Motivation*. Lincoln: University of Nebraska Press. *207*

Bandura, A. (1963) The role of imitation in personality development. *J. Nursery Educ.*, **18**, 48–58. *207*

Bandura, A., Ross, D. and Ross, S. (1963a) Imitation of film-mediated aggressive models. *J. abn. soc. Psychol.*, **66**, 3–11. *207*

Bandura, A., Ross, D. and Ross, S. (1963b) Vicarious reinforcement and imitative learning. *J. abn. soc. Psychol.*, **67**, 527–534, *207*.

Bandura, A. and Walters, R. H. (1963) *Social learning and personality development*. New York: Holt, Rinehart & Winston. *207, 211, 233*

Barendregt, J. P. (1961) *Research in psychodiagnostics*. The Hague: Mouton. *37*

Barker, G. (1942) An experimental study of the resolution of conflict by children. In: McNemar, L. and Merrill, S. (Eds.) *Studies in Personality*. New York: McGraw-Hill. *64*

Barker, J. C. *et al.* (1961) Behaviour therapy in a case of transvestism. *Lancet*, **1**, 510. *151*

Barrett, B. H. (1962) Reduction in rate of multiple tics by free-operant conditioning methods. *J. nerv. ment. Dis.*, **135**, 187–195. *122, 172, 224, 225, 262*

Beach, F. A. (1951) Instinctive behaviour: reproductive activities. In: S. S. Stevens, (Ed.) *Handbook of Experimental Psychology*. New York: Wiley. *143, 157*

Becker, W. C. (1960) Cortical inhibition and extraversion-introversion. *J. abnorm. soc. Psychol.*, **61**, 52–66. *38*

Becker, W. C. and Matteson, H. G. (1961) GSR conditioning, anxiety and extraversion. *J. abnorm. soc. Psychol.*, **62**, 427–430. *38*

Beech, R. (1960) The symptomatic treatment of writer's cramp. In: Eysenck, H. J. (Ed.) *Behaviour Therapy and the Neuroses*. Oxford: Pergamon Press. *110, 138, 169*

Beech, R. and Adler, F. (1963) Some aspects of verbal conditioning in psychiatric patients. *Behav. Res. Ther.*, **1**, 273–282. *178*

Behrle, F. *et al.* (1956) Evaluation of a conditioning device in the treatment of nocturnal enuresis. *Pedaetrics*, **17**, 849–855. *198*

Bender, L. and Cottington, F. (1942) The use of amphetamine sulfate in child psychiatry. *Amer. J. Psychiat.*, **99**, 116–121. *55*

Bender, M. B. (1952) *Disorders in perception*. Springfield: Thomas. *35*

Bentler, P. M. (1962) An infant's phobia treated with reciprocal inhibition therapy. *J. Child. Psychol. Psychiat.*, **3**, 185–189. *210, 257*

Berkson, G. *et al.* (1963) Situation and stimulus effects on stereotyped behaviors of chimpanzees. *J. comp. physiol. Psychol.*, **56**, 786–792. *130, 131*

Berlyne, D. E. (1960) *Conflict, arousal and curiosity*. New York: McGraw-Hill. *34*

Bijou, S. W. (1961) Discrimination performance as a baseline for individual analysis of young children. *Child Develpm.*, **32**, 163–170. *193, 235*

Bijou, S. and Baer, D. (1960) The laboratory-experimental study of child behaviour. In: Mussen, P. H. (Ed.) *Handbook of Research Methods in Child Development*. London: Wiley. *241*

Blakemore, C. B. (1963) Personal communication. *172*

Blakemore, C. B. *et al.* (1963a) Application of faradic aversion conditioning in a case of transvestism. *Behav. Res. Ther.*, **1**, 26–35. *131, 153, 162*

Blakemore, C. B. *et al.* (1963b) Follow-up note. *Behav. Res. Ther.*, **1**, 191. *156*

Boardman, W. (1962) Rusty: A brief behavior disorder. *J. consult. Psychol.*, **26**, 293–297. *196*

Bond, I. and Hutchison, H. (1960). Application of reciprocal inhibition therapy to exhibitionism. *Canad. M. A. J.*, **83**, 23–25. *135, 145*

Bradley, C. (1937) The behavior of children receiving benzedrine. *Amer. J. Psychiat.*, **94**, 577–585. *55*

Bradley, C. (1950) Benzedrine and dexedrine in the treatment of children's behavior disorders. *Pedaetrics*, **5**, 24–37. *55*

Bradley, C. and Bowen, M. (1941) Amphetamine (benzedrine) therapy of children's behaviour disorders. *Amer. J. Orthopsychiat.*, **11**, 92–103. *53*

Bradley, P. B. (1948) The central action of certain drugs in relation to the reticular formation of the brain. In: Jasper, H. H. (Ed.) *Reticular Formation of the Brain.* Boston: Little, Brown. *49*

Brady, J. and Lind, D. L. (1961) Experimental analysis of hysterical blindness. *Arch. gen. Psychiat.*, **4**, 331–339. *97, 224, 236, 262*

Brady, J., Pappas, N., Tausig, T. and Thornton, D. R. (1962) M.M.P.I. correlates of operant behavior. *J. clin. Psychol.*, **18**, 67–70. *223*

Brebner, J. M. T. (1957) An experimental investigation of the relationship between conditioning and introversion-extraversion in normal subjects. Aberdeen: Unpublished M.A. thesis. University of Aberdeen Library. *37*

Broadhurst, P. L. (1959) The interaction of task difficulty and motivation. The Yerkes-Dodson law revived. *Acta Psychol.*, **16**, 321–338. *56*

Broadhurst, P. L. (1960) Abnormal animal behaviour. In: H. J. Eysenck (Ed.) *Handbook of Abnormal Psychology.* London: Pitmans. *63*

Burnett, A. and Ryan, E. (1963) The application of conditioning techniques in psychotherapy in a day-care treatment hospital. (To be published.) *247*

Canestrari, R. (1957) Sindromi psichiatriche e rigidita percettiva. *Riv. exp. di Freniatria*, **81**, 1–10. *42*

Cattell, R. B. (1957) *The sixteen personality factor questionnaire.* Champaign, Ill.: Institute for Personality and Ability Testing. *21*

Cattell, R. B. and Scheier, I. H. (1961) *The meaning and measurement of neuroticism and anxiety.* New York: Ronald Press. *18*

Case, H. W. (1960) Therapeutic methods in stuttering and speech blocking. In: H. J. Eysenck (Ed.) *Behaviour Therapy and the Neuroses.* Oxford: Pergamon Press. *119, 194*

Chazan, M. (1962) School phobia. *Brit. J. educ. Psychol.*, **32**, 209–217. *213, 216, 217, 218*

Cherry, C. and Sayers, B. (1960) Experiments on the total inhibition of stammering. In H. J. Eysenck (Ed.) *Behaviour Therapy and the Neuroses.* Oxford: Pergamon Press. *194, 264*

Chittenden, G. (1942) An experimental study in measuring and modifying assertive behavior in young children. *Monogr. Soc. Res. Child Develpm.* **7**, No. 1. *207*

Church, R. (1963) The varied effects of punishment. *Psychol. Rev.*, **70**, 369–402. *164, 166*

Claridge, G. (1960) The excitation-inhibition balance in neurotics. In: H. J. Eysenck (Ed.) *Experiments in Personality.* London: Routledge & Kegan Paul. *42, 43*

Clark, D. F. (1963a) Fetishism treated by negative conditioning. *Brit. J. Psychiat.*, **109**, 404–407. *151, 152*

Clark, D. F. (1963b) Treatment of a monosymptomatic phobia by systematic desensitization. *Behav. Res. Ther.*, **1**, 89–104. *152, 258*

Clark, D. F. (1963c) Letter to *Brit. J. Psychiat.*, **109**, 695–696. *152*

293

Clark, D. F. (1963d) The treatment of hysterical spasm and agoraphobia by behaviour therapy. *Behav. Res. Ther.*, **1**, 245–250. *114*

Clein, L. (1959) A follow-up of non-attenders at the Maudsley Hospital Children's Department. Dissertation, University of London. *273*

Cohen, J., Dearnaley, E. J. and Hansel, C. E. M. (1958) The risks taken in driving under the influence of alcohol. *Brit. Med. J.*, **1**, 1438. *51*

Cooper, A. J. (1963) A case of fetishism and impotence treated by behaviour therapy. *Brit. J. Psychiat.*, **109**, 649–653. *152, 158*

Cooper, J. E. (1961) Some aspects of the use of behaviour therapy in psychiatry. Dissertation, University of London. *249*

Cooper, J. E. (1963) A study of behaviour therapy in thirty psychiatric patients. *The Lancet*, **1**, 411–415. *249, 257*

Costello, C. G. (1957) The control of visual imagery in mental disorder. *J. ment. Sci.*, **103**, 840–849. *43*

Costello, C. G. (1961) The effects of meprobromate on time perception. *J. ment. Sci.*, **107**, 67–73. *50*

Costello, C. G. (1963) Behaviour therapy: Criticisms and confusions. *Behav. Res. Ther.*, **1**, 159–162. *257*

Cowden, R. and Ford, L. (1962) Systematic desensitization with phobic schizophrenics. *Amer. J. Psychiat.*, **119**, 241–245. *175, 178, 262*

Cowie, V. (1961) The incidence of neurosis in the children of psychotics. *Acta Psychiat. Scand.*, **37**, 37–87. *27*

Cummings, J. D. (1946) A follow-up study of emotional symptoms in school children. *Brit. J. educ. Psychol.*, **16**, 163–177. *272*

Cutts, K. K. and Jasper, H. H. (1949) Effect of benzedrine sulfate on behavior-problem children with abnormal electro-encephalograms. *Arch. Neurol. Psychiat.*, **41**, 1138–1145. *51*

Das, J. G. (1957) An experimental study of the relation between hypnosis, conditioning and reactive inhibition. Univ. of London: Unpublished Ph.D. thesis. *37*

Davidson, J. and Douglass, E. (1950) Nocturnal enuresis: a special approach to treatment. *Brit. Med. J.*, **1**, 1345–1347. *196, 198*

Davidson, P. O., Payne, R. W. and Sloane, R. B. (1964) Introversion, neuroticism, and conditioning. *J. abnorm. soc. Psychol.*, **68**, 136–143. *38*

Davies, B. and Morgenstern, F. (1960) A case of cysticercosis, temporal lobe epilepsy, and transvestism. *J. neurol. neurosurg. Psychiat.*, **23**, 247–249. *151*

Davis, D. R. (1946a) The disorganization of behaviour in fatigue. *J. neurol. Psychiat.*, **9**, 23–29. *106*

Davis, D. R. (1946b) Neurotic predisposition and the disorganization observed in experiments with the Cambridge cockpit. *J. neurol. Psychiat.*, **9**, 119–124. *106*

Davis, D. R. (1948) *Pilot Error—Some Laboratory Experiments*. London: H.M. Stationery Office. *42*

Davis, D. R. (1949) Increase in secondary drive as a cause of disorganization. *Quart. J. exp. Psychol.*, **1**, 136–142. *106*

Davison, G. S. (1964) A social learning therapy programme with an autistic child. *Behav. Res. Ther.* (in press) *224*

Denker, R. (1946) Results of the treatment of psychoneuroses by the general practitioner. *New York State J. Med.*, **46**, 2164–2166. *5*

Devadasan, K. (1963) Personality dimensions: a critical study. Unpublished Ph.D. thesis, Univ. of Kerala. *27*

Dews, P. B. (1956) Modification by drugs of performance on simple schedules of positive reinforcement. *Ann. N.Y. Acad. Sci.*, **65**, 268–281. *223*

Diamond, S., Balvin, R. S. and Diamond, F. R. (1963) *Inhibition and choice*. New York: Harper and Row. *34*

Dittes, J. (1957) Extinction during psychotherapy of GSR accompanying "embarrassing" statements. *J. abn. soc. Psychol.*, **54**, 187–191. *90*

Dodge, R. (1931) *Human variability.* New Haven: Yale Univ. Press. *33*

Dollard, J. and Miller, N. E. (1950) *Personality and Psychotherapy.* New York: McGraw Hill. *102*

Drew, G. C., Colquhoun, W. P. and Long, H. A. (1959) *Effect of small doses of alcohol on a skill resembling driving.* M.R.C. Memorandum No. 38, London: H.M. Stationery Office. *51*

Dunlap, K. (1932) *Habits, their Making and Unmaking.* New York: Liveright. *116, 118*

Edlin, J. V. *et al.* (1945) Conditioned aversion treatment in chronic alcoholism. *Amer. J. Psychiat.*, **101**, 806–809. *163*

Edmondson, B. and Amsel, A. (1954) The effects of massing and distribution of extinction trials. *J. comp. physiol. Psychol.*, **47**, 117–123. *124*

Efron, R. (1957) The conditioned inhibition of uncinate fits. *Brain*, **80**, 251–262. *115, 116*

Eisenberg, L. (1958) School phobia. *Amer. J. Psychiat.*, **114**, 712–718. *213, 217, 218*

Eisenberg, L., Lackman, R. Molling, P. A., Lockner, A., Mirelle, J. D. and Conners, C. K. (1963) A psychopharmacologic experiment in a training school for delinquent boys: methods, problems, findings. *Amer. J. Orthopsychiat.*, **33**, 431–447. *54*

Ellis, N. (1962) Amount of reward and operant behaviour in mental defectives. *Amer. J. ment. Def.*, **66**, 595–599. *223*

Eriksen, C. W. (1954) Psychological defences and "ego-strength" in the recall of completed and incompleted tasks. *J. abnorm. soc. Psychol.*, **49**, 45–50. *42*

Erwin, W. J. (1963) Confinement in the production of human neuroses; The Barber's Chair Syndrome. *Behav. Res. Ther.*, **1**, 175–184. *86, 232*

Eysenck, H. J. (1947) *Dimensions of Personality.* London. Routledge, Kegan Paul. *18, 21, 42*

Eysenck, H. J. (1950) Criterion analysis—an application of the hypothetico—deductive method to factor analysis. *Psychol. Rev.*, **57**, 38–53. *17*

Eysenck, H. J. (1952a) *The Scientific Study of Personality.* London: Routledge, Kegan Paul. *18*

Eysenck, H. J. (1952b) The effects of psychotherapy. *J. Cons. Psychol.* **16.** 319–324. *268*

Eysenck, H. J. (1954) *The Psychology of Politics.* London: Routledge, Kegan Paul. New York: Praeger. *42, 43*

Eysenck, H. J. (1955a) Psychiatric diagnosis as a psychological and statistical problem. *Psychol. Rep.*, **1**, 3–17. *26, 27*

Eysenck, H. J. (1955b) Cortical inhibition, figural after-effect and the theory of personality. *J. abnorm. soc. Psychol.*, **51**, 94–106. *42*

Eysenck, H. J. (1956) The inheritance of extraversion-introversion. *Acta psychol.*, **12**, 95–110. *30, 42*

Eysenck, H. J. (1957) *The dynamics of anxiety and hysteria.* London: Routledge, Kegan Paul. *33, 35, 37, 42, 49, 50, 82, 124, 228, 263*

Eysenck, H. J. (1959a) Learning theory and behaviour therapy. *J. ment. Sci.* **105**, 61–75. *11*

Eysenck, H. J. (1959b) Personality and verbal conditioning. *Psychol. Reports*, **5**, 520. *42*

Eysenck, H. J. (1959c) Personality and the estimation of time. *Percept. Mot. Skills*, **9**, 405–406. *42*

Eysenck, H. J. (1959d) *The Maudsley Personality Inventory.* London: University of London Press. San Diego: 1962. Educ. & Indust. Testing Service. *20*

Eysenck, H. J. (1959e) Personality and problem-solving. *Psychol. Reps.*, **5**, 92, *43*

Eysenck, H. J. (Ed.) (1960a) *Handbook of abnormal psychology*. London: Pitman·
New York: Basic Books. *2, 5, 25, 82, 85, 86, 105, 173, 236, 268, 277*

Eysenck, H. J. (Ed.) (1960b) *Behaviour Therapy and the Neuroses*. Oxford: Pergamon
Press. *4, 94, 96, 97, 98, 108, 110, 118, 119, 138, 148, 153, 169, 262, 272, 278*

Eysenck, H. J. (1960c) *The structure of human personality*. New York: Macmillan.
London: Methuen. *17, 18, 19, 20, 22, 23, 32*

Eysenck, H. J. (Ed.) (1960d). *Experiments in personality*. London: Routledge, Kegan
Paul. New York: Praeger, *35*

Eysenck, H. J. (1960e) Levels of personality, constitutional factors and social
influences: an experimental approach. *Internat. J. soc. Psychiat.*, **6**, 12–24. *41, 82*

Eysenck, H. J. (1960f) Classification and the problem of diagnosis. In: Eysenck,
H. J. (Ed.) *Handbook of Abnormal Psychology. 25*

Eysenck, H. J. (1960g) The effects of psychotherapy. In: *Handbook of Abnormal
Psychology* (Ed. Eysenck, H. J.), London: Pitman. *5*

Eysenck, H. J. (1960h) Symposium: The development of moral values in children.
vii. The contribution of learning theory. *Brit. J. educ. Psychol.*, **30**, 11–21. *7*

Eysenck, H. J. (1960i) Reminiscence as a function of rest, practice and personality.
Percept. Mot. Skills, **11**, 91—94. *106*

Eysenck, H. J. (1962a) Conditioning and personality. *Brit. J. Psychol.*, **53**, 299–305.
36

Eysenck, H. J. (1962b) Reminiscence, drive and personality—revision and extension of a theory. *Brit. J. soc. clin. Psychol.*, **1**, 127–140. *42*

Eysenck, H. J. (Ed.) (1963a) *Experiments with Drugs*. Oxford: Pergamon Press.
35, 47, 48, 49, 50, 51, 199

Eysenck, H. J. (1963b) Biological basis of personality. *Nature*, **199**, 1031–1034.
16, 46

Eysenck, H. J. (1963c) Behaviour therapy, extinction and relapse in neurosis.
Brit. J. Psychiat., **109**, 12–18. *199, 272, 281, 282, 287*

Eysenck, H. J. (1963d) Funktion und Anwendung der Statistik in der Psychiatrie
in, *Psychiatrie der Gegenwart*. Band. Zeil 2, 249–273. Berlin: Springer. *23*

Eysenck, H. J. (1963e) Behaviour therapy, spontaneous remission and transference
in neurotics. *American J. Psychiat.*, **119**, 867–871. *271*

Eysenck, H. J. (1964a) *Experiments in Behaviour Therapy*. Oxford: Pergamon Press.
4

Eysenck, H. J. (1964b) *Crime and personality*. London: Routledge, Kegan Paul.
Boston: Houghton Mifflin. *7, 21, 31, 266*

Eysenck, H. J. (1964c) *Experiments in motivation*. London: Pergamon Press. New
York: Macmillan. *56, 57*

Eysenck, H. J. and Aiba, S. (1957) Drugs and Personality. V. The effects of stimulant
and depressant drugs on the suppression of the primary visual stimulus. *J. ment.
Sci.*, **103**, 661–665. *50*

Eysenck, H. J., Casey, S. and Trouton, D. S. (1957) Drugs and Personality. II. The
effect of stimulant and depressant drugs on continuous work. *J. ment. Sci.*,
103, 645–649. *51*

Eysenck, H. J. and Claridge, G. (1962) The position of hysterics and dysthymics
in a two-dimensional framework of personality description. *J. abnorm. soc.
Psychol.*, **69**, 46–55. *23, 24*

Eysenck, H. J. and Easterbrook, J. A. (1960a) Drugs and Personality. VI. The
effects of stimulant and depressant drugs upon body sway (static ataxia). *J.
ment. Sci.*, **106**, 831–834. *51*

Eysenck, H. J. and Easterbrook, J. A. (1960b) Drugs and Personality. VII. The
effects of stimulant and depressant drugs upon pupillary reactions. *J. ment. Sci.*,
106, 835–841. *50*

Eysenck, H. J. and Easterbrook, J. A. (1960c) Drugs and Personality. VIII. The effects of stimulant and depressant drugs on visual after-effects of a rotating spiral. *J. ment. Sci.*, **106**, 842–844. *50*

Eysenck, H. J. and Easterbrook, J. A. (1960d) Drugs and Personality. X. The effects of stimulant and depressant drugs upon kinaesthetic figural after-effects. *J. ment. Sci.*, **106**, 852–854. *50*

Eysenck, H. J. and Eysenck, S. B. G. (1963) *The Eysenck Personality Inventory.* San Diego. Educ. & Indust. Testing Service 1963. London: University of London Press. *21*

Eysenck, H. J., Holland, H. C. and Trouton, D. S. (1957) Drugs and Personality. III. The effects of stimulant and depressant drugs on visual after-effects. *J. ment. Sci.*, **103**, 650–655. *50*

Eysenck, H. J., Holland, H. C. and Trouton, D. S. (1957) Drugs and Personality. IV. The effects of stimulant and depressant drugs on the rate of fluctuation of a reversible perspective figure. *J. ment. Sci.*, **103**, 656–660. *50*

Eysenck, H. J. and Prell, D. (1951) The inheritance of neuroticism: an experimental study. *J. ment. Sci.*, **97**, 441–465. *30*

Eysenck, H. J., Tarrant, M. and England, L. (1960) Smoking and personality. *Brit. Med. J.*, **1**, 1456–1460. *43*

Eysenck, S. B. G. (1956) Neurosis and psychosis; an experimental analysis. *J. ment. Sci.*, **102**, 517–529. *27*

Eysenck, S. B. G., Eysenck, H. J. and Claridge, G. (1960) Dimensions of personality, psychiatric syndromes and mathematical models. *J. ment. Sci.*, **106**, 581–589. *18, 23, 43*

Farber, I. E. (1948) Response fixation under anxiety and non-anxiety conditions. *J. ex. Psychol.*, **38**, 111–131. *129, 211*

Farber, I. E., Spence, K. W. and Bechtoldt, N. P. (1957) Emotionality, introversion-extraversion and conditioning. Paper presented at the Midwestern Psychol. Assn. Chicago. *37*

Felsinger, J. N., Lasagna, L. and Beecher, H. K. (1953) The persistence of mental impairment following a hypnotic dose of a barbiturate. *J. Pharmacol. Ther.*, **109**, 284–291. *50*

Ferster, C. B. (1958) Reinforcement and punishment in the control of human behaviour by social agencies. *Psychiat. Res. Rep.*, **10**, 101–118. *173, 232, 233, 257*

Ferster, C. B. (1961) Positive reinforcement and behavioral deficits of autistic children. *Child Developm.*, **32**, 437–456. *193, 225*

Ferster, C. B. and de Meyer, M. (1961) The development of performances in autistic children in an automatically controlled environment. *J. chronic Dis.*, **13**, 312–345. *224, 225, 230, 235, 237, 241*

Ferster, C. B. and de Meyer, M. (1962) A method for the experimental analysis of the behaviour of autistic children. *Amer. J. Orthopsychiat.*, **32**, 89–98. *224*

Field, J. G. and Brengelmann, J. C. (1961) Eyelid conditioning and three personality parameters. *J. abnorm. soc. Psychol.*, **63**, 517–523. *37*

Flanagan, B., Goldiamond, I. and Azrin, N. (1958) Operant stuttering—the control of stuttering behaviour through response—contingent consequences. *J. exp. anal. Behav.*, **1**, 173–177. *224*

Fonberg, E. (1956) On the manifestation of conditioned defensive reactions in stress. *Bull. Soc. Sci. Lettr. Lodz.*, **7**, 1. *125*

Forster, F. and Chun, R. (1964) Conditioned reflex factors in epilepsy. Proc. First Int. Cong. Soc. Psychiat. London. *116*

Forster, F. *et ali.* (1964) The modification by extinction techniques of stroboscopic—induced seizure discharges. Trans. Amer. Neuro. Assoc. (in press). *116*

Fort, J. G. (1961) Secondary reinforcement with pre-school children. *Child Develpm.* **32**, 755–764. *234*

Foulds, G. A. (1953) A method of scoring the T.A.T. applied to psychoneurotics. *J. ment. Sci.*, **99**, 235–246. *42*

Foulds, G. A. (1956) The ratio of general intellectual ability to vocabulary among psychoneurotics. *Int. J. Soc. Psychiat.*, **1**, 5–12. *42*

Foulds, G. A. (1959) The relative stability of personality measures compared with diagnostic measure. *J. ment. Sci.*, **105**, 783–787. *43*

Franks, C. M. (1956) Conditioning and personality; a study of normal and neurotic subjects. *J. abnorm. soc. Psychol.*, **52**, 143–150. *36, 38, 42*

Franks, C. M. (1957) Personality factors and the rate of conditioning. *Brit. J. Psychol.*, **48**, 119–126. *36, 42*

Franks, C. M. (1958) Alcohol, alcoholism and conditioning. *J. Ment. Sci.*, **104**, 14–33. Reprinted in 1960 in Eysenck's (Ed.) *Behaviour Therapy and the Neuroses*. Oxford: Pergamon Press. *160, 163*

Franks, C. M. (1963) Behaviour therapy, the principles of conditioning and the treatment of the alcoholic. *Quart. J. Stud. Alcohol.*, **24**, 511–529. *160*

Franks, C. M. and Laverty, S. G. (1955) Sodium amytal and eyelid conditioning. *J. Ment. Sci.*, **101**, 654–663. *50*

Franks, C. M. and Leigh, D. (1959) A theoretical and experimental application of a conditioning model to a consideration of bronchial asthma in man. *J. psychosom. Res.*, **4**, 88–98. *37*

Franks, C. M. and Trouton, D. S. (1958) Effects of amobarbital sodium and dexamphetamine sulfate on the conditioning of the eyeblink response. *J. comp. physiol. Psychol.*, **51**, 220–222. *50, 52*

Freeman, H. and Kendrick, D. (1960) A case of cat phobia. *Brit. Med. J.*, **2**, 497–502. *278*

Freund, K. (1960) Problems in the treatment of homosexuality, in *Behaviour Therapy and the Neuroses*. (Ed. Eysenck, H. J.) Oxford: Pergamon Press. *147, 148, 286*

Gantt, W. H. (1944) Experimental Basis for Neurotic Behaviour. *Psychomat. Med. Monogr.*, **3**, *82, 211*

Gantt, W. H. (1949) Psychosexuality in animals. *Psychosexual Development in Health and Disease*. New York: Grune & Stratton. *141, 142, 157*

Gantt, W. H., Newton, J. and Royer, F. (1962) Development of experimental neurosis. *Proc. III World Congress Psychiat.*, Montreal. *82*

Gellhorn, E. (1953) *The Physiological Foundations of Neurology and Psychiatry*. Mineapolis: U. Minnesota Press. *92*

Geppert, T. (1953) Management of nocturnal enuresis by the electric alarm. *J. Amer. Med. Ass.*, **52**, 381–383. *196, 198*

Gewirtz, J. (1956) A program of research on the dimensions and antecedents of emotional dependence. *Child Develpm.*, **27**, 205–222 *233*

Gewirtz, J. L. and Baer, D. M. (1958a) The effect of brief social deprivation on behaviour for a social reinforcer. *J. abn. Soc. Psychol.*, **56**, 49–56 *233*

Gewirtz, J. L. and Baer, D. M. (1958b) Deprivation and satiation of social reinforcers as drive conditions. *J. abn. Soc. Psychol.*, **57**, 165–172. *233*

Gewirtz, J., Baer, D. and Roth, C. (1958) A note on the similar effects of low social availability of an adult and brief social deprivation on young children's behaviour. *Child Develpm.*, **29**, 149–152. *233*

Gillison, T. and Skinner, J. (1958) Treatment of nocturnal enuresis by the electric alarm. *Brit. Med. J.*, **2**, 1268–1272. *196, 198*

Glover, E. (1955) *The Technique of Psychoanalysis*. London: Balliere *269*

Glynn, J D. and Harper, P. (1961) Behaviour therapy in transvestism. *Lancet*, **1**, 619. *152*

Gottesman, I. I. (1963) Heritability of personality: a demonstration. *Psychol. Monogr.* No. 572. *30*

Gray, J. (1964) *Pavlov's typology: recent theoretical and experimental developments from the laboratory of B. M. Teplov*. Oxford: Pergamon Press. *45*

Grinker, R. R. and Spiegel, J. P. (1945). *Men under stress*. London: Churchill. *63, 66, 90, 103*

Gwinn, G. T. (1949) The effects of punishment on acts motivated by fear. *J. exp. Psychol.*, **39**, 260–269. *169*

Hagman, C. (1932) A study of fears of children in pre-school age. *J. exp. Psychol.*, **1**, 110–130. *204, 206, 211*

Halberstam, J. L. (1961) Some personality correlates of conditioning, generalization and extinction. *Psychosom. Med.*, **23**, 67–76. *38*

Hamilton, V. (1962) Personal communication. *180*

Haslerud, G., Bradbard, L. and Johnstone, R. (1954) Pure guidance and handling as components of the Maier technique for breaking fixations. *J. Psychol.*, **37**, 27–30. *129, 130, 138, 258*

Hastings, D. W. (1958) Follow-up results in psychiatric illness. *Amer. J. Psychiat.*, **114**, 1057–1066. *177*

Hebb, D. O. (1955) Drive and the C.N.S. (conceptual nervous system). *Psychol. Rev.*, **62**, 243–254. *56*

Hersov, L. (1960a) Persistent non-attendance at school. *J. Child Psychol. and Psychiat.*, **1**, 130–136. *213, 216, 217*

Hersov, L. (1960b) Refusal to go to school. *J. Child Psychol. Psychiat.*, **1**, 137–142. *213, 216, 217*

Hilgard, E. R. (1958) *Theories of Learning*. New York: Appleton-Century-Crofts. *287*

Hilgard, E. R., Jones, L. V. and Kaplan, S. J. (1951) Conditional discriminations as related to anxiety. *J. exper. Psychol.*, **42**, 94–99. *39*

Hilgard, E. and Marquis, D. (1940, 1961) *Conditioning and Learning*. Revised edition by G. A. Kimble. London: Methuen. *93, 95*

Hill, D. (1947) Amphetamine in psychopathic states. *Brit. J. Addiction*, **44**, 50–54. *55*

Himmelweit, H. T. (1945) The intelligence-vocabulary ratio as a measure of temperament. *J. Person.*, **14**, 93–105. *42*

Himmelweit, H. T. (1946) Speed and accuracy of work as related to temperament. *Brit. J. Psychol.*, **36**, 132–144. *42*

Himmelweit, H. T. (1947) A comparative study of the level of aspiration of normal and neurotic persons. *Brit. J. Psychol.*, **37**, 41–59. *42*

Holland, H. C. (1960a) Drugs and Personality: XII. A comparison of several drugs by the flicker fusion method. *J. ment. Sci.*, **106**, 858–861. *51*

Holland, H. C. (1960b) The effects of sodium amylobarbitone and dexamphetamine sulphate on the peripheral visual field. *J. ment. Sci.*, **106**, 1438–1442. *51*

Holland, J. G. (1957) Technique for behavioural analysis of human observing. *Science*, **125**, 348–350. *223*

Holmes, F. (1935) An experimental study of fear of young children. In: Jersild, A. and Holmes, F. *Children's Fear*. Child Developm. Monogr. No. 20. *203, 204, 207*

Hovland, C. and Sears, R. R. (1938) Experiments on motor conflict. *J. ex. Psychol.*, **23**, 477–493. *64*

Hull, C. L. (1943) *Principles of Behaviour*. New York: Appleton, Century, Crofts. *33, 281, 285*

Humphery, J. and Rachman, S. (1963) Case data. *137*

Hussain, A. (1963) The results of behaviour therapy in 105 cases. (To be published). *246, 262, 265*

Ingham, J. G. (1959) Variations in cross-masking with frequency. *J. exp. Psychol.*, **58**, 199–205. *35*

Isaacs, W., Thomas, J. and Goldiamond, I. (1960) Application of operant conditioning to reinstate verbal behaviour in psychotics. *J. Speech Hearing Dis.*, **25**,
842. *182, 230, 238*

Ivanov-Smolensky, A. G. (1927) Methods of examining the conditioned reflexes
in children and in mental disorders. *Brain*, **50**, 138–141. *241*

Jacobson, E. (1938) *Progressive Relaxation.* Chicago: Chicago U. Press. *67*

Jacubczak, L. and Walters, R. H. (1959) Suggestibility as dependency behaviour.
J. abn. Soc. Psychol., **59**, 102–107. *233*

James, B. (1962) Case of homosexuality treated by aversion therapy. *Brit. Med. J.*,
1, 768–770. *148*

Jaspers, K. (1962) *General Psychopathology.* Trans. J. Hoenig and M. Hamilton.
Manchester: Manchester Univ. Press. *158*

Jenkins, W. O. and Stanley, J. C. (1950) Partial reinforcement. A review and
critique. *Psychol. Bull.*, **47**, 193–234. *234*

Jersild, A. T. (1950) *Child Psychology.* New York: Prentice Hall. *200, 206, 207, 211*

Jersild, A. T., Goldman, B. and Loftus, J. (1941) A comparative study of the
worries of children. *J. exper. educ.*, **9**, 323–326. *215*

Jersild, A. and Holmes, F. B. (1935) Children's Fears. *J. Psychol.*, **1**, 75. *200*

Jersild, A. T. and Holmes, F. (1935a) *Children's Fears.* Child Develpm. Monogr.
No. 20. *200, 201, 212*

John, E. (1941) A study of the effects of evacuation and air-raids on pre-school
children. *Br. J. Educ. Psychol.*, **11**, 173–179. *204, 211*

Jones, H. E. (1930) The galvanic skin reflex in infancy. *Child Develpm.*, **1**, 106–110.
83

Jones, H. G. (1956) The application of conditioning and learning techniques to
the treatment of a psychiatric patient. *J. abn. soc. psychol.*, **52**, 414–420. *119*

Jones, H. G. (1960a) The behavioural treatment of enuresis nocturna in *Behaviour Therapy and the Neuroses* (Ed. Eysenck, H.J.). Oxford: Pergamon Press.
196, 197, 198, 262, 286

Jones, H. G. (1960b) Learning and Abnormal Behaviour. In: *Handbook of Abnormal
Psychology.* (Ed. Eysenck, H. J.) London: Pitman. *193.*

Jones, M. C. (1924) A laboratory study of fear: The case of Peter. *Pedagog. Sem.*,
31, 308–315. *67, 192, 194, 208, 209, 211*

Jones, M. C. (1925) A study of the emotions of pre-school children. *School and Soc.*
21, 755–780. *192, 204, 207, 211*

Kamin, L. J. (1957) The gradient of delay of secondary reward in avoidance
learning. *J. comp. physiol. psychol.*, **50**, 450–456. *165*

Kamin, L. J. (1959) The delay of punishment gradient. *J. comp. physiol. Psychol.*,
52, 434–437. *166, 167*

Kanner, L. (1960) *Child Psychiatry.* Oxford: Blackwell. *213, 290*

Kassebaum, G. G., Couch, A. S., and Slater, P. E. (1959) The factorial dimensions
of the M.M.P.I. *J. Consult. Psychol.*, **23**, 226–236. *18*

Keehn, J. P. (1956) Unrealistic reporting as a function of extraverted neurosis.
J. clin. Psychol., **12**, 61–63. *43*

Kennedy, T. (1964) Treatment of chronic schizophrenia by behaviour therapy;
Case Reports. *Behav. Res. Th..*. (in press). *184*

Kerenyi, A. B. (1959) Sedation threshold, conditioning, introversion, extraversion
and manifest anxiety. Univ. of McGill, unpublished Diploma thesis. *37.*

Kimble, G. (1961) *Conditioning and Learning.* Revised ed. Hilgard and Marquis.
London: Methuen *63, 82, 124, 154*

Kimble, G. A. and Kendall, J. W. (1953) A comparison of two methods of producing experimental extinction. *J. ex. Psychol.*, **45**, 87–90. *208*

King, G. F. (1956) Withdrawal as a dimension of schizophrenia; an exploratory
study. *J. Clin. Psychol.*, **12**, 373–375. *224, 236*

King, G. F., Armitage, S. and Tilton, J. (1960) A therapeutic approach to schizophrenics of extreme pathology. *J. abn. soc. Psychol.*, **61**, 276–286. *178, 181, 223, 224, 236, 262*

King, G. F., Merrell, D., Lovinger, E. and Denny, M. (1957) Operant motor behaviour in acute schizophrenics. *J. Pers.*, **25**, 317–326. *224*

King, M. S., Kimble, G. A., Gorman, J. and King, R. A. (1961) Replications report: two failures to reproduce effects of anxiety on eyelid conditioning. *J. exper. Psychol.*, **62**, 532–533. *39*

Klee, J. B. (1944) The relation of frustration and motivation to the production of abnormal fixations in the rat. *Psychol. Monogr.* **56**, (4. No. 257). *165, 168*

Klein, E. (1945) The reluctance to go to school. *Psychoanalytic Study Child*, **1**, 263–292. *213*

Knight, R. P. (1941) Evaluation of the results of psychoanalytic therapy. *Amer. J. Psychiat.*, **98**, 434–444. *76, 243*

Knopfelmacher, F. (1952) Some effects of reward on the strength of position stereotypes. *Quart. J. exp. Psychol.*, **4**, 7–86. *130*

Knopfelmacher, F. (1953) Fixations, position stereotypes and their relation to stress. *Quart. J. exp. Psychol.*, **5**, 108–127. *130, 131*

Krasner, L. (1958) Studies of the conditioning of verbal behaviour. *Psychol. Bull.*, **55**, 148–170. *223*

Krasnagorski, N. I. (1933) Conditioned reflexes in psychopathology of childhood. *Amer. J. Dis. Child.*, **45**, 355–370. *241*

Kurtz, K. and Walters, G. (1962) The effects of prior experiences of an approach-avoidance conflict. *J. Comp. physiol. psychol.*, **55**, 1075–1078. *83*

Lacey, J. I. (1950) Individual differences in neurotic response patterns. *J. comp. physiol. Psychol.*, **43**, 338–350. *32*

Lacey, J. I. and Lacey, B. C. (1958) Verification and extension of the principle of autonomic response specificity. *Amer. J. Psychol.*, **71**, 50–73. *32*

Lacey, J. I. and van Lehn, R. (1952) Differential emphasis on somatic response to stress. *Psychosom. Med.*, **14**, 71–81. *32*

Lake, M. and Levinger, G. (1960) Continuance beyond application interviews in a child guidance clinic. *Soc. Casewk.*, **91**, 303–309. *273*

Landreth, C. (1958) *The Psychology of Early Childhood.* New York: Knopf. *210*

Lang, P. J. and Lazovik, A. D. (1963) The experimental desensitization of a phobia. *J. abn. soc. Psychol.*, **66**, 519–525. *249, 250, 252*

Lapouse, R. and Monk, M. (1959) Fears and worries in a representative sample of children. *Amer. J. Orthopsychiat.*, **29**, 803–818. *203, 214*

Lashley, K. S. (1930) The mechanism of vision. *J. genet. Psychol.*, **37**, 453–460. *128*

Lauber, M. V. and Denhoff, E. (1957) Hyperkinetic behaviour syndrome in children. *J. Pediat.*, **50**, 463

Lauber, M. V., Denhoff, E. and Rubini, E. Z. (1957) Photometrazol activation in children. *E.E.G. Clin. Neurophysiol.*, **6**, 1–8. *55*

La Verne, A. (1953) Rapid coma technique of carbon dioxide inhalation therapy. *Dis. Nerv. Syst.*, **14**, 141–152. *92*

Lawson, R. (1960) *Learning and Behavior.* New York: Macmillan. *239*

Lazarus, A. (1960) The elimination of children's phobias by deconditioning, in *Behaviour Therapy and the Neuroses* (Ed. Eysenck, H. J.). Oxford: Pergamon Press. *210*

Lazarus, A. (1961) Group therapy of phobic disorders. *J. abn. soc. Psychol.*, **63**, 504–512. *208, 250, 255*

Lazarus, A. (1963) The results of behaviour therapy in 126 cases of severe neurosis. *Behav. Res. Ther.*, **1**, 65–78. *92, 101, 245, 249, 262, 264*

Lazarus, A. (1963b) The treatment of chronic frigidity by systematic desensitization. *J. Nerv. Ment. Dis.*, **136**, 272–278. *145*

Lazarus, A. A. (1964) Crucial procedural factors in desensitization therapy. *Behav. Res. Ther.* (in press). *78, 256*

Lazarus, A. and Abramovitz, A. (1962) The use of "emotive imagery" in the treatment of children's phobias. *J. Ment. Sci.,* **108,** 191–195. *210*

Lazarus, A. and Rachman, S. (1960) The use of systematic desensitization psychotherapy, in *Behaviour Therapy and the Neuroses* (Ed. Eysenck, H. J.). Oxford: Pergamon Press. *87, 140*

Lazowik, A. and Lang, P. (1960) A laboratory demonstration of systematic desensitization. *J. Psychol. Stud.,* **11,** 238–247. *208, 249, 250*

Lehner, G. F. J. (1960) Negative practice as a psychotherapeutic technique. Reprinted in Eysenck's (Ed.) *Behaviour Therapy and the Neuroses.* Oxford: Pergamon Press. *118, 119*

Lemere, F. and Voegtlin, W. (1950) An evaluation of the aversion treatment of alcoholism. *Quart. J. Stud. Alcoh.,* **11,** 199–204, *161, 162*

Lesser, G. and Abelson, R. (1959) Personality correlates of persuasibility in children. In *Personality and persuasibility.* (Ed. Janis, I. L. and Holland, C. I.). New Haven: Yale Univ. Press. *233*

Levitt, E. E. (1957) The results of psychotherapy with children. *J. Consult. Psychol.,* **21,** 189–195. *270, 273*

Levitt, E. E. (1963) Psychotherapy with children: A further evaluation. *Behav. Res. Ther.,* **1,** 45–51. *216, 270, 271, 277*

Lewis, D. J. (1960) Partial reinforcement: A selective review. *Psychol. Bull.,* **57,** 1–28. *234*

Lichtenstein, P. E. (1950) The production of a feeding inhibition in dogs. *J. comp physiol. Psychol.,* **43,** 16–29. *165, 211*

Liddell, H. (1944) Conditioned reflex method and experimental neurosis, in *Personality and the Behaviour Disorders.* (Ed. J. McV. Hunt.) New York: Ronald Press. *63, 82, 85*

Lienert A. and Reisse, H. (1961) Ein korrelationanalytischer Beitrag zur genetischen determination des Neurotizismus. *Psychol. Beitr.,* **7,** 121–130. *30*

Lindsley, D. B. and Henry, C. E. (1942) The effects of drugs on behaviour and the electro-encephalograms of children with behaviour disorders. *Psychosom. Med,* **4,** 140–149. *52*

Lindsley, O. R. (1956) Operant conditioning methods applied to research in chronic schizophrenia. *Psychiat. Res. Repts.,* **5,** 118–139. *178, 179, 193, 223, 241*

Lindsley, O. R. (1960) Characteristics of the behaviour of chronic psychotics as revealed by free-operant conditioning methods. *Dis. Nerv. System.,* **21,** 66–78. *178, 179, 180, 193, 223, 227, 229*

Lindsley, O. R. (1961a) Free-operant conditioning, persuasion and psychotherapy. Paper read at A.P.A. Meeting, Chicago. *178, 223*

Lindsley, O. R. (1961b) Direct measurement and functional definition of vocal hallucinatory symptoms in chronic psychosis. Paper read at 3rd World Congress of Psychiatry, Montreal. *178, 223*

Lindsley, O. R. (1962a) Operant conditioning methods in diagnosis, in *The First Hohnemann Symposium on Psychosomatic Medicine.* New York: Lea & Febiger. *223*

Lindsley, O. R. (1962b) Operant conditioning techniques in the measurement of psychopharmacologic response, in *The First Hohnemann Symposium.* New York: Lea & Febiger. *223*

Lindsley, O. R. (1963) Experimental analysis of social reinforcement. *Amer. J. Orthopsychiat.,* **33,** 624–633. *223*

Lippmann, R. (1957) Quoted by Waldfogel *et al.* (1957) *216, 218*

Liversedge, L. and Sylvester, J. (1955) Conditioning techniques in the treatment of writers' cramp. *Lancet*, pp. 1147–1149. Reprinted in Eysenck's (Ed.). *Behaviour Therapy and the Neuroses. 108*

Long, E. R. (1959) The use of operant conditioning techniques in children, in *Child Research in Psychopharmacology*. (Ed. Fisher, S.). Thomas: Springfield. *235*

Long, E. R. (1962) Additional techniques for producing multiple-schedule control in children. *J. exp. Anal. Behav.*, **5**, 443–455. *235*

Long, E. R., Hammack, J. T., May, F. and Campbell, B. J. (1958) Intermittent reinforcement of operant behaviour in children. *J. exp. anal. Behav.*, **1**, 315–339. *234*

Lovaas, O. I. (1960) The control of operant responding by rate and content of verbal operants: Preliminary report. Unpublished paper. *236*

Lovaas, O. I. (1961a) Interaction between verbal and non-verbal behaviour. *Child Develpm.*, **32**, 329–336. *193, 236*

Lovaas, O. I. (1961b) The control of food-intake in three children by reinforcement of relevant verbal behaviour. Unpublished paper. *193, 233, 236*

Lovibond, S. H. (1961). *Conditioning and Enuresis*. Ph.D. thesis, Univ. Adelaide. *197, 234, 285*

Lovibond, S. (1963) The mechanism of conditioning treatment of enuresis. *Behav. Res. Ther*, **1**, 1–8. *197, 198, 262*

Lovibond, S. H. (1963b) Intermittent reinforcement in behaviour therapy. *Behav. Res. Ther.*, **1**, 127–132. *197, 198, 235*

Lovibond, S. N. (1964) Personal communication. *197*

Luria, A. R. (1932) *The Nature of Human Conflict*. New York: Liveright. *113*

Lykken, D. T. (1957) A study of anxiety in the sociopathic personality. *J. abnorm. soc. Psychol.*, **55**, 6–10. *38*

Macfarlane, J. W., Allen, L. and Honzik, M. (1954) *A developmental study of the behaviour problems of normal children*. Berkeley: U. Calif. Press. *201, 202, 203, 273, 274, 275, 276*

Mackworth, H. (1948) *Research in the Measurement of Human Performance*. M.R.C. Special Report No. 268. London: H.M.S.O. *50*

Maier, N. R. F. (1949) *Frustration*. New York: McGraw-Hill. *126*

Maier, N. (1956) Frustration theory: restatement and extension. *Psychol. Rev.*, **63**, 370–388. *129*

Maier, N. and Ellen, P. (1955) The effect of three reinforcement patterns on positional stereotypes. *Amer. J. Psychol.*, **68**, 83–95. *130*

Maier, N. and Klee, J. (1943) Studies of abnormal behaviour in the rat. *J. exp. Psychol.*, **33**, 377–398. *127*

Maier, N. and Klee, J. (1945) Studies of abnormal behaviour in the rat XVII. *J. Psychol.*, **19**, 133–163. *127*

Malan, D. H. (1963) *A Study of Brief Psychotherapy*. London: Tavistock Publications. *269*

Malmo, R. B. (1959) Activation: a neurophysiological dimension. *Psychol. Rev.*, **66**, 367–386. *55*

Malmo, R. B., Davis, J. F. and Barza, S. (1960) Total hysterical deafness: an experimental case study. Reprinted in *Behaviour Therapy and the Neuroses* (Ed. Eysenck, H. J.). Oxford: Pergamon Press. *96*

Malmo, R. B., Shagass, C. and Davis, F. N. (1950) Symptom specificity and bodily reactions during psychiatric interview. *Psychosom. Med.*, **12**, 362–376. *32*

Martin, B. (1963) Reward and punishment associated with the same goal response. *Psychol. Bull.*, **60**, 441–451. *126, 170, 173*

Martin, I. (1960a) Somatic reactivity. In H. J. Eysenck (Ed.) *Handbook of abnormal psychology*. London: Pitman. *34*

Martin, I. (1960b) The effects of depressant drugs on palmar skin resistance and adaptation. In Eysenck, H. J. (Ed.) *Experiments in Personality. 38, 51*

Martin, I. (1960c) The effects of depressant drugs on reaction time and "set". In Eysenck, H. J. (Ed.) *Experiments in Personality*. London: Routledge, Kegan Paul. *51*

Masserman, J. H. (1943) *Behaviour and Neuroses*. Chicago: Chicago U. Press. *165, 168, 211, 258*

Max, L. (1935) Breaking a homosexual fixation by the conditioned reflex technique. *Psychol. Bull.*, **32**, 734. *148*

May, R. (1950) *The Meaning of Anxiety*. New York: Ronald Press. *204*

McGuire, R. J. and Vallance, M. (1964) Aversion therapy by electric shock; a simple technique. *Brit. Med. J.*, **1**, 151–152. *149, 151, 163*

Meehl, P. (1954) *Clinical versus Statistical Prediction*. Minneap. Univ. Minnesota Press. *235*

Metzner, R. (1961) Learning theory and the therapy of the neuroses. *Brit. J. Psychol. Monogr. Suppl.* **33**, *62, 82, 83, 84, 85, 102, 124, 211*

Metzner, R. (1963) Some experimental analogues of obsession. *Behav. Res. Ther.*, **1**, 231–236. *125, 134, 153, 158*

Meyer, V. (1957) The treatment of two phobic patients on the basis of learning theory. *J. abn. soc. Psychol.* **55**, 261–265. *262*

Meyer, V. (1963) Unpublished case material. *232*

Meyer, V. and Gelder, M. G. (1963) Behaviour therapy and complex disorders. *Brit. J. Psychiat.*, **109**, 19–28. *257*

Meyer, V. and Mair, J. (1963) A new technique to control stammering: a preliminary report. *Behav. Res. Ther.*, **1**, 251–254. *194, 264*

Miller, D. R. (1951) Responses of psychiatric patients to threat of failure. *J. abnorm. soc. Psychol.*, **46**, 378–387. *42*

Miller, N. E. (1944) Experimental studies of conflict. In: J. McV. Hunt *Personality and the Behaviour Disorders*. New York: Ronald Press. *63, 64, 65*

Miller, N. (1951) Learnable drives and rewards. In: S. S. Stevens (Ed.) *Handbook of Experimental Psychology*. New York: Wiley. *83, 84*

Miller, N. E. (1960) Learning resistance to pain and fear. *J. exp. Psychol.*, **60**, 137–142. *66, 83, 168*

Mitchell, J. V. and Pierce-Jones, J. (1960) A factor analysis of Gough's California Psychological Inventory. *J. consult. Psychol.*, **24**, 453–456. *18*

Morgan, J. and Witmer, F. (1939) The treatment of enuresis by the conditioned-reaction technique. *J. Genet. Psychol.*, **55**, 59–65. *198*

Morgenstern, F., Pearce, J. and Davies, B. (1963) The application of aversion therapy to transvestism. Paper read at Reading Conference of British Psychol. Society. *151, 173*

Morris, H. H., Escoll, P. J. and Wexler, R. (1955) Aggressive behaviour disorders of childhood: a follow-up study. *Amer. J. Psychiat.*, **112**, 991–997. *271*

Morris, D. P., Soroker, E. and Burrus, M. (1954) Follow-up studies of shy, wthdrawn children. I. Evaluation of later adjustment. *Amer. J. Orthopsychiat.*, **24,** 743–754. *272*

Mowrer, O. H. (1939) Stimulus-response theory of anxiety. *Psychol. Rev.*, **46**, 553–565. *84*

Mowrer, O. H. (1950) *Learning theory and personality dynamics*. New York: Ronald Press. *3, 7, 9*

Mowrer, O. H. (1959) *The Crisis in Psychiatry and Religion*. New York: Van Nostrand. *269*

Mowrer, O. H. (1960) *Learning theory and Behaviour*. New York: Wiley. *82, 84*

Mowrer, O. H. and Jones, H. M. (1943) Extinction and behaviour variability as a function of effortfulness of task. *J. exp. Psychol.*, **33,** 369–386. *124*

Mowrer, O. H. and Mowrer, W. (1938) Enuresis: A method for its study treatment. *Amer. J. Orthopsychiat.*, **8**, 436–459. *192, 196, 198, 262*

Mowrer, O. H. and Viek, P. (1948) An experimental analogue of fear. *J. abn. Soc. Psychol.*, **43**, 193–200. *85*

Muenzinger, K. F. (1934) Motivation in learning. *J. comp. Psychol.*, **17**, 267–277. *169*

Murray, E. J. (1962) Paper read at A.P.A. Conv. St. Louis. Quoted by Costello, C. G. (1963). *257*

Neale D. H. (1963) Behaviour therapy and encopresis in children. *Behav. Res. Ther.*, **1**, 139–150. *231*

Nichols, R. C. and Schnell, R. O. (1963) Factor scales for the California Psychological Inventory. *J. consult. Psychol.*, **27**, 228–235. *18*

O'Neal, P. and Robins, L. N. (1958) The relation of childhood behaviour problems to adult psychiatric status. *Amer. J. Psychiat.*, **114**, 961–969. *271*

Orlando, R. and Bijou, S. W. (1961) Single and multiple schedules of reinforcement in developmentally retarded children. *J. exper. anal. Behav.*, **3**, 339–348. *223, 237*

Oswald, I. (1962) Induction of illusory and hallucinatory voices with consideration of behaviour therapy. *J. Ment. Sci.*, **108**, 196–212. *163*

Pasamanick, B. (1951) Anti-convulsant drug therapy of behaviour problem children with abnormal E.E.G. *Arch. Neurol. Psychiat.*, **65**, 752. *55*

Pavlov. I. P. (1927) *Conditional reflexes*. Oxford Univ. Press. *33*

Pavlov, I. P. (1941) *Conditioned Reflexes and Psychiatry*. Trans. by W. H. Gantt. *New York. Internat. Publ.* *103*

Peak, H. *et alia*. (1941) Positive and negative practice in the correction of spelling errors. *J. Psychol.*, **11**, 103–114. *119*

Pearce, J. (1964) Personal communication. *156*

Peterson, D. (1961) Behaviour problems of middle childhood. *J. Consult. Psychol.*, **25**, 205–209.

Petrie, A. (1952) *Personality and the frontal lobes*. London: Routledge, Kegan Paul. *55*

Poindexter, A. (1936) The factor of repetition in learning to type, quoted by Lehner. (1960). *119*

Popper, K. A. (1948) *The logic of scientific discovery*. London: Routledge, Kegan Paul. *40*

Popper, K. R. (1963) *Conjectures and refutations*. London: Routledge, Kegan Paul. *40*

Porter, J. (1939) Experimental extinction as a function of the interval between successive unreinforced elicitations. *J. gen. Psychol.*, **20**, 109–134. *124*

Poser, E. (1958) Kinaesthetic figural after-effects as a measure of cortical excitation and inhibition. *Amer. Psychologist*, **13**, 334–335. *50*

Prugh, D. (1953) A study of the emotional reactions of children and families to hospitalization. *Amer. J. Orthopsychiat.*, **22**, 70–106. *206*

Rachman, S. (1956) Psychological conflict. *Proc. S. A. Psychol. Assn.* (Abstract). *64*

Rachman, S. (1958) Objective psychotherapy: Some theoretical considerations. *S. Afri. Med. J.*, **33**, 19–21. *77, 253*

Rachman, S. (1961) *Psychomotor behaviour and personality*. Thesis, University of London. *107, 114*

Rachman, S. (1961a) Effect of a stimulant drug on extent of motor responses. *Percept. Mot. Skills*, **12**, 186. *50*

Rachman, S. (1961b) Sexual disorders and behaviour therapy. *Amer. J. Psychiat.*, **118**, 235–240. *153, 162*

Rachman, S. (1962) Learning theory and child psychology: therapeutic possibilities. *J. Child. Psychol. Psychiat.*, **3**, 149–163. *226, 262, 289*

Rachman, S. (1963) *Critical essays on psychoanalysis*. Oxford: Pergamon Press. *2, 80, 81*

Rachman, S. (1963b) Inhibition and disinhibition in schizophrenics. *Arch. gen. Psychiat.*, **8**, 91–98. *175*

Rachman, S. (1963c) Introduction to behaviour therapy. *Behav. Res. Ther.*, **1**, 4–15. *262*

Rachman, S. and Costello, C. G. (1961) The aetiology and treatment of children's phobias. A review. *Amer. J. Psychiat.*, **118**, 97–105. *80, 81*

Rafi, A. A. (1962) Learning theory and the treatment of tics. *J. Psychosom. Res.*, **6**, 71–76. *121*

Ray, O. S. (1959) Personality factors in motor learning and reminiscence. *J. abnorm. soc. Psychol.*, **59**, 199–203. *43*

Raymond, M. (1956) Case of fetishism treated by aversion therapy. *Brit. Med. J.*, **2**, 854–856. *148, 149*

Raymond, M. (1964) The treatment of addiction by aversion conditioning with apomorphine. *Behav. Res. Ther.*, **2**, 287–292. *150, 161, 163*

Razran, G. (1961a) The observable unconscious and the inferable conscious in current Soviet psychophysiology. *Psychol. Rev.*, **68**, 81–147. *34*

Razran, G. (1961b) Recent Soviet phyletic comparisons of classical and operant conditioning. *J. Comp. Physiol. Psychol.*, **54**, 357–365. *241*

Rheingold, H. Gewirtz, J. and Ross, J. (1959) Social conditioning of vocalizations in the infant. *J. comp. physiol. Psychol.*, **52**, 68–73. *232*

Robertson, J. B. S. (1958) Operant conditioning of speech and drawing in schizophrenic patients. *Swiss Rev. Psychol.*, **17**, 309–315. *184, 230*

Robertson, J. B. S. (1961) Effects of different rewards in modifying the verbal behaviour of disorganized schizophrenics. *J. Clin. Psychol.*, **17**, 399–402. *184*

Robinson, N. and Robinson, H. (1961) A method for the study of instrumental avoidance conditioning with young children. *J. comp. Physiol. Psychol.*, **51**, 20–23. *241*

Rosenthal, D. (1962) Book Review. *Psychiatry*, **25**, 377–380. *178, 268*

Ross, A. and Lacey, H. (1961) Characteristics of terminators and remainers in child guidance treatment. *J. cons. Psychol.*, **25**, 420–424. *273*

Sainsbury, P. and Gibson, J. J. (1950) Symptoms of anxiety and tension and the accompanying physiological changes in the muscular system. *J. Neurol. Psychiat.*, **17**, 216–224. *32*

Salter, A. (1950) *Conditioned reflex therapy*. New York: Creative Age Press. *87, 143, 157*

Salzinger, K. (1959) Experimental manipulation of verbal behaviour: A review. *J. Gen. Psychol.*, **61**, 65–94. *178, 223*

Salzinger, S., Salzinger, K., Pisoni, S., Eckman, J., Mathewson, P., Deutsch, M. and Zubin, J. (1962) Operant conditioning of continuous speech in young children. *Child Develpm.*, **33**, 683–695. *224, 227, 230, 234, 236*

Salzinger, L. *et al.* (1962b) Verbal behaviour of schizophrenic and normal subjects. Unpublished manuscript. *224, 225*

Sanderson, R. E., Campbell, D. and Laverty, S. G. (1963) Traumatically conditioned responses acquired during respiratory paralysis. *Nature*, **196**, 1235–1236. *63, 82*

Sarason, I. G. (1958) Inter-relationships among individual difference variables, behaviour in psychotherapy, and verbal conditioning. *J. abnorm. soc. Psychol.*, **56**, 339–344. *42*

Sears, R. R. and Cohen, L. H. (1960) Hysterical anaesthesia, analgesia and astereognosis. Reprinted in *Behaviour Therapy and the Neuroses*. (Ed. Eysenck, H. J.). Oxford: Pergamon Press. *93, 94*

Shagass, C. (1956) Sedation threshold: a neurophysiological tool for psychosomatic research. *Psychosom. Med.*, **18**, 410–419. *42*

Shagass, C. and Kerenyi, A. B. (1958) Neurophysiologic studies of personality. *J. nerv. ment. Dis.*, **126,** 141–147. *37*

Shagass, C. and Naiman, J. (1956) The sedation threshold as an objective index of manifest anxiety in psychoneurotics. *J. Psychosom. Res.*, **1,** 49–57. *50*

Shapiro, M. B. (1961) The single case in fundamental clinical psychological research. *Brit. J. Med. Psychol.*, **34,** 255–262. *235*

Sheehan, J. (1951) The modification of stuttering through non-reinforcement. *J. abn. soc. Psychol.*, **46,** 51–63. *194*

Sheehan, J. and Voas, R. B. (1957) Stuttering as conflict. Comparison of therapy techniques involving approach and avoidance. *J. Speech. Hearing Dis.*, **22,** 714–723. *194*

Shields, J. (1962) *Monozygotic twins brought up apart and brought up together.* Oxford: Univ. Press. *30, 31*

Shorvon, H. J. (1945) Use of benzedrine sulphate by psychopaths. The problem of addiction. *Brit. Med. J.*, **2,** 285–286. *55*

Shorvon, H. J. (1947) Benzedrine in psychopathy and behaviour disorders. *Brit. J. Addict.*, **44,** 58–63. *55*

Sidman, M. (1956) Drug Behaviour Interaction, in Dews and Skinner, B. F. (Eds.) *Ann. N.Y. Acad. Sci.*, **65,** 281–295. *239, 240*

Sidman, M. (1962) Operant Techniques, in *Experimental Foundations of Clinical Psychology.* (Ed. Bachrach, A. J.). New York: Basic Books. *241*

Simmons, M. W. and Lipsitt, L. P. (1961) An operant discrimination apparatus for infants. *J. exp. Anal. Behav.*, **4,** 233–235. *241*

Singh, S. D. (1958) Conditioned emotional response in the rat: I: Constitutional and situational determinants. *J. Comp. physiol. Psychol.*, **52,** 574–578. *51*

Singh, S. D. (1961) Conditioned emotional response in the rat: II. Effects of stimulant and depressant drugs. *J. Psychol. Res.*, **5,** 1–11. *51*

Singh, S. D. and Eysenck, H. J. (1960) Conditioned emotional response in the rat: III. Drug antagonism. *J. gen. Psychol.*, **63,** 275–285. *51*

Sinha, S. N., Franks, C. M. and Broadhurst, P. L. (1958) The effect of a stimulant and a depressant drug on a measure of reactive inhibition. *J. exp. Psychol.*, **56,** 349–354. *51*

Skinner, B. F. (1948) "Superstition" in the pigeon. *J. ex. Psychol.*, **38,** 168–172. *134, 135*

Skinner, B. F. (1957) *Verbal Behaviour.* New York: Appleton Century Crofts. *223*

Skinner, B. F. (1959) *Cumulative Record.* New York: Appleton Century. *193, 223*

Skinner, B. F., Solomon, H. C. and Lindsley, O. R. (1954) A new method for the experimental analysis of the behaviour of psychotic patients. *J. Nerv. Ment. Dis.*, **120,** 403–406. *193, 237*

Slater, E. (1939) Responses to a nursery school situation. *Soc. Res. Child Devop. Monogr.*, *4,* **2,** *204, 205*

Solomon, R. L. (1948) Effort and extinction rate: A confirmation. *J. comp. physiol. Psychol.*, **41,** 93–101. *124*

Solomon, R. L. and Wynne, L. (1953) Traumatic avoidance learning. *Psychol. Monogr.*, **67,** 4. *63, 170, 171*

Solomon, R. L. and Wynne, L. (1954) Traumatic avoidance learning: the principles of anxiety conservation and partial irreversibility. *Psychol. Rev.*, **61,** 353–385. *168, 279*

Spearman, C. (1927) *Abilities of Man.* London: Macmillan. *285*

Spence, K. W. (1956) *Behaviour theory and conditioning.* New Haven: Yale Univ. Press. *38*

Spence, K. W. (1964) Anxiety (drive) level and performance in eyelid conditioning. *Psychol. Bull.*, **61**, 129–139. *39*

Spence, K., and Spence, Janet T. (1964) Relation of eyelid conditioning to manifest anxiety, extraversion, and rigidity. *J. abnorm. soc. Psychol.*, **68**, 144–149. *37*

Spiker, C. C. (1960) Research methods in children's learning, in *Handbook of Research Methods in Child Development* (Ed. Mussen, P. H.). New York: Wiley and Sons. *223*

Spradlin, J. E. (1961) Operant conditioning of severely retarded children. Unpublished paper. *193, 223, 225, 237, 238*

Spradlin, J. E. (1962) Effects of reinforcement schedules on extinction in severely mentally retarded children. *Amer. J. Ment. Def.*, **66**, 634–640. *224, 234, 241*

Staats, A. W. and Staats, C. K. (1962) Personal communication. *226*

Staats, A. W. and Staats, C. K. (1962b) A comparison of the development of speech and reading behaviour. *Child Developm.*, **33**, 831–846. *227*

Staats, A. W., Staats, C. K., Heard, W. G. and Finley, J. R. (1962) Operant conditioning of factor analytic personality traits. *J. Gen. Psychol.*, **66**, 101–114. *223*

Stern, G. G. (1962) The measurement of psychological characteristics of students in learning environments. In: S. Messick and J. Ross (Eds.), *Measurement in personality and cognition*. London: J. Wiley & Sons, 27–68. *18*

Stevenson, H. W. (1954) Latent learning in children. *J. exp. Psychol.*, **47**, 17–22. *288*

Stevenson, I. and Wolpe, J. (1960) Recovery from sexual deviations through overcoming non-sexual neurotic responses. *Amer. J. Psychiat.*, **116**, 737–742. *87, 148, 157*

Summerfield, A. and Steinberg, H. (1957) Reducing interference in forgetting. *Quart. J. exp. Psychol.*, **9**, 146–154. *51*

Sweetbaum, H. A. (1963) Comparison of the effects of introversion-extraversion and anxiety on conditioning. *J. abn. soc. Psychol.*, **66**, 249–254. *37*

Sylvester, J. and Liversedge, L. A. (1960) Conditioning and the occupational cramps. In: H. J. Eysenck (Ed.) *Behaviour Therapy and the Neuroses*. Oxford: Pergamon Press. *108, 262*

Symon, Sheena M. (1958) *An investigation of the relationship between conditioning and introversion-extraversion in normal students*. Aberdeen: Unpublished M.A. thesis, Univ. of Aberdeen Library. *37*

Talbot, M. (1957) Panic in school phobia. *Amer. J. Orthopsychiat.*, **27**, 286–295. *216, 217, 218*

Tafts, R. and Coventry, J. (1958) Neuroticism, extraversion and the perception of the vertical. *J. abnorm. soc. Psychol.*, **56**, 139–141. *43*

Taylor, J. (1956) Drive theory and manifest anxiety. *Psychol. Bull.*, **53**, 302–320. *38*

Taylor, J. G. (1963) A behavioural interpretation of obsessive-compulsive neurosis. *Behav. Res. Ther.*, **1**, 237–244. *132, 139*

Teplov, B. M. (1956, 1959) *Typological features of higher nervous activity in man*. (2 vols.). Moscow: Acad. Ped. Sci. *33*

Teplov, B. M. (1957) Differences psychologiques individuelles et les propriétés typologiques du système nerveux. *J. de psychol. appliquèe*, **54**, 151–161. *45*

Thimann, J. (1949) Conditioned reflex treatment of alcoholism I. *New Engl. J. Med.*, **241**, 368–370. *163*

Thimann, J. (1949) Conditioned reflex treatment of alcoholism II. *New Engl. J. Med.*, **241**, 406–410. *163*

Thistlethwaite, D. (1951) A critical review of latent learning. *Psychol. Bull.*, **48**, 97–112. *287*

Thorpe, J., Schmidt., E., Castell, D. (1964) A comparison of positive and negative (aversive) conditioning in the treatment of homosexuality. *Behav. Res. Ther.*, **1**, 357–362. *149*

Thorpe, J. G., Schmidt, E., Brown, P., and Castell, D. (1964) Aversion relief therapy: A new method for general application. *Behav. Res. Ther.*, **1**, 71–82. *159*

Tolman, E. C. and Honzik, H. C. (1930) Introduction and removal of reward and maze performance in rats. *Univ. Calif. Publ. Psychol.*, **4**, 257–267. *288*

Tong, J. G., and Murphy, I. C. (1960) A review of stress reactivity research in relation to psychopathology and psychopathic behaviour disorders. *J. ment. Sci.*, **106**, 1277–1295. *38*

Treadwell, E. (1960) The effects of depressant drugs on vigilance and psychomotor performance. In Eysenck, H. J. (Ed.), *Experiments in Personality.* London: Routledge, Kegan Paul. *50*

Trouton, D. and Eysenck, H. J. (1960) The effect of drugs on behaviour, in *Handbook of Abnormal Psychology* edited by Eysenck, H. J. London: Pitmans. *50*

Turner, L. and Solomon, R. L. (1962) Human traumatic avoidance learning. *Psychol. Monographs*, **76**, No. 40. *170, 172, 173*

Uttal, W. R. (1960) Inhibitory interaction of responses to electrical stimuli in the fingers. *J. comp. physiol. Psychol.*, **52**, 47–51. *35*

Ullman, A. D. (1951) The experimental production and analysis of a compulsive eating syndrome. *J. comp. physiol. Psychol.*, **44**, 575–581. *170*

Venables, P. H. (1955) Change in motor response with increase and decrease in task difficulty in normal industrial and psychiatric patient subjects. *Brit. J. Psychol.*, **46**, 101–110. *42, 43, 106*

Vernon, P. E. (1953) *Personality tests and assessments.* London: Methuen. *18*

Verplanck, W. S. (1956) Operant conditioning of human motor behaviour. *Psychol. Bull.*, **53**, 70–83. *212*

Voegtlin, W. and Lemere, F. (1942) The treatment of alcohol addiction. *Quart. J. Stud. Alcohol*, **2**, 717–803. *161*

Vogel, M. D. (1960) The relation of personality factors to GSR conditioning of alcoholics: an exploratory study. *Canad. J. Psychol.*, **14**, 275–280. *38*

Vogel, M. D. (1961) GSR conditioning and personality factors in alcoholics and normals. *J. abn. Soc. Psychol.*, **63**, 417–421. *38, 162*

Voronin, L., Sokolov, E. and Bao-Khua, U. (1959) Type features of the orienting response in man. *Voprosy Psrkhologic.*, **5**, 73–88. *107*

Waldfogel, S., Coolidge, J. C. and Hahn, P. (1957) The development, meaning and management of school phobia. *Amer. J. Orthopsychiat.*, **27**, 754–758. *213, 218*

Waldfogel, S., Tessman, E. and Hahn, P. B. (1959) A programme for early intervention in school phobia. *Amer. J. Orthopsychiat.*, **29**, 324–332. *217*

Wallerstein, R. S. *et alia.* (1957) *Hospital treatment of alcoholism.* Menninger Clinic Monogr. Series No. 11. London: Imago Press. *163*

Walters, G. C. (1963) Frequency and intensity determinants of fearfulness. *Canad. J. Psychol.*, **17**, 412–419. 83, *207*

Walters, R. and Demkow, L. (1963) Timing of punishment as a determinant of response inhibition. *Child. Develpm.*, **34**, 207–214. *121*

Walton, D. (1960) Strengthening of incompatible reactions and the treatment of a phobic state in a schizophrenic patient, in *Behaviour Therapy and the Neuroses* (Ed. Eysenck, H. J.). Oxford: Pergamon Press. *176*

Walton, D. (1960a) The application of learning theory to the treatment of a case of neurodermatitis, in *Behaviour Therapy and the Neuroses* (Ed. Eysenck, H. J.). Oxford: Pergamon Press. *97*

Walton, D. (1961) Experimental psychology and the treatment of a ticqueur. *J. Child Psychol. Psychiat.*, **2**, 148–155. *119, 121, 195, 262*

Walton, D. (1963) The interaction effects of drive, reactive and conditioned inhibition. *Behav. Res. Ther.*, **1**, 55–64. *137*

Walton, D. and Black, D. A. (1960) The application of learning theory to the

treatment of chronic hysterical aphonia, in *Behaviour therapy and the Neuroses*. (Ed·
Eysenck, H. J.). Oxford: Pergamon Press. *98*

Walton, D. and Mather, M. D. (1963) The application of learning principles to
the treatment of obsessive compulsive states. *Behav. Res. Ther.*, **1**, 163–174. *131,
138*

Warren, A. H. and Brown, R. H. (1943) Conditioned operant response phenomena
in children. *J. genet. Psychol.*, **28**, 1–14. *241*

Watson, J. B. and Rayner, R. (1920) Conditioned emotional reactions. *J. exp.
Psychol.*, **3**, 1–14. *81, 192*

Watson, J. B. (1930) *Behaviourism*. London: Kegan Paul. *14*

Weinstock, H. I. (1959) Paper read at the Maudsley Hospital, London. *268, 269*

Weisberg, P. (1963) Social and non-social conditioning of infant vocalizations.
Child Develpm., **34**, 377–388. *232*

Wenger, M. A. (1948) Studies of autonomic balance in Army Air Forces personnel.
Comp. Psychol. Mon., **19**, 1–111. *32*

White, J. G. (1959) The use of learning theory in the psychological treatment of
children. *J. Clin. Psychol.*, **15**, 229–233. *194*

Wickes, I. G. (1958) Treatment of persistent enuresis with the electric buzzer.
Arch. Dis. Childhood, **33**, 160–164. *196, 198*

Wilcoxon, H. (1952) "Abnormal fixations" and learning. *J. exp. Psychol.*, **44,**
324–333. *129*

Wilde, G. J. S. (1962) *Neurotische labiliteit gemetan volgens de Vragenlijstmethode.*
Amsterdam: Unit g. F. van Rossen. *30*

Willett, R. A. (1960a) The effects of psychosurgical procedures on behaviour. In
Eysenck, H. J. (Ed.) *Handbook of Abnormal Psychology*. London: Pitman. *55*

Willett, R. A. (1960b) The effects of depressant drugs on learning and conditioning. In Eysenck, H. J. (Ed.) *Experiments in Personality*, London: Routledge,
Kegan Paul. *37, 50*

Willett, R. A. (1960c) Measures of learning and conditioning. In Eysenck, H. J.
(Ed.) *Experiments in Personality. Vol. 2*. New York: Praeger. *43, 50*

Willett, R. A., Holland, H. C. and Eysenck, H. J. (1960) The excitation-inhibition
balance in normals. In Eysenck, H. J. (Ed.) *Experiments in Personality*. London:
Routledge, Kegan Paul. *41*

Williams, C. D. (1959) The elimination of tantrum behaviour by extinction procedures. *J. abn. Soc. Psychol.*, **59**, 269–270. *119, 173, 195*

Willmuth, R. and Peters, J. E. (1964) Recovery from traumatic experience in rats:
specific "treatment" vs. passage of time. *Behav. Res. Ther.* (In Press). *278*

Willoughby, R. (1934) Norms for the Clarke-Thurstone Inventory. *J. Soc. Psychol.*,
5, 91–95. *69*

Wolf, M., Risley, T. and Mees, H. (1964) Application of operant conditioning
procedures to the behaviour problems of an autistic child. *Behav. Res. Ther.* **1**,
305–312. *173, 224, 226*

Wolpe, J. (1952) Experimental neuroses as learned behaviour. *Brit. J. Psychol.*, **43,**
243–261. *63, 129, 208, 243*

Wolpe, J. (1958) *Psychotherapy by Reciprocal Inhibition*. Stanford: Stanford Univ.
Press. *66, 78, 79, 81, 82, 85, 86, 90, 101, 104, 131, 132, 134, 136, 140, 142,
145, 146, 192, 193, 208, 211, 212, 236, 243, 244, 253, 262, 263, 272, 281, 284,
286*

Wolpe, J. (1961) The systematic desensitization treatment of neuroses. *J. Nerv.
Ment. Dis.*, **132**, 189–203. *194*

Wolpe, J. (1962a) Experimental foundations of some new psychotherapeutic
methods, in *Experimental Foundation of Clinical Psychology*. (Ed. Bachrach, A. J.).
New York: Basic Books. *82*

Wolpe, J. (1962b) Isolation of a conditioning procedure as the crucial psycho-therapeutic factor. A case study. *J. Nerv. Ment. Dis.*, **134,** 316–329. *258*

Wolpe, J. (1963a) Quantitative relationships in the systematic desensitization of phobias. *Amer. J. Psychiat.*, **119,** 1062–1068. *258, 259, 261, 262*

Wolpe, J. (1963b) Behaviour therapy in complex neurotic states. *Br. J. Psychiatry,* **110,** 28–34. *79, 136, 264*

Wolpe, J. (1964) Personal communication. 147

Wolpe, J. and Rachman, S. (1960) Psychoanalytic evidence: A critique based on Freud's case of Little Hans, in *Critical Essays on Psychoanalysis* (Ed. Rachman, S.). Oxford: Pergamon Press. *80, 81, 213*

Woodward, J. (1959) Emotional disturbances of burned children. *Brit. Med. J.,* **1,** 1009–1013. *82*

Wundt, W. (1903) *Grundzuge der Physiologischen Psychologie.* Leipzig: W. Engelmann. 5th Ed. Vol. 3. *17*

Yates, A. (1958) The application of learning theory to the treatment of tics. *J. abn. Soc. Psychol.*, **56,** 175–182. *116, 193, 262*

Yates, A. (1960) Abnormalities of Psychomotor Functions, in *Handbook of Abnormal Psychology.* (Ed. Eysenck, H. J.). London: Pitmans. *105, 114*

Yates, A. (1960a) Symptoms and symptom substitution. In *Behaviour Therapy and the Neuroses.* (Ed. Eysenck, H. J.). Oxford: Pergamon Press. *198*

Yates, A. (1962) *Frustration and Conflict.* London: Methuen. *84, 127, 128, 129, 130*

Yorkston, N. (1963) Personal communication. *114*

Young, G. C. (1963) *Enuresis: Aetiology, Treatment and Learning Theory.* M.D. Dissert. Univ. Wales. *198*

Zimmerman, E. and Zimmerman, J. (1962) The alteration of behaviour in a special classroom situation. *J. exp. anal. Behav.*, **5,** 59–60. *196*

SUBJECT INDEX